FLAMES IN THE FIELD

Rita Kramer was born and brought up in midwestern USA. She graduated from the University of Chicago and studied English literature at Columbia University, before working as an editor for various New York publishing houses. She began a career in journalism writing for the *New York Times Magazine* and has since published articles and reviews in the *Wall Street Journal*, *American Heritage*, *Commentary*, the *American Spectator*, the *Wilson Quarterly*, *City Journal*, and various other newspapers, magazines and anthologies in the United States, Britain and Europe.

Maria Montessori: A Biography has been reprinted in many editions and translated into several languages since it first appeared in 1977. Her subsequent books have included *In Defence of the Family*, *At a Tender Age* and *Ed School Follies*. She has also published short stories in literary quarterlies in the USA and Canada.

Flames in the Field was researched and written after Rita Kramer came upon the names of the four woman SOE agents who died at Natzweiler, and she set out to tell their story. When not travelling in connection with her writing, she lives with her husband in New York City.

Flames in the Field

The Story of Four SOE Agents
in Occupied France

RITA KRAMER

First published by Michael Joseph 1995
Published in Penguin Books 1996
1 3 5 7 9 10 8 6 4 2

The author and publishers would like to thank Faber and Faber Ltd for permission to reproduce extracts from the following copyright material: 'Gare du Midi' from *Collected Poems* by W. H. Auden, edited by Edward Mendelson; 'September 1, 1939' from *The English Auden*, edited by Edward Mendelson; 'Gerontion' from *Collected Poems 1909–1962* by T. S. Eliot

Contents

Part Three: Sifting the Ashes

Illustrations

(*Copyright holders are indicated in italics*)

Winston Churchill to the Commons, reviewing the first year of the war:

'... that the British Empire stands invincible, and that Nazidom is still being resisted, will kindle again the spark of hope in the breasts of hundreds of millions of down-trodden or despairing men and women throughout Europe, and ... from these sparks there will presently come cleansing and devouring flame.'

Churchill, *War Speeches 1938–1941*

Major SOE Networks in France, June 1943

Preface

January 20, 1988

Dear Vera Atkins,

Peter Williams of TVS has kindly offered to forward my letter to you. I appreciate his reluctance to give out your address to someone unknown to either of you, and so I will tell you how I come to be writing to you and with what purpose in mind.

Four years ago my husband and I, driving through Alsace on our way to Italy, stumbled on Struthof-Natzweiler. A sign on the road pointed in two directions – one way to the bar-restaurant, the other way to the gas chamber. We decided to investigate and found ourselves at the gate with the word *Konzentrationslager* on the wooden sign above it. There was no English-speaking guide at the camp that day, so we were given the guide's text, printed on several worn sheets of paper, and we walked through the camp, each of us by turn reading aloud until we could not go on, then handing it to the other one. You will know what we read. As we walked and read, we passed groups of French school-children and groups of tourists, mostly German. Both the children and the grown-ups were talking casually, occasionally laughing, just like visitors to any tourist attraction.

When we came to the crematorium we stood in front of the oven, looking at the stretcher, the wooden shoes, and forgot to move. A large woman pushed my husband aside with a peremptory '*Bitte*' and snapped a picture of the crematorium.

In that room we saw a plaque with the names of four women on it. I remember that we noticed two of them had English-sounding names, one was French and one Slavic. It must have been in the English-language visitors' guide to the camp that we learned that the four had been captured while on a mission into occupied France. We stood there a while, not quite able to go back to the outside world, the pleasant end-of-summer day, the tourists, our own trip, hotels, meals . . . and we wondered who they were, those four women.

After we left and re-entered our own lives, we talked about Natzweiler, some of our impressions, and some of the things that had occurred to us there. How small it was, for one thing. How surprisingly small for the amount of evil and pain. I had always imagined the camps as enormous, the towers as reaching the sky, but it was possible to do those things in a very small place . . .

We went on wondering about those young women. Once in a while we would be reminded of the place and we would think of them, or we would tell someone about the trip and then about the camp and the plaque we'd seen. I thought of finding out about the four – who they were, where they came from, what brought them to that place – but I didn't know where to begin. And I was immersed in writing a book at the time. And then one night in November, shortly after I'd finished this last book, we came home from dinner with friends and switched on the TV set to catch the late news, and there was a documentary narrative voice saying words that caught me and pictures that were familiar first in a general way and then in a particular way and I recognized Natzweiler. I sat there, hardly believing what I was seeing, when you were introduced and began to speak about those four young women . . .

I would like to write a book about them. About who they were and what they did. I think they deserve to be remembered. History, after all, is what we choose to remember. I cannot think of anything I would rather learn about and write about than their stories, which must eventually become one story, the way the stories of Achilles and Agamemnon and Ulysses become one story. Would you help me by telling me what you know about them and how I could learn more about their lives? I would come over there to see you and whoever else might be able to give me information and to visit places they grew up in and meet friends or relatives who remember them.

I am sending along some things I've written by way of introduction.

I must apologize for the length of this letter. I wanted to tell you everything I could that would explain my request. (It took me several weeks to track down the name of the producer of the programme I had seen in order to find a way of getting in touch with you.) It only remains for me to thank you for your patience, to salute you, and to assure you that I will look forward with great eagerness to hearing from you.

Sincerely yours,

(signed) Rita Kramer

6 February 88

Dear Mrs Kramer

Thank you for your most interesting letter of 20 January and the literature which will be returned to you via TVS. It gave me the opportunity to judge the quality of your writing and your attitude to some problems of today.

As regards the book you wish to write, I shall be pleased to give you all the information that I have – and it is quite a lot! – if we can meet. I have to deal with a very voluminous and varied correspondence and will not attempt to brief you in writing. Moreover, I am going abroad on the 12th and will be away until Easter.

If you are coming over here in the summer, we could agree on dates to meet in London or down here.

With kind regards,

(signed) Vera Atkins

Well, that is how it began. The following summer I went to Winchelsea, on the East Sussex coast, to meet Vera Atkins, a remarkable woman who has lived an extraordinary life. She does not talk about herself, but told me a great deal about the women I had come to ask her about, the organization to which they had belonged, and what had become of them. She suggested some books for me to read, official history as well as personal memoirs of others in the organization who had known and worked with 'my' women, and referred me to some of their fellow agents still living in England and in France.

And so began a journey of such complexity that, if I had known then what I know now, I probably would not have begun it – but I would have missed the most fascinating quest of my life. The organization, a secret one, was part of the story, but the more I read and the more I talked with those who had been part of it, the more the stories of unique individuals emerged. Some were proud, some were bitter, all had stories to tell of adventure, honour, and betrayal. Many disagreed with each other's versions. And that was only among those Vera Atkins had led me to and the trail I'd followed from there. I was also eventually to get in touch with others, in France, whose view of things was still different – dramatically so – and to find myself in the midst of a mystery that may never be solved but still persists unabated after half a century. Material flooded in on me. I wrote hundreds of letters, some of which were not answered, some of which received perfunctory replies, some of which led me to encounters with unforgettable men and women. I made several trips to England and to France, interviewing former agents and those who had known them and been involved in those long-ago events they remembered so vividly, and consulting archives, both official and unofficial.

To anyone who has followed the stream of publications concerning SOE which have appeared in England over the years it will be obvious what a debt I owe to the many writers who have preceded me on this terrain. I have listed in the bibliography at the end of this book all those whose contributions I have found useful in one way or another. However, I must mention more particularly those books which weigh most heavily in having contributed to this one because they are part of the story, like Elizabeth Nicholas' *Death Be Not Proud* and Jean Overton Fuller's several volumes. Above all I must stress the extent of my gratitude to M.R.D. Foot. No one who writes about SOE in France escapes the obligation of acknowledging a unique debt to Professor Foot, whose works on resistance in general and on escape and evasion are second only to his history of the French Section itself in providing the background necessary to an understanding of events in occupied France.

I owe a very special kind of thanks to those men and women, English and French, who entrusted their recollections to me so many years after those events. First was Vera Atkins, who marked the beginning of the trail for me. Francis Cammaerts was a generous source of much valuable information and patiently corrected errors and misunderstandings in an early draft of parts of the manuscript. Among other former F Section agents I talked with who helped me understand the nature of the resistance effort and the parts they had played in it I wish to thank especially Lise de Baissac Villameur, Brian Stonehouse, Odette Sansom Churchill Hallowes and Arthur Watt.

Mark Chetwynd-Stapylton made available both his own memories and documents relating to his cousin Diana Rowden. Serge Olschanezky revisited his family's past and produced numerous photographs and other mementos of his sister Sonia. Mme Léone Borrel Arend received me warmly and allowed me access to letters and photographs recording her sister Andrée's life before and during the war. John Nicholas kindly made available to me the papers of his late wife Elizabeth Nicholas including her notes for *Death Be Not Proud* and correspondence relating to it. I am grateful for information provided in letters from Jacqueline Bolton, the daughter of V.A.D. Clark, Vera Leigh's half brother and designated next of kin.

Typical of French villagers who had been early members of the resistance, Odette Mathy Fournier and her husband, George, were eager to talk about Diana Rowden and others they had worked with in admiring detail, but little and only modestly about themselves. I am grateful for their cooperation and that of other members of the Association nationale des anciennes déportées et internées de la résistance and of the Fédération nationale des déportés et internés résistants et patriotes.

My thanks are due to Larry Collins for his suggestions about the research and for his generosity in sharing some of his own material, particularly transcripts of his 1983 interviews with Harry N. Sporborg, Hugh Verity, and Maurice Buckmaster. My friend Tereska Torres did invaluable research for me in the Paris archives of the Institut Charles de Gaulle, where she turned up signs that pointed down some new paths. One of them, through historian Henri Noguères, led me to Pierre Raynaud, who graciously opened his home and his voluminous files to me. Ferdinand Rodriguez provided correspondence with Jean-Bernard Badaire of the Fédération nationale libre résistance, the 'Amicale Buck', and described his life as an agent in the field and his experiences in prison in a way that contributed to my understanding of both when we met at Natzweiler. My presence at the ceremonies on my third visit there was greatly enhanced by the arrangements and travelling companionship of Nigel F.C. Smith, MBE, whose efforts had been responsible for the placement of the memorial plaque that first called my attention to the history of the four women at Natzweiler.

My dear friends Walter and Patricia Wells read through early drafts of the manuscript, bringing their knowledge of French life and French politics to bear on it in many ways both large and small and invariably helpful. They have cheered me on since their Paris debriefing after my first research trip and helped me track down some of the figures from the past still living on the Continent. Robin Smyth shared his memories of the controversies surrounding the publication of the book by Elizabeth Nicholas, his 'angel with a fiery sword', and Antony Terry's correspondence proved as stimulating and as suggestive to me as it had to her thirty-five years earlier.

John Taylor of the Military Reference Branch of the National Archives in Washington, DC helped me locate individuals and records that provided interesting background. In London Mark Seaman of the Imperial War Museum's Research and Information Office identified relevant resources in the Museum's holdings and gave me valuable suggestions as to how to make use of them.

Gervase Cowell, the SOE advisor of the Foreign and Commonwealth Office, provided me with much factual information gleaned from the extant files. I want to thank him for his painstaking help and sympathetic encouragement in the early stages of this project when it was much needed, while making it clear that neither he nor Her Majesty's Government bear any responsibility for the interpretations I have made of the facts. Nothing in this book purports to reflect an official view, any more than it does the views of any of the men and women I have thanked.

Over the years in which I pursued my subject, I have selected and rejected from what I found before me in written as well as spoken communications, and in the end no one other than myself is responsible for the way I have told this story or what I have made of it.

Many details have been omitted, many stories left untold, many individuals left unmentioned here, in order to simplify a tale of such Byzantine complexity that the mind numbs trying to keep track of all the people involved. For this reason only, many people who were there when these things happened, and sometimes deeply affected by them, even in some cases having gone to their deaths because of them, have been left out of this account. Names like Burney, Cowburn, Heslop, the Newtons, Trotobas, and Peulevé of F Section and Yeo-Thomas of RF Section are not to be found in these pages not because they were not worthy of mention but because it was possible to tell this story without them. Also in the interests of helping the reader to follow these often hopelessly tangled threads I have left some of the threads lying where I found them. I apologize for that and can only refer the reader to the many volumes listed at the end of this book, in each of which various parts of the vast puzzle can be found.

To my husband, Yale Kramer, I owe a debt it would be hard to do justice to in a formal acknowledgement such as this. He has been a partner in this enterprise from the very beginning and a constant source of support as well as of criticism. It would be hard to say which was the more valuable. In the end, this book is not mine but ours.

Rita Kramer
New York, 1994

PART ONE

Striking the Sparks

Defenceless under the night
Our world in stupor lies;
Yet, dotted everywhere,
Ironic points of light
Flash out wherever the Just
Exchange their messages:
May I, composed like them
Of Eros and of dust,
Beleaguered by the same
Negation and despair,
Show an affirming flame.

From W.H. Auden, 'September 1, 1939'

CHAPTER I

Prologue: Into the Darkness

The guidebook describes the picturesque villages in the pleasant resort area of the Vosges mountains in Alsace, the region of western France known as the Bas Rhin. In this idyllic place, it says, 'there is not much to do except rest and take long walks through the pine woods.' However, the traveller furnished with Michelin map number 87, having followed one of the main roads out of Strasbourg or Colmar, can take the road marked D392 to the town of Schirmeck, and there pick up the D130 south to the village of Rothau, with its quaint railroad station. From there it is only a few minutes' drive along the twisting mountain road past deep green forest broken by occasional glimpses of bright blue sky and wind-blown puffs of white cloud until the spot where in the late 1980s a signpost directed motorists and climbers the way 'To Bar Restaurant' and, below that, 'To Gas Chamber'.

The bar-restaurant is inside a small hotel described in the red Michelin guide as 'pleasant, quiet, and well-situated'. It is across the road from the tile-roofed building that was the gas chamber, before the war a restaurant serving inexpensive meals to skiers. Here, in August of 1943, inside the former restaurant, which had been extensively renovated for the purpose, lethal gas was administered to eighty-seven Jews, fifty-seven men and thirty women, who were selected to be brought here to France from Auschwitz for the purpose of 'medical experimentation'. A little glass panel enabled doctors to observe the reactions of the men and women inside. After gassing, the bodies were kept in three deep tile-lined tanks designed to preserve them until they could be used as cadavers for dissecting by medical students. The skulls and skeletons were to become part of a collection being assembled by SS doctors and professors of the Faculty of Medicine at the Institute of Anatomy in the University of Strasbourg Municipal Hospital.

Just a few minutes further along the mountain road, well marked today and much travelled by cars and by school and tourist buses, is Struthof-Natzweiler. Unlike the nondescript façade of the '*maison rustique*' that served as its gas chamber, the silhouette of the Natzweiler camp is immediately identifiable to a visitor as that of a concentration camp. Konzentrationslager Natzwiller, as it was officially identified on the wooden sign above the gate, looks no different from the photographs of other death camps and slave-labour holding pens that dotted the Polish countryside and stood beside bustling towns in eastern Germany. Here in France this one still stands, with its heavy gates and square watchtowers, surrounded by double fences of barbed wire. Inside, at the top of a slope, you can look past the gallows on its stagelike platform, over the site of the razed barracks, the outlines of their foundations still visible on the ground, down towards the still-standing punishment-cell bunker and the adjacent crematorium with its tall black chimneys. Beyond the surrounding barbed wire there is a clear view of the magnificent mountains and above them the endless sky with its wind-driven clouds.

Just outside the gates of the camp, on the afternoon of 6 July 1944, a work detail of prisoners digging ditches under heavy guard witnessed an extraordinary thing. A car drove up to the gate and out of it soldiers led four people, who were brought within the gates and shortly afterwards led down the stepped path to the prison block. They wore decent clothes and carried personal belongings and were not like the usual prisoners transferred from other camps, starved, emaciated, broken, hobbling, sometimes shoeless, in remnants of civilian clothes or uniforms. That much was unusual. What was truly extraordinary – so much so that, in the few minutes it took for the new arrivals to walk from the gate down the path to the blockhouse, every detail could be remembered clearly years afterwards by those who had witnessed the scene – was that the four were women.

Natzweiler was a camp for men, held no women prisoners, had no facilities for women, and the thirty women who had been brought there as human guinea pigs and asphyxiated in the gas chamber outside the camp gates had never lived in the camp proper. This was the first glimpse of ordinary women, dressed in ordinary clothes, that prisoners at Natzweiler had seen, some of them for months, some for years.

Struthof-Natzweiler was the only extermination camp on French soil. It lay among the wooded ravines of a territory west of the Rhine over which Germany and France had fought repeatedly for centuries and in which loyalties were deeply divided by language and national allegiance. In the Second World War the provinces of Alsace and Lorraine were not considered to be an occupied part of a conquered enemy like other parts of France; the victorious Germans considered the area to have been reabsorbed into the Reich, like Austria at the time of the Anschluss.

In 1939 the spot, on a hill bordering the pine forests of Natzweiler and Barembach, havens for hikers and mushroom gatherers, had been a popular ski resort. Its north and west exposures brought icy winds all year, and its gentle slopes were covered by the heavy swirling snows of winter. Postcards of the thirties show winter-sports enthusiasts in front of the hotel with their wide wooden skis and toboggans. Towards the end of the first year of the German occupation of France, late in 1940, German officials installed themselves in the former Hôtel de Tourisme and asked the local authorities to provide workers to build a road – which would later be known as the 'Route du Désespoir' – up to the summit of the Struthof hill from the station at Rothau, so that materials and prisoners could be transported there to construct the camp. Described by a survivor as 'walking skeletons in rags', they carried up on their backs the stones and beams to build their own prison. Only a handful of them were still there when the camp was liberated four years later by the US Seventh army.

The camp existed for the purpose of inflicting suffering and death. It was intended that those who were sent there should disappear, in circumstances as brutal and degrading as possible, after being used to work in the nearby quarries and underground munitions factories until their strength gave out. They were kept on a starvation diet, were barely clothed in the icy winter, received no medical attention except for those who were experimented on, and were constantly subject to the whims of sadistic guards.

The overcrowded barracks were ruled over by prisoners who had been transferred from the civil jails, many of them those who had been convicted of violent crimes. Prisoners were made to stand at attention for hours in their thin striped uniforms during roll calls in the freezing pre-dawn or winter evenings, when the outlines of the surrounding mountains and thoughts of life beyond them kept some of them on their feet and drove others mad. Those who dropped were left to lie there. Those who tried to escape were hanged slowly in front of the assembled prisoners; those guilty of other infractions, such as trying to smuggle letters out of the camp or trading food for a pair of shoes, were tied to a wooden rack and beaten with a whip by a fellow prisoner until they were unconscious, or placed in solitary confinement for up to three days in a cagelike space too small to stand up or lie down in. To amuse themselves, guards might force a prisoner out of the line of march on the way to the quarries, then machine-gun him 'for attempting to escape'. On occasion they organized hunts, setting hungry attack dogs on prisoners selected for the sport.

Fewer than a hundred SS guards were needed to oversee the thousands of prisoners in the camp, since escape past the double high-voltage electrified fencing was next to impossible and since the violent criminals among them were made responsible for maintaining discipline over the rest, weakened by hunger and broken by physical punishment. Most of the specially trained

German personnel had volunteered for the concentration camp assignment. It was considered preferable to being at the Russian front. The prisoners themselves were made to perform most of the work, including the loading of bodies into the crematorium. All in all, it was a system designed to meet the needs of Nazi policy, including being economically profitable,* and did not vary much from the regime at all the other camps to the east.

Aside from geography, one thing set Natzweiler in France apart from those other extermination camps to the east. It was not the brutality systematically practised, not the human misery endured, or even the utter hopelessness of those within or the indifference of those outside. Those were the same in all the places designed to carry out German policy of the time, the Nazi doctrine of superior and inferior races. The difference had to do with the prisoner population, with who was sent there to be obliterated and why.

By 1944, on any given day, among the three to four thousand prisoners crowded three to a bunk in Natzweiler were men, or the shadows of those who had once been men, of every national-ity. Most were Poles, Russians, and French; some were Germans, Italians, Lithuanians, Hungarians, Yugoslavians. At various times there were a few British. About three-quarters of those in the camp were political prisoners. Among the rest were civilians from Poland, Russia, and France who had been conscripted for forced labour in Germany, had tried to escape and been recaptured.

What all of these men had in common was some sense of the reason they were there. Unlike the Jews in Germany and the conquered countries of the greater Reich who had been herded

---

* The SS, the most fanatic of the Nazis, were volunteers whose attitude and training specially fitted them for running the concentration camps. These killing factories financed the SS by means of the slave labour they provided while at the same time eliminating its enemies. Profits also accrued from what the murdered left behind: clothing and other personal possessions such as watches, jewellery and eyeglasses as well as their hair.

into boxcars and delivered to the killing factories in the east, what happened to these men had at least a logic of evil. The Jews of Europe had done nothing but be what they were born, and could do nothing to influence their fate. Their persecutors looked on them with loathing, with contempt, as less than human.

The prisoners at Natzweiler, especially the 'politicals', knew at least – and it does not minimize their suffering to recognize the fact – that they had done something, committed some act, made some decision they could look on as a moral choice or a spiritual necessity, in some way an expression of their individuality. What had brought them to this was a voluntary act of will. Their tormentors looked on them not with disgust but with hatred. They feared them. And in so doing left them at least their pride, their self-respect.

In addition to the physical abuse inflicted at the time they were shaved and disinfected and stripped of all personal belongings on being admitted to the camp, the prisoners at Natzweiler were classified by the Germanically methodical camp administrators according to various categories. Each wore an identifying symbol, in the case of the largest numbers a green triangle for the ordinary convicts, with a special point on that for dangerous criminals, and a red triangle for the condemned political prisoners, with a letter indicating the prisoner's nationality. The smaller groups were identified by purple triangles for conscientious objectors (Jehovah's Witnesses), pink for homosexuals, and black for 'antisocials', who, along with the greens, were put in charge of the work gangs.

A special category was reserved for captured maquis partisans and members of other resistance organizations. These prisoners, classified as 'NN', were identified by a red cross on the back of their uniforms and red stripes on the trousers and a yellow patch with three black circles making a convenient target over the heart.

NN stood for *Nacht und Nebel*, or night and fog (*la nuit et le brouillard* in French), a phrase that was the inspiration of a particularly cultured Nazi official fond of Goethe and of Wagner, in whose admired operas he found the appropriate term for those who were meant to disappear without trace. The NN prisoner was considered to have no further rights nor even any longer any legal existence. He was not permitted to receive or send mail or packages, and his name was written in the camp records in pencil, so it could be erased and any memory of him obliterated when he finally disappeared, as was intended, into the night and fog.

For all prisoners, admittance to Natzweiler was tantamount to a death sentence. Those who were physically strong enough to withstand the slave labour and were not shot or hung could expect to succumb to psychological and moral disintegration, disease and malnutrition. The life expectancy of a prisoner was not worth reckoning. It took a combination of extraordinary will and extraordinary luck to survive.

One who did was a British officer who had been caught while engaged in resistance work. Classified as an NN prisoner, he was on a work detail digging trenches for a pipeline near the gate of the camp on the afternoon the four women were brought there.

Brian Stonehouse was a young conscript gunner who before the war had been an art student. He had an artist's eye, trained to pay close attention to the details of features, form and dress of models sketched in class. On that afternoon he went on digging under the eye of the guard with a machine gun beside the electrified barbed-wire fence, while managing to pay close attention to the women as they were marched through the gate and down the steps leading past the barracks to the bunker. He remembered what they had looked like, what they had been wearing, what they carried with them. The memory stayed with him through the remaining months of his imprisonment in Natzweiler and Dachau. And after his liberation and return to England, his detailed recollections of the four women would become a matter of some importance in establishing who they were and what had happened to them.

On that day at the camp he had no idea where they came from or why they had been brought there, and no idea of what connected them with him, other than their presence in this forsaken place. He noted that one of them was tall and looked typically English, with a bit of tartan plaid ribbon in her hair. One looked older than the others, fortyish he would guess, with the others in their twenties. One carried a small suitcase, another had a rather ratty-looking fur coat over her arm. When asked, he would be able to describe their faces, their colouring, little details that would individualize them. He would remember that they all looked pale, as though they had been indoors for a long time, and seemed tired, as though after a journey, but not starved, like the camp inmates. They looked incongruously like people 'from the real world'. He managed to observe them for what could not have been more than a minute or two before they disappeared into the bunker at the bottom of the stone steps. He never saw them again, but he would be able to sketch their likenesses, recognizably, later.

His talent for sketching recognizable likenesses was one of the things that helped him stay alive in the camps. He traded his sketches for cigarettes, the camp currency, which he was able to exchange for extra bits of food. Another talent, his ability to speak French, was one of the things that had brought him there.

Until his family moved back to England when he was fourteen, Brian Stonehouse had been brought up and educated in France. Between the wars, a British income went further in France than it did in England, and, like a number of Englishmen, Brian's father established his family in the French countryside, where they could live better than they could have at home. An engineer, he worked in England much of the time, visiting when he could at the seaside villa in the north of France. Brian was perfectly bilingual and his fluency in the two languages, which might have remained a social asset, was recognized as a strategic one when war came. He was twenty years old, an officer cadet serving as a gunner in the artillery, when he was approached about his willingness to put himself and his command of French to use in a more dangerous capacity. Although it would not be spelled out until later, it was a matter of being dropped by parachute into enemy-occupied France, as an agent of British resistance to the Nazi conquest of Europe.[1]

CHAPTER 2

Schooling for Subterfuge

On the very day – 10 May 1940 – that Winston Churchill took office as Britain's wartime coalition prime minister, Hitler launched a devastating armada of 2,500 heavily armoured Panzer tanks, 136 army divisions, and 3,000 modern aircraft in an end-run around the northern end of the 'impregnable' Maginot Line, through the 'untankable' Ardennes forest into Belgium, heading for Holland, the Channel coast, and France. Within a month the French army was in chaotic retreat and the small and demoralized British army was huddled on the beach at Dunkirk waiting to be evacuated. France fell on 22 June.

What the British left behind at Dunkirk was not only their arms but a feeling on the part of many of the French that their allies had let them down and run out on them. The English, went a saying of the time, were prepared to fight to the last Frenchman.

In the French army itself there was little will to fight. Many on the French General Staff preferred the Germans to the Popular Front elected in 1936 and its leftist and/or Jewish leaders such as Léon Blum. Everywhere, officers deserted, leaving their men behind to surrender to the onrolling Panzers. France's political leaders were intent on their own squabbles, unable to unite in common cause even against the invader. It wasn't hard to find French politicians who were more anti-Communist than anti-German. They could see that what the Communists planned was a socialist revolution; they managed to close their eyes to what it was the Germans planned. Almost no one resisted.

By the 10 June, with the panzers at the outskirts of Paris, the

French government left for Tours to the south. In their wake followed an exodus of Parisians, young and old, in cars and on bicycles, pushing baby carriages and wagons with mattresses and pots and pans strapped to them, leaving Paris practically deserted when the Germans entered the city on 14 June.

Churchill urged the French government to fight on, but the anti-war faction won out and appointed Marshal Philippe Pétain, the aging First World War hero of the battle of Verdun, to head the government and negotiate with the Germans for an armistice. Churchill brought across the Channel a very junior French army general who had supported him in his determination to resist to the end and on 18 June Charles de Gaulle broadcast a radio appeal 'to all Frenchmen' in which he claimed that, although France had lost a battle, it had not lost the war and called on them to join him 'in action, in sacrifice and in hope' to save their country.

De Gaulle believed in France's mission, to represent civilization to the world, and in his own, to restore that civilization with honour. He had no official position, held no command and spoke with no authority but his own when he broadcast to a defeated people that 'the flame of French resistance must not and shall not go out'. He assured them that the enemy would eventually be crushed, and declared it his aim that France should be 'present at the victory' he envisioned.

Meanwhile, defeat was the reality. France fell in less than six weeks. By the terms of the armistice, the French continued to administer a sizable part of their country. Paris and the north of France and the entire Atlantic coast were to be administered by the German military command, while a so-called 'free zone' south of the Loire would be administered by the French under Marshal Pétain. His collaborationist headquarters was set up at Vichy, a sleepy spa in the Auvergne, chosen primarily for the number and size of its hotels. Alsace-Lorraine was incorporated into Germany while Vichy retained control of France's overseas possessions, including North Africa.

On 3 July the British sank the French fleet at Mers el-Kebir in Algeria to keep it from falling into German hands. The French were understandably bitter; more than a thousand French sailors were killed, and to many Frenchmen the British began to seem worse than the Germans, who were still on good behaviour as occupiers.

They could afford to be. Many of the French proved all too willing to do the Germans' dirty work for them, rounding up first anti-Nazi refugees, then Communists and foreign-born Jews, and finally French Jews, for transport to 'the east'. Among the occupied countries of Europe, the French enjoyed the distinction of providing for the Nazis a record number of informers.

France's defeat, both physical and moral, was total. It was an abject nation, demoralized, resigned. There was no active resistance, only a few clandestine newspapers and pamphlets being mimeographed and distributed; most people chose to go on with their lives, conducting business as usual.

Thus, by July of 1940 the German army had swept everything before it and the Nazis and their Axis allies controlled all of Europe. England, across the narrow Channel, stood alone, braced for invasion.

It was at this moment and in this atmosphere that Churchill, faced with crucial decisions about how to organize for the immediate defence of the island, as well as with enormous issues of long-range strategy, established the organization that would bring Brian Stonehouse to France and eventually to Natzweiler.

The organization was known as Special Operations Executive and its Churchillian mandate was to 'set Europe ablaze'.[1] 'Known' is misleading; SOE was known to no one except the handful of men and women who worked in it and a few others – members of the air services that supplied its transportation needs and the intelligence department that often competed with it. It existed in what its official historian called a 'dense fog of secrecy'[2] and even half a century after it was disbanded arguments rage about its methods, its purposes, and its ultimate worth. It had become clear that long-range British strategy would require fomenting and supporting revolt in German-occupied territories, and a special organization would have to be created 'to coordinate all action by way of subversion and sabotage, against the enemy overseas'.[3]

Hugh Dalton, the Minister of Economic Warfare under whose aegis the early plans for the conduct of 'irregular warfare' were laid, described the function of such an organization as 'to co-ordinate, inspire, control and assist the nationals of the oppressed countries who must themselves be the direct participants' and added that 'we need absolute secrecy, a certain fanatical enthusiasm, willingness to work with people of different nationalities, complete political reliability'[4] wherever they were to be found. As it turned out, the enthusiasm would be easier to come by than the secrecy.

Through an unfortunate oversight, probably a result of the confusion inherent in forming a secret organization, its establishment remained a secret from Stewart Menzies, the head of MI6, the existing intelligence service, setting the stage for a resentment and a rivalry that would plague the new organization in the long months and short years ahead of it. MI6 considered the upstart organization unprofessional, a motley collection of amateur agents, and a danger, in the conspicuous 'bangs' that called attention to its sabotage actions, to MI6's agents in the field, whose need was for a silence in which they could collect secret information.[5]

By October 1940 the SOE staff was headquartered in an office building at 64 Baker Street, not far from Sherlock Holmes's fictional address across the Marylebone Road at number 221B. A brass plate on the door of number 64 identified the premises as those of the 'Inter-Services Research Bureau'. As it grew, the offices of SOE's various country-section offices came to occupy other buildings in the area, including a flat in Orchard Court, Portman Square, used by F, the British-run French Section; and the offices in Dorset Square of RF, the Gaullist-run French Section, not far from the Gaullist Free French headquarters in Duke Street. In the shorthand of the special services, those place names would become synonymous with the sections housed there.

Each country in enemy-held territory had its own section with its own head. The French Section's staff was headed from the end of 1941 by Maurice Buckmaster, a man who was more often praised for affability than for keenness of mind, but it has passed into legend that the show was really run by his civilian aide, Vera Atkins, who was officially his intelligence officer.

Country-section agents were supposed to be fluent enough in the language of the country and familiar enough with its customs to pass for natives. If they possessed that requirement – and sometimes a degree of compromise was necessary – they would be accepted for training. The two French sections – one British-run, the other run by de Gaulle's staff – among the largest of the country sections, each sent more than four hundred agents into enemy-occupied territory.

The new organization was looked on askance by the traditional branches of the government and the armed forces. Eccentric, amateur, schoolboyish, lunatic were only some of the politer epithets used to refer to it by its rivals and enemies in the other services. More than unconventional, it was considered disreputable.

Initially, those selected for the SOE staff were drawn mainly from the public-school and university old-boy network, the charmed prewar inner circle of those who had gone from schools like Eton, Harrow and Winchester to the most prestigious colleges at Oxford and Cambridge. Some had had military training at Sandhurst and some were academics, but most held influential positions in the City, London's centre of business, finance, and the courts of law. This was natural enough, given the needs for secrecy and security. Staff members recommended people they knew and trusted.

Patrick Howarth, a writer who came to SOE via Rugby and St John's College, Oxford, would later note that 'the public schools, with their adherence to the prefect system and to the concept of the survival of the fittest', and with a curriculum he characterized as 'a kind of prolonged assault course',[6] had produced young men with habits of mind and conduct that enabled them as SOE officers not only to survive, but to assume quasi-ambassadorial, quasi-military responsibility over large areas in which guerrilla warfare was being waged.

As time went on and the organization grew, its agents, a far more diverse group than the staff, came to include a diverse cast of characters with wide-ranging backgrounds in worlds as far apart as the theatrical and the criminal. The ability to play a part and the ability to forge a ration book or an identity card were both invaluable skills in the undercover organization Churchill referred to as 'the ministry of ungentlemanly warfare'.

Interviews with prospective recruits to SOE's F Section were held in a small dark back room in the old Victoria Hotel in Northumberland Avenue, then a War Office annexe, although nothing on the outside identified it as such.[7] There they would find themselves talking with one of the recruiting officers. It might be Lewis Gielgud, the brother of the actor, or Selwyn Jepson, a prolific author of mysteries (among his titles: *I Met Murder*, *Keep Murder Quiet*) and screenplays (*The Riverside Murders*, *The Scarab Murder*).

Jepson's interviews took place under a naked light bulb in the dingy little hotel room, in which a bare table and two hard kitchen chairs were the only furnishings besides a blackout curtain. Prospects summoned to this bleak setting had no idea at first why they were there. After a moment or two of introductory conversation, Jepson would begin to speak French. He was making a judgement about whether the candidate's command of the language and knowledge of the country was good enough for he or she to pass for French, and also making an assessment of his or her character and motivation for responding to the invitation to be considered for some kind of special duty.

If the candidate passed muster on French, did not appear to be running away from an unhappy personal life or courting danger too impulsively, and if a background check turned up nothing unfavourable, Jepson would invite the applicant back for another meeting, at which he would give some idea of what it was all about. At this point he would indicate that it was not a question of working as an interpreter but of actually being sent behind enemy lines in France in a capacity still not specified. Only the danger was made explicit, and he would ask the prospective agent to think it over before returning with the decision to volunteer or not. One thing was made clear. It was essential to keep the matter a secret, to arrive at a decision alone, without discussing it with anyone else, not even a parent or closest friend.

The recruits were a motley crew of bankers and dons, music hall entertainers and barristers, West End playboys and public school masters, salesgirls and aristocrats, playwrights and accountants, restaurant chefs and taxi drivers. Some were impelled by loyalty to England, some by a love of France, some by their hatred of Nazism. The only thing they all had in common was that they were amateurs at the dangerous business in which they were to be 'specially employed', one of the many euphemisms used to disguise the organization they would refer to as the Racket, the Outfit or the Firm. One MI6 officer has been quoted as saying, 'The British were quite good at clandestine life because their boarding-school education was a constant battle against authority from the age of seven on.'[8]

The recruiting officers were looking for individuals who not only spoke unaccented French fluently and had the ability to pass for natives in a French locale and among French people, but who exhibited a certain combination of prudence and initiative, toughness and imagination, that they could only guess at intuitively. Sometimes, inevitably, they guessed wrong. And sometimes they bent the requirements in the case of a recruit who possessed some specially useful talent or skill.

Those who were found acceptable and agreed to join the outfit were now about to begin a rigorous course of training designed to teach them what they would have to know to survive in a hostile environment and do the work they were sent there to do. It was also designed to weed out those who were not up to the rigours or who in some other way revealed characteristics not considered suitable for the job at hand. Being reckless was one; talking too much while under the influence was another.

When the war broke out the government had requisitioned many of the great English country houses. So many of them were used as special training schools that someone said that SOE stood for 'Stately 'Omes of England'. It was in one of these great houses, at around the time that the servants whose livelihood it had been to run it went off to war, that F Section's recruits were sent for the first stage – usually three or four weeks – of their training.

Wanborough Manor was a gracious sixteenth-century house set on its own parkland on the Hog's Back near Guildford in Surrey. There the F Section recruits were looked after by women, most of them young, some of them titled, who were members of the posh First Aid Nursing Yeomanry. The FANYs started out doing their bit for the war effort by acting as hostesses, cooks, housekeepers and providers of comradeship and comfort to the trainees who came and went at the special schools, but as the war went on their membership became less exclusive and they took on more serious tasks as well. FANYs were trained as secretaries and typists, code clerks and wireless operators, and eventually staffed most of the wireless telegraphy (W/T) stations that sent and received signals to and from agents in the occupied countries.

The prospective agents came to Wanborough via a circuitous route in closed vehicles. The idea was that those who didn't make this first cut and were not asked to go on would not be able to say where they had been. Nor would they be told the purpose of the training they were undergoing until later. The premises were strictly guarded by Field Security police and while there the students at this special school had no contact with their families or friends on the outside, although they were not totally isolated from the surrounding world. At least one former agent remembers that the daily exercise run continued outside the grounds along the road that led to the local pub.

The senior officer in charge at Wanborough was Roger de

Wesslow, a major in the Coldstream Guards who epitomized the public-school and Oxbridge aura of the elite Guards and liked to compare notes on continental cuisine and vintage wines with French Section recruits who had lived in France. The daily schedule included some military drill interspersed between hours of lectures by specialists in the various skills an agent might need to be able to call on in the field; they included intelligence officers, sappers, ordnance men, and detectives from Scotland Yard.

A film made at Wanborough while the war was still on[9] shows a setting not unlike those of prewar drawing-room dramas, except that, instead of ladies in flowing frocks being waited on by butlers and courted by gentlemen in white flannels on the terraced grounds, young men and women in gym outfits are doing PT exercises and starting out on cross-country runs. In addition to physical fitness, there was some training in map-reading and the use of firearms, and a good deal of observation of an informal kind, with the staff officers in charge taking note not only of the trainees' grasp of the material being taught but of their characteristics and behaviour as well.

John Goldsmith, an agent who operated in the south of France up until the liberation, later described this phase of his training as 'a cross between going back to school and staying in a series of first-class hotels where shooting, hunting and even fishing were free'.[10]

Those who made it through this preliminary stage were sent on to be toughened up for the kind of physical endurance required by commando units. In the rugged wilds of the Scottish highlands at Arisaig and Meoble, accessible only on foot over a mountain track, men and women alike trekked over the rough country in bad weather, wading through cold rushing streams and creeping through undergrowth to hide from other groups of trainees sent out in patrols to hunt for them. Here on the desolate western coast of Inverness they learned to handle arms and ammunition, practising how to assemble, dismantle and shoot rifles, pistols, and Sten and Bren guns, the weapons most often dropped to resisters, and how to instruct others in their use. For occasions in which their skill at hitting a target with a Sten submachine gun was not the appropriate one, they mastered the techniques of unarmed combat, including, when necessary, that of silent killing.

There was instruction in the use of explosives and in various methods of industrial and railroad sabotage, and by the time the course was over they had carried out simulated sabotage actions. The bleak and barren area was off limits to anyone but SOE personnel, who were isolated there during their training. John Goldsmith would describe Arisaig as the place where 'we played deadly forms of Boy Scout games'.[11]

No distinction was made between the men and the women who eventually joined them there as trainees. They too learned to handle various types of small arms and machine guns, set explosive charges, and kill silently. The training of women for operational roles as couriers and radio operators was unprecedented and their presence in the field would not become a matter of public knowledge until well after the war had ended, when it was still considered controversial.

Those men and women whose nerve and stamina held out, and who had mastered the skills of underground warfare so far, were by now a hardy and self-confident lot. More specialized courses lay ahead for them.

At Wanborough and in the highlands, former agent Francis Cammaerts says, 'programmes consisted of a bit of everything. They were generalist, not specialist. The idea was to see if you had any particular skills of any kind and the energy and self-confidence necessary.'[12] Then came parachute training at Ringway, near Manchester – now that city's airport – and, 'after a jump or two', training in intelligence and security.

Those who had made it this far found themselves returned to a country-house setting for the final stage of their training. The finishing course was at Beaulieu, the ancestral home of the Lords Montagu in the New Forest, where the new agents were housed in cottages on the grounds of the estate. Even with the wartime alterations, it was a beautiful place, and agents later remembered the setting at Beaulieu as a kind of romantic paradise, despite the intense concentration that was required of them. It was certainly an easing off compared to the fierce conditions they had left behind in the highlands.

Life at Beaulieu was a graduate course in survival in an occupied country. Members of the French Section would have to be familiar with German army uniforms and insignia and the various branches of the Nazi intelligence services as well as with the Vichy police. And the Milice, a volunteer paramilitary organization of French fascists, would be as great a danger to them once they landed in France as the Gestapo. In some cases, the Milice were even more of a danger, given their familiarity with their own country and its customs, and their ability to perceive subtler differences in language and behaviour than the Germans. There was repeated practice in how to withstand interrogation without giving oneself away, how to keep one's cover story in mind at a sudden road check, how to act naturally when challenged unexpectedly, how to remain inconspicuous, above all how to appear to be a French man or woman in France.

There was instruction in coding and in passing messages surreptitiously in public places, in shaking off a pursuer when being followed, and lectures on what was known – not much at first – about conditions in occupied France and what to expect there. John Goldsmith would remember, 'There was so much to pick up since my last visit to France in 1938 ... facts about politics; what it was practical to ask for in the shops; who the latest film stars and what the songs of the moment were'.[13] And such things as the *jours sans*, the days on which spirits were not available, and asking for a vermouth cassis in a café instead of ordering ersatz coffee or a lemonade could mark you more certainly than carrying forged papers.

The customs of the country would be new even to those who had grown up in France. They had not had to deal with ration books when making purchases, show their identity papers when challenged, pass through a snap control at a rail station. By 1943 any adult man moving around in France could be required to produce, in addition to his photo identity card stating the particulars of his cover data, a work permit, a ration card, a tobacco card, a permit if in a coastal or frontier zone, as well as demobilization papers and a medical certificate establishing his exemption from forced labour in Germany. Each forgery of these papers in the possession of an agent had to be the up-to-date official form, correctly signed and stamped.

Lectures in the great hall were devoted to such details in addition to all aspects of security measures to be taken in the field and there was intensive instruction in map reading and the various techniques of coding information. At Beaulieu the prospective agents were given their new identities, like a new skin they had to learn to live in, and met their conducting officers, who would act as their guides and mentors from now until they left on their assigned missions.

They learned the tricks of the clandestine trade at Beaulieu, making contacts, locating safe houses, setting up mail drops, locating and preparing suitable dropping grounds and arranging for receptions of agents and arms. They learned to use their false papers and how to hide documents so they couldn't be found by the Scotland Yard inspectors who searched them, and they underwent interrogation sessions that came as close to the real thing as possible without involving actual physical torture. They were screamed at, shoved around, kept standing under bright lights and questioned for hours without letup, often looking down a gun barrel. Later, over a drink, they would hear a critique of their performance, with some tips to keep in mind in the eventuality of having to face the real thing some time in the future.

The final exam at the end of the course was a simulation of what might be expected of them later. They were assigned, like the heroes in fairy tales, tasks that had to be fulfilled, trophies that had to be brought back if they were to win the prize, in this case not the princess and half the kingdom but a chance to undertake further dangers. Groups of two or three would have to lay a dummy explosive charge on a railway track or steal a police car and bring it back. If caught, they were to rely on their cover story or escape. Only as a last resort would they be bailed out by the SOE staff.

With their basic training over, some agents were sent on for more specialized courses to the wireless-training school at Thame Park in Oxfordshire or to a school for sabotage where they would study engineering in reverse, learning how to use explosives to destroy bridges and railway engines.

Once training was successfully behind them, the finished agents might go home on leave – with strict instructions to reveal nothing to relatives or friends about the nature of the work they had been prepared for – or, if they had no home in Britain, might be put up somewhere near the departure grounds in East Anglia. Now it was a matter of waiting until the moon and the weather and the availability of aircraft made the Channel crossing possible.

Tempsford, west of Cambridge in Bedfordshire, was the base at which the pilots of 138 Special Duties Squadron stood at the ready to make the dangerous trip over, carrying the passengers they called 'Joes', whose real names and identities they never knew, whom they would drop over France along with containers of arms and supplies. Or an agent's final destination before leaving might be another RAF station, Tangmere, near Chichester, which was used for Lysanders, the small planes flown by pilots of the 161 Squadron. These were the flights that carried the agents who would be landed rather than parachuted. Hugh Verity, a Special Duty Squadron pioneer much decorated for the number of flights he made into France – over thirty in 1943 alone – wrote that when he joined the Lysander flight, 'there was an atmosphere of cinematic stunt-riding about the whole thing'.[14] Special Duties fliers had an *esprit de corps* special even for RAF pilots, all of whom felt themselves members of a happy few who faced danger and death every time they went up. They prided themselves on the safe delivery of the Joes they flew over and those they brought back in their 'Lizzies', sometimes with bottles of Chanel No. 5 and Moët et Chandon in hand. After the war they learned that among the names of the French they had brought out to England were those of Auriol, d'Astier de la Vigerie, Malraux, Mitterrand.

All the while they waited, in Orchard Court, at Tempsford or Tangmere, the agents continually went over the details of the life of the person they had become, the person named on the identity cards and ration books they carried, so that names of family members, schools attended, birth dates and anniversaries, professional identity and job history, the names of the streets in the towns they came from would automatically be produced instead of their real ones when they were questioned.

Vera Atkins saw all of the agents who left for France, making arrangements for letters to be sent to relatives while they were out of touch, taking charge of the wills they drew up and of personal possessions left behind, and briefing them on what to expect once they landed. She continually collected bits of information about changes in the necessary documents and the conditions of daily life – regulations about curfew, travel, the workplace – first from refugees, later from agents returning from the field, hoping to send new agents into action as well prepared as possible to pass as ordinary citizens of an occupied country. It took an enormous amount of research to prepare someone to be unobtrusive – particularly when that someone was not a native of the country or had not lived there for long periods of time. Something as simple as looking the wrong way before crossing the street or the way you used your knife and fork could arouse suspicion.

What you sounded like was part of it; what you looked like was crucial too. The way you did your hair, what you carried, most of all what you wore could give you away. Continental and English styles of clothing were unmistakably different, and the tiniest details – the way lapels were stitched, the label on your underwear – could betray you on inspection. A Jewish refugee from Vienna headed up a staff of tailors and seamstresses at a factory hidden away near Oxford Circus, turning out clothing

made to European specifications. He made the rounds of syna-
gogues and persuaded other refugees to part with used suits or
dresses from which the labels could be removed and copied for
an added touch of authenticity.

At the last minute Vera Atkins or a conducting officer would
go through the agent's pockets to make sure there were no
overlooked English coins or hotel matchbooks or West End
ticket stubs. She collected all sorts of ephemera to add to the
supposed French citizen's wallet: photos of putative relatives,
postmarked letters from old friends in other cities, Métro tickets,
sales slips from a *grand magasin*. No one ever knew how she
came by these scraps of corroborating material, only that they
were reassuring to have in one's possession.

These final touches were part of the routine of the last hours
an agent spent before leaving for the unknown and they were
spent in an apartment in Orchard Court in Portman Square, not
far from Marble Arch. There was a butler named Park, the soul
of tact and the epitome of the vanishing breed of gentleman's
gentleman, brigadier's batman, or Oxford undergraduate's scout.
His job was to receive the agents and manage the traffic so that
they came in contact with each other as little as possible. It had
all of the elements of a drawing-room farce, especially since the
arriving agents sometimes outnumbered the available rooms,
necessitating the use of the bathroom, a black-tiled art deco
affair complete with onyx bidet, for briefings. Agents bound for
France were sometimes taken out for dinner at a smart French
restaurant like La Coquille where they practised French table
manners in the company of conducting officer André Simon,
scion of the famous wine family. It was considered part of the
training.

Buckmaster's gift to departing agents was a gold compact for
the women, gold cufflinks for the men. The idea was that these
items could be pawned if the agent ran out of money. It was also
the kind of stylish gesture that appealed to the unconventional
side of many SOE agents.

All this drama, the romance of it, helped to keep the darker possibilities, the risk, the fear, the danger, the loneliness, at bay. Brian Stonehouse, like many of the agents only in his early twenties at the time, remembers thinking in the car on the way to the airfield to take off for occupied France, 'My God, what the hell am I doing here? How did I get myself into this?' He went anyway.[15]

CHAPTER 3

The Sparks Ignite

The first agent dropped into France by F Section was parachuted just south of the demarcation line in May 1941, just a year after the German onslaught on western Europe. His name was George Bégué and he landed near the town of Valencay, where a memorial to the men and women of F Section would be dedicated exactly fifty years later.

Although there was an occasional landing by fishing boat or submarine, most agents reached enemy territory by air.[1] Some were dropped by parachute from twin-engine Whitley or four-engine Halifax bombers, which were used to drop heavy cylindrical metal containers of arms and ammunition as well as agents. Other agents were landed on the ground from a Hudson or a Lysander. The Hudson was a two-engine low-wing monoplane originally designed by Lockheed in the US as a small airliner and converted for military reconnaissance and escort purposes. It could carry ten passengers and their luggage. The Lysander was a small, light monoplane with shorter range than the Hudson but which could land in a flat field as little as four hundred and fifty yards long and take off a few minutes later after letting out a couple of passengers and some letters and taking on two or, at a pinch, three returning agents and some London-bound messages.

The two RAF special duty squadrons that flew the agents over – the 138 Squadron based at Tempsford that dropped the parachutists and the containers and wireless sets and the 161, closer to France from its base at Tangmere, that made the landings and pickups – were known as the Moon Squadrons because they could make the flights across the channel and find the dropping zones only during the two-week period before and after the full moon. Even during that time they were limited by weather conditions on one side or the other, most often the notorious English fog.

Moon-phase and weather conditions permitting takeoff, pilots of the unarmed Lysanders would navigate their 'Lizzies' themselves by moonlight while flying at low altitudes and slow speeds over such landmarks as rivers and fields, looking for an identifying bridge or a bend in the river. Avoiding enemy flak while consulting the Michelin map on which the landing field had been identified by Baker Street from references to an identical map by agents in the field, the pilot would look for the signal lights of the reception committee on the ground, a flare-path laid out in the shape of an inverted L and an agreed letter flashed in morse. If the lights were not there, or the correct letter was not signalled, the pilot would have to turn round and head back.

The agent about to parachute from a Whitley or a Hudson, once alerted by the dispatcher, sat with legs dangling through a hole in the floor of the plane's fuselage, and then, at a hand signal from the dispatcher and the sight of a red light turning green, pushed off down through the hole. The chute would be opened automatically when the weight of the parachutist's body pulled a static line attached within the plane. Once clear of the slipstream the agent floated down to be met by a reception committee, typically consisting of agents already in the area and local volunteers willing to risk the penalties of being out after curfew and the heavier ones of being caught receiving, transporting, or hiding arms and ammunition, usually in barns on nearby farms.

Many of the special arms and sabotage equipment came from SOE's 'toyshop', hidden away in the basement of the Natural History Museum in South Kensington. Here a scientific and technical staff designed and tested secret devices for use in sabotage and evasion. It later became the model for the fictional world of James Bond, whose creator, Naval Intelligence officer Ian Fleming, had a brother, Peter Fleming, in SOE.

The most important of the experimental weapons and equipment invented and perfected were plastic explosive and time fuses for bombs. Successful sabotage actions by SOE agents in the field were carried out using the delayed detonator for explosive charges, called a time pencil because of its size and shape. One of the more imaginative applications of plastic explosive was exploding horse or cow dung – imitation animal droppings to be left on the road until a passing car or truck set them off. Another contribution to resistance work brought into the field by SOE was the light machine gun called the Sten, inexpensive to manufacture, simple to assemble and easy to operate, which proved invaluable in the kind of close-range house-to-house combat engaged in by urban guerrillas.

Before each drop, reception committees were alerted as to when and where to expect a delivery of agents and/or supplies by the BBC – listening to which was in itself a crime punishable by deportation. After the evening news bulletins read in French, the BBC announcer would repeat a series of *messages personnels* called *avis*. It was George Bégué who thought up the stratagem of using this feature of the BBC French Programme to send coded messages into France.

These seemingly innocuous messages followed the news reports broadcast from Bush House on the Strand in the heart of London every night at 7.30 and again at 9.15. Men and women all over occupied France listened surreptitiously to the broadcasts, which were introduced by the opening measure of Beethoven's Fifth Symphony, which sounded the rhythm of the morse code signal for V, the dot-dot-dot-dash which had become synonymous with V-for-victory and the image of an indomitable Churchill holding up two fingers in a V as he inspected rubble-strewn London. The expressionless but perfectly pronounced sentences, read in the manner of a French schoolmaster's *dictée*, followed the opening words, '*Et maintenant, voici quelques messages personnels . . .*'

The items of trivia (*Louise est en vacance à la campagne*) or lines of poetry (*Je me souviens des jours anciens*) that followed were actually coded information. Scattered among the sentences flowing in the announcer's measured cadences might be phrases previously agreed on as signals announcing arrangements for a Hudson operation: *Moïse dormira sur les bords du Nil* (Moses will sleep on the banks of the Nile) and *L'Ange rompera le sceau de cire rouge* (The angel will break the seal of red wax).

The listener would be alerted by the agreed-on message in the early evening broadcast; if it was repeated on the later programme he would spring into action, rounding up volunteers to wait for the plane. When they were not caught – and many, too many, were – the enterprise was a great morale booster, a proof that they were not abandoned by the powers that were fighting on and an indication that liberation could be anticipated.

Even riskier than taking part in reception committees for agents and arms was providing a place for wireless operators to send from. There was no chance of getting away; it was one's own house in which the set was found. Many Allied sympathizers who had provided hospitality for agents who were caught sending W/T transmissions from their houses joined them on the trains to the camps and never came back.

As time went on, radio communications would provide a strategic link between Allied command and resisters in occupied countries, enabling them to plan and coordinate sabotage efforts for the time of invasion. But, from the first, short-wave morse wireless telegraphy was the main and the indispensable means of communication between London and agents in the field, and the W/T operator had the most dangerous job of all. By 1943 a radio operator in the field could expect to last about six weeks.

In the beginning, the sets they had to carry were heavy and cumbersome. The first ones consisted of two separate boxes. The one that contained the transmitter with its morse key and battery weighed forty-five pounds and a separate box was necessary to hold the receiver. George Bégué, when he landed in 1941, brought with him such a wireless set – the only one working out of France for most of 1941.

The next improvement was an all-in-one transceiver, which even together with its power pack weighed considerably less. A quartz crystal, necessary for tuning to a particular wavelength to establish a frequency, was carried in a separate little box. Eventually the ingenious SOE technical staff developed a set which looked like the small suitcase or attaché case of the fibreboard type with reinforced corners commonly used in Europe at the time, that could send and receive, but still weighed about thirty pounds. Anything much smaller and lighter in those pre-transistor days did not have a long enough range to be really useful.

Direction-finder vans, alerted by Gestapo headquarters on the Avenue Foch in Paris, which monitored all wavelengths, could take their bearings and close in on an operator still on the air within half an hour of his first signal on a particular frequency. It was essential not to stay on the air too long, but not until the winter of 1943–44 was the order given that no wireless transmission was to last longer than five minutes. Until then, and occasionally even afterwards, operators were known to run the risk of transmitting for long periods at a time, sometimes even for hours. They were the ones, like Brian Stonehouse, who were caught at it.

The radio sets used in the field had to be powered by electricity and, lacking batteries or generators, this necessitated being connected to the local source of power. One of the most chilling sights in occupied France was the mobile detection van making its way slowly down the street, closing in on a hapless radio operator concentrating on his transmission, unaware that the power was being switched off block by block until his exact location was revealed by the silence.

In the beginning, until the spring of 1942, MI6 handled SOE's wireless traffic at Bletchley Park, the site of the Government Code and Cipher School. It was here that MI6 began receiving SOE's messages, decoding them, and relaying them to section headquarters in Baker Street, an arrangement which, given the friction between the two services, might have been expected to cause trouble.

MI6's chief, Stewart Menzies, and his deputy, Claude Dansey, held particular animus for SOE. Before the war the Secret Intelligence Service – later designated MI6 – had sole and unchallenged authority to carry out irregular operations overseas. Unprepared for the lightning war that swept over Europe, SIS had been left bereft of agents anywhere in occupied territory. Smarting from its failures on the Continent, MI6 was dealt a further blow to its prestige by the creation of an independent agency for special operations without its knowledge and outside its control. It did what it could to maintain some hold over its upstart antagonist, but eventually had to relinquish control of SOE's wireless communications. By that time, however, it had bagged bigger game in the wireless wars, a matter that would not come to light until decades after the war had ended.

That MI6 had been privy to all of SOE's clandestine wireless messages to and from the field until mid-1942, when SOE finally began to use its own codes and ciphers and receive its signals at its own station at Grendon Underwood, would assume noteworthy, if not sinister, significance later.

George Bégué was soon joined by a fellow Frenchman, Pierre de Vomécourt, who set up a group known as AUTOGIRO in the Paris area. Others followed, making their way to various towns and villages, looking for sympathizers to organize into groups called circuits in English or *réseaux* in French and establishing contact for them with London on Bégué's wireless. It was an effort without precedents to guide its workings, and the few rules which should have been rigidly followed, those pertaining to security and requiring strict separation of groups and constant mobility of individuals, seem to have melted away in the heat and confusion of the moment. Once in the field, agents did not always remember to keep apart from each other, keep on the move – especially important for wireless operators – and know as little as possible about activities beyond their own. And a series of disasters overtook the early efforts of SOE in France.

De Vomécourt was introduced to a woman named Mathilde Carré who had been part of INTERALLIÉ, an early resistance organization led by a Polish officer in Paris connected with MI6. Impressed with her experience, contacts, and seeming know-how, he took her into his group and put her in touch with London. Unfortunately, he was unaware of the full extent of her experience and the exact nature of some of her contacts. Betrayed by an informer, she had been arrested by an official of the Abwehr, German military intelligence, named Hugo Bleicher, who was to play a significant role in the affairs of SOE.

Bleicher was a persuasive ladies' man who easily convinced Carré that switching sides was a preferable alternative to imprisonment and interrogation by the Gestapo. She was turned round in record time – it took a single night during which she remained unharmed in a jail cell to convince her of where her true interests lay. As a double agent, she reported to Bleicher and arranged a series of rendezvous with unsuspecting agents she was fingering for arrest. La Chatte, the Cat, as she was called, eventually offered her services to the Allied side again, making it clear that, whatever her motivations, they were not ideological.

Bleicher had been led to INTERALLIÉ by an agent named Raoul Kieffer, known as Kiki, another of those he had been able to persuade to work for him after arresting them. Reflecting in his memoirs on those he had succeeded in turning traitor, Bleicher commented, 'It was my experience that educated persons succumbed more easily to the bribe of freedom than simple people did'.[2] The betrayals engineered by Bleicher drew in such an impressive catch of agents that he was rewarded with a posting to Paris, where he took up his duties in March of 1942 to continue his surveillance of resistance groups, which he saw beginning to spring up everywhere, 'Like mushrooms overnight'.[3]

During the winter of 1941–42 agents in the south had reported the existence of a group called CARTE, led by an artist named André Girard who claimed to control a secret army of some

300,000 only waiting to be armed and led to rise up against the Germans. In the early months of 1942 F Section dispatched agent Peter Churchill (no relation to Winston Churchill) to the Riviera to look into the CARTE business. He was favourably impressed with the signs of potential resistance activity, although in the end it turned out that CARTE's activities amounted to little more than talk among an enthusiastic bunch of students, artists, musicians and hangers-on living the bohemian life on the Riviera and that the 'secret army' existed only on the paper on which Girard had drawn up lists of potential members.*

Churchill was less impressed with the squabbling between the leaders of the organization, Girard and his deputy Henri Frager. He would have been even less impressed – horrified in fact – if he had known that one of the forms Girard had drawn up neatly listing hundreds of potential *résistants*, with full particulars identifying, locating, and describing each of them in detail, had been in a briefcase carried by one of Girard's assistants on the train from Marseilles to Paris one day in November 1942. The courier, André Marsac by name, dozed off during the journey and woke to find that his briefcase and the two hundred names and addresses it contained had disappeared. It appeared that an agent of the Abwehr, less susceptible to the lulling effect of train wheels, had made off with it. From that moment on, there was reason to suppose that every one of those names was that of a marked man or woman, a supposition that does not seem to have been taken into account by Baker Street.

* According to Francis Cammaerts, the early British agents were seduced by Carte (Girard's code name) and his handful of associates because they seemed to them 'people like us'. The background of the first agents the British sent over was similar enough to that of the artists, intellectuals, students, and upper-class bohemians who gathered around Girard, and their style of life familiar enough to lend them a certain credibility in the eyes of men like Peter Churchill and his fellow agent Nicholas Bodington. They felt no such affinity for those like the trade unionists who would later prove to be far more dependable allies but who were looked on with some suspicion in the early days as hardly suitable for the enterprise at hand.[4]

In any case, between the ineptitude in CARTE and the handiwork of Hugo Bleicher, by spring of 1942 de Vomécourt's circuit AUTOGIRO had been destroyed, leaving agents in the occupied zone without a centre of operations in the capital. New agents were arriving, and new radios were transmitting, and it would be necessary to start up a new circuit in the Paris area. It would be called PROSPER and its leader also took the code name of Prosper, after a fifth-century Christian preacher of the doctrine of predestination. It would prove an apt choice of name.

While French Section was establishing its presence, a counter force was also stepping up efforts to put an end to the resistance. Among the agents who arrived in the summer of 1942 was young Brian Stonehouse. He had been in the field four months when he was caught, and it was in the month following his arrest that the Germans launched their operation ATTILA in response to Montgomery's victory over Rommel's seemingly invincible Afrika Korps at El Alamein. In the first week of November a combined force of British and American troops had landed in North Africa and Vichy troops surrendered. In retaliation, on 11 November the Germans crossed the demarcation line that had divided France and marched into the previously designated unoccupied zone, taking over the remainder of metropolitan France.

In Vichy France fifteen separate French police organizations willingly did the Germans' bidding. After the Germans took over the previously unoccupied zone the forty-five thousand fanatic French neo-Nazis who made up the Milice came to be as feared as the Gestapo, being even more adept at spotting strangers and sniffing out irregularities the foreign occupiers might have missed. All across the country, the dangers were escalating in ways that were obvious and in some that were not.

Many French men and women – no one will ever be able to say with exactitude how many – were corrupted by their complicity in the occupation and its laws. The black market thrived and informing became something of a profession, a free-lance occupation. It paid. Thousands of French men and women worked with the Gestapo. French double agents infiltrated resistance networks, and French informers hunted out Jews and betrayed deserters from the compulsory work crews sent off to Germany. Thugs, hoodlums, gangs of criminals of the kind who can be found at the fringes of any society came into their own under a political system that empowered those who were good at the uses of violence and terror. They joined the Milice or became *V-Männer* – for those the Nazis referred to as *Vertrauensmänner*, 'trusted ones' – or volunteered to serve in the Waffen-SS.

With the Gestapo and its many helpers tightening the vice all over the country, it became even riskier for *résistants*, especially British agents. Young men of military age stood out on the street and in public places, particularly after the forced labour system went into effect. Why are you not at work in Germany? Papers, please. The trip to Germany could be arranged. Increasing numbers of sudden roundups, the *rafles*, and strictly enforced curfews emptied France's busy streets. Those who tried to avoid conscription, the *réfractaires*, faced heavy penalties.

It was a situation for which the recruitment and training of women agents seemed a partial solution. Women were less conspicuous as they walked or bicycled around. It was normal for them to be out, shopping for what food there might be, standing in line for bread, for soap, doing household errands that needed to be done even in wartime. And, at first, they were not suspect. Women in this role were an innovation, something the Germans had not anticipated. This was after all a society in which women had neither the right to the vote nor even a right to the cigarette ration. Women's papers would be given a more cursory glance, a smile from one might cause an officer to wave her through a control, her presence accompanying a man made him somehow more domestic, less problematic. At least until, inevitably, it became known that the British were using women as agents and that French women were aiding in the efforts of what local resistance there was.

As 1942 drew to an end, Germany controlled all of Europe, from the Atlantic coast to the borders of the Don. Hitler's planned cross-Channel invasion of the British Isles had had to be called off because the RAF kept the Luftwaffe from gaining command of the skies. The Battle of Britain was fought in the air and won by the young British pilots so many of whom died defending the air space and keeping it from ever becoming a battle on the land. But across the Channel the Continent remained a fortress, seemingly impregnable.

Pétain's puppet government supplied forced labour, and countenanced the establishment of the Milice, which all but outdid the Gestapo in searching out Jews, *résistants* and *réfrectaires*. When there were not enough volunteers for *la relève*, the French police began to round up men between eighteen and fifty to be sent to Germany to work under the February 1943 law known as *Service du travail obligatoire* (STO). The unintended consequence of the law was to create a partisan force. It was STO that sent young men into hiding in groups that called themselves the maquis, the name for the brush that grows wild in the Corsican hill country where bandits once hid.

It was in 1943, too, that SOE's French Section really got off the ground. Nineteen forty-one and 1942 were years spent establishing circuits, with more or less success here and there. Although things were easier in the Vichy zone, run by Nazi sympathizers if not by the occupiers themselves, much time was lost and energy diverted in pursuit of what turned out to be a pipe dream, the illusory secret army of Carte. One agent later contrasted 'the melodramatic days of 1942 when everyone was learning the business' with '1943 when the tension was at its height and the German counter-measures at their best'.[5]

Despite setbacks, by the spring of 1943 there were effective circuits operating in Provence and in various parts of central France, in the industrial area around Lille and among the railway workers around Montauban and Lyon. Successful sabotage operations were being carried out and recruits were being trained in preparation for the anticipated invasion of the Atlantic coast. To escape forced labour in Germany, thousands of young men had taken to the hills, forming the makeshift clandestine army of the maquis. And from Paris and its *banlieux* out to the surrounding countryside the large circuit led by the organizer known as Prosper was in place, receiving agents and large and frequent drops of arms and ammunition. It was here that disaster would strike in mid-year.[6]

In July of 1943 the Allies invaded Sicily and Mussolini was deposed. The Allies landed in southern Italy in September and, with the Russian victories on the eastern front, a Nazi defeat began to appear a distinct possibility. By the end of 1943 resistance activities were in full swing, in anticipation of the Allied invasion which was thought to be imminent.

And when it did come, they were ready. On the night of 5/6 June, Operation NEPTUNE, the initial assault phase of the invasion, established a bridgehead for OVERLORD, the return to western Europe of the Allied forces. But the invasion of Normandy did not succeed easily. The Germans did not give up the way the French had four years earlier. They fought like cornered animals, and after a month were still holding off the Americans and the British in western Normandy. But the end was clearly at hand. German reinforcements were not arriving in anything like the numbers needed, largely because of SOE-armed and trained resisters, and at their rear they were feeling the sting of sabotage as the local peasantry joined in support of the agents of the invading armies.

At this time a kind of rage took hold of the officials who had signed on for a thousand years of domination and saw the Reich crumbling after less than five years of war. Random killings were stepped up, the dying were marched out of extermination camps to perish on the roads, and prisoners were disposed of either so that they could not live to tell what they might have seen or learned or simply in a frenzy of Teutonic efficiency. No loose ends were to be left behind. And in the chaos, the flames, the mud, the fear, things happened that some would spend their lives trying to forget and others trying to remember.

The end of the war brought with it a mood of euphoria and an attitude of denial. Effort and sacrifice were going to pay off in the brave new world. And few among the British and Americans wanted to hear the unbearable facts, to be confronted with what had gone on in supposedly civilized Europe during those years just past and how little had been done to stop it.

The French, now united under de Gaulle, had their own reasons for going after the traitors in their midst. The Republic was to be purified so it might resume the belief in its tradition of glory. To do so it would be necessary not just to purify, but to construct the myth of widespread French resistance to conquest and occupation from the beginning, and of the French having liberated themselves, with a little help from their friends. The Americans and British allowed the French General Leclerc to enter Paris first, leading his columns down the Champs Élysées to the cheers of tumultuous crowds, and within a few days after the Normandy landings de Gaulle himself, having followed the liberating armies into Paris, was travelling from town to town, reviewing local officials who came out to greet him, wearing uniforms and insignia that suggested a number of resistants that would have greatly surprised the agents who came trying to find them in the early days of occupation.

Politics reemerged with peace, and those who had no resistance record invented one. Many who had collaborated enthusiastically went on to enjoy positions of power and influence in the postwar governments for years to come. The real resisters, the farmers and country priests, proprietors of village cafés and small garages who had provided hiding places for organizers, let wireless operators hang aerials out of their windows, and stored ammunition and supplies on their premises, expressed little bitterness, or even surprise. About what they had done, they shrugged and said, '*C'est une chose normale*'. About the aftermath, the lack of recognition of their efforts as medals were handed out to the *naphthalinés*, those who took their uniforms out of mothballs and became *résistants* at the last minute, they smiled and said, '*Enfin, j'ai le coeur tranquil*'. And went on with their lives.

48

De Gaulle greeted the populace like a conquering hero, a liberator, which is what they felt him to be. He was preceded by delegations of civilian administrators who skilfully took over communications and other essential services as they arrived, thus assuring that it was the Gaullists and not the Communists who were in control. In many towns and cities collaborators were identified and made a public example of in an orgy of finger-pointing that was like a mirror image of the informing that had gone on all the while the Germans were in charge. And everywhere he found them, the general greeted the British agents who had organized the earliest resistance efforts in France with the news that they were no longer welcome there. To F Section agent Roger Landes, who had organized and led over two thousand armed men around the Bordeaux area in time for D Day, he said, 'You are English? Your place is not here,' and gave him two hours to leave the country.[7]

The British were sick of war and privation, and the Americans longed to get back home. There appeared to be a new enemy now, as the Uncle Joe of wartime became the Stalin whose troops occupied the 'liberated' nations of eastern Europe. SS officers were interrogated by the Americans, primarily for whatever information might be of use against the Soviets, then allowed to slip away to other parts of the world to start new lives. Scientists who had developed weaponry for the Nazis with full knowledge of the slave labour used to produce it were invited to continue their work in the United States. Only the military lawyers occupied themselves with the evidence of what had been done and how it had been done, to whom and by whom.

For most people, the camps were too horrible to contemplate, the fate of the men and women who entered them beyond understanding. For most of those who managed to survive them, those events were too painful to look back on. How to deal with the rage and shame, at what had been done to them, at what they had become. In fact, it would be years, many years, before the survivors and just what they had survived would be widely talked about and written about.

At the moment in which the horrors were first revealed, the most common impulse was not to look. Except for the lawyers, who had the job of putting together for the international military courts the case against war criminals and those guilty of what had been defined as crimes against humanity. And except for a few other individuals with a special interest. One of them was Vera Atkins of SOE's French Section.[8]

One of the first things the new postwar Labour prime minister Clement Attlee did on assuming office was to give orders to have the Special Operations Executive disbanded. The staff was given forty-eight hours in which to wind up its affairs. Records were packed up and files vetted under the supervision of MI6, still run by its wartime head, Menzies, SOE's old rival, and his second-in-command Claude Dansey. Boxes of papers were taken away to storage and remain locked away to this day in the archives of the Foreign Office. An unspecified number are said to have been destroyed in a fire soon after the offices in Baker Street were closed down and all SOE activity officially ceased in mid-January 1946.

Unofficial activity, however, was another story. F Section had sent over four hundred agents into the field. When the war ended, 118 of them had not returned. Thirteen of them had been among the thirty-nine women sent into the field. Vera Atkins was not about to close up shop and turn things over to MI6 before finding out what had happened to the missing agents, men and women she had known, briefed for their missions, accompanied to the planes that would take them into France, for whom she had written letters to their parents and children offering reassurance that there continued to be 'good news' when there was no news or even bad news, but still reason for hope. Now she would set out to find what had happened to that hope.

CHAPTER 4

The Hunt

Vera Atkins had so many responsibilities in F Section that it is hard to describe her job. She helped to make the decisions about who would be sent into the field as an organizer (almost always men) or a radio operator (women as well as men) or a courier. Couriers were almost always women, who would be less conspicuous bicycling around the countryside or riding on a train or walking on city streets than the young men liable for army service or forced labour in Germany.

She had come to know the prospective agents while they were still students at the special training schools. Sometimes she was asked to give her opinion when there was a question about a student's performance or suitability for the job. When they came to London on leave she often manoeuvred round the regulations to arrange advances on their minuscule pay. She had handled their personal affairs when it was time for them to leave, helping to draw up their wills and collecting the letters and postcards that would be sent off to their families at regular intervals while they were in the field. She also helped prepare them for the tests they would face once they got there. Writing about her years later, George Millar, whom she had helped prepare to go into the field in 1944, described her as 'wonderfully soothing in her difficult job . . . a tough, clever, thorough staff officer'.[1]

She had made it part of her job as F Int (Int stood for intelligence but she liked to say it stood for interference) to circulate every scrap of information she had gathered from returning agents, refugees, clandestine publications and official German publications that came her way about conditions in occupied France – what people were wearing, what they were eating, when to apply for a bread or tobacco ration, the days when alcoholic drinks weren't served in the cafés, what was no longer available in stores – a daily summary of intelligence material she called 'Tidbits' which was distributed on a restricted basis among staff officers and a more general mimeographed sheet called 'Comic Cuts' circulated among F Section agents and those of the various other European country-sections to provide them with whatever tips came her way.

Sometimes she made use of the BBC *messages personnels* to pass on a vital bit of family news to an agent in the field. In one case the phrase agreed on ahead of time to let an agent in occupied France know that his wife in England had given birth was *Joséphine réssemble à sa grandmère* if the baby was a girl and, if it was a boy, *Joseph réssemble à son grandpère*.

She accompanied as many of the F Section agents as she could to the airfield to see them off when they left for France and was there to meet as many as she could when they returned after the war.

Some did not return at all. The fate of many of these was known. In some cases agents who came back were able to report on what had happened to others with whom they had worked. But at war's end there were a number of British F Section agents unaccounted for, simply 'missing'. And Vera Atkins, who knew every one of them, sometimes better than their own families, was determined to find out what had happened to them.

She had some clues she was anxious to follow up but SOE had for all practical purposes ceased to exist. Denied official permission, Vera Atkins set about her undertaking anyway, with the help of some well placed and like-minded friends – Captain Yurka Galitzine and Major E.W. 'Bill' Barkworth.

Early in December 1944 a three-man intelligence-gathering team for the Political Warfare Department of Supreme Headquarters Allied Expeditionary Force arrived at the gate of Natzweiler. The camp had been evacuated three months earlier, most of the prisoners forced eastwards, ahead of the Allied advance, to camps within Germany.

One of the team was a twenty-one-year-old British officer, son of a White Russian nobleman and an English mother, named Yurka Galitzine, who made a number of discoveries. He found all of the camp records intact in the administration building; he heard that there had been some British men in the camp and that some women described as well-dressed spies had been brought there, and he carefully put together a record of the systematic shootings, hangings and gassings, the medical experiments carried out on live prisoners, the conditions of slave labour on starvation rations, the brutal punishments randomly inflicted by sadistic criminals put in charge of the barracks, and other details of daily life in the camps that had been intended to pave the way for the New Order promised by the Third Reich. No one would believe him. Only when Bergen-Belsen and Dachau were entered by Allied troops the following April, four months later, would it be possible to conceive of systematic atrocities carried out on such an unprecedented scale.

In Galitzine's report, ignored and effectively suppressed by SHAEF headquarters, it was noted that one of the English prisoners had left behind some drawings he had made while in Natzweiler. He had given them to one of the civilian foremen employed by a local firm of stonemasons that had contracted with the Germans to supervise the prisoners who slaved in the quarry. The drawings were signed 'B.J. Stonehouse'.

Frustrated by the official indifference to his report, and unable to forget what he had learned at Natzweiler, Galitzine also saw the approach of peace bring with it a widespread desire to bury the past, to forget about the horrors that had taken place. At war's end he accepted a transfer to the branch of the War Office assigned to investigate war crimes. Eventually his path would cross that of Major Bill Barkworth.

In mid-August of 1944, with the Americans advancing across northern France toward the Rhine, commandos of the Special Air Service, known as the SAS, were dropped in the countryside not far from Struthof-Natzweiler. Their mission was to disrupt the communications of the Germans, who were thought to be retreating from the vicinity, and to make contact with and give support to the maquis and other members of the resistance in the area.

The mission proved to have been based on a miscalculation. The Germans, still strong in the region of the Vosges, mounted a punitive action they called Waldfest, which means something like a picnic in the woods. In it, with the help of local informers, they captured many of the British airmen and numerous French civilians, partisan fighters as well as farmers who had hidden the British. Although they were uniformed members of regular forces, all of the British were shot. The locals, as well as the entire male populations of their towns and villages, were deported, some to Natzweiler, others to Dachau, Bergen-Belsen, and Auschwitz.

When the war in Europe finally ended some nine months later, some of these men were still alive and they came back to their villages, several of which had been burned to the ground by the Germans before they left the area. The bodies of the British dead were buried in the churchyard at Moussey, one of the villages that had suffered the heaviest reprisals, but their commanding officer and the other members of the detachment who had managed to escape and return to England were unaware of their fate. They were listed as missing in action.

By the end of 1945 the SAS no longer officially existed. But the commanding officer of the team that had carried out the doomed operation in the Vosges was determined to find out what had happened to those of his men who had not returned. Equally determined – some said obsessed – was Major Bill Barkworth, who had been their intelligence officer and had become head of the SAS war crimes investigation team. A half-dozen men who had known the missing men personally set out early in the summer of 1945 for what was then the French zone of Germany. There and back in France in the area of Moussey they found and identified the bodies of their dead comrades, who had been betrayed by French men and women cooperating with the Gestapo, tortured, killed, and buried in mass graves with other Allied servicemen captured towards the end of the war.

Now they were determined to find those responsible and bring them to justice. When the SAS was officially disbanded, it was Galitzine who managed, in the administrative confusion of the time, to keep the team going. He saw to it that their pay and supplies continued so they could complete their investigation, track down the murderers of their fellow airmen and bring them to trial. In the ensuing months, Barkworth's team stumbled on evidence of a number of other crimes. The trail eventually brought them to Struthof-Natzweiler, where they established the identities of several of the SS staff who had run the camp.

When Vera Atkins decided to find out what had happened to the missing F Section agents, she was aware of Galitzine's report on Natzweiler. She called on him at his office in Eaton Square and showed him a list of names of missing women agents, hoping he might recognize some of them. He didn't, but he did the next best thing. He agreed to support her efforts and helped her get to Karlsruhe in Germany, where she was able to establish that several Englishwomen had been imprisoned there before being sent off together in a convoy.

Convinced that she was on to something, she used the connections she had made with RAF brass to obtain a temporary commission as a squadron officer in the WAAF. This would give her the authority necessary for dealing with the military in the various zones of occupation. She also made use of her connection with Galitzine to get the War Office to agree to attach her to the War Crimes Investigation Unit in the British Zone. With the judicial process already underway, she had a limited time in which to carry out investigations that might have been expected to take years. She had three months.

Among the clues she had to go on, in addition to the Galitzine report, was the information provided by the SAS team that had been to Natzweiler, and it was with Natzweiler that she decided to begin.

A few survivors of the camps were trickling back. One of them was Odette Sansom, who was captured in the south of France with fellow agent Peter Churchill in April 1943 and had convinced her captors that he was the nephew of the prime minister and that she was his wife. Neither was true, but the deception is probably what saved her life. She had travelled from Paris to Karlsruhe with a party of British agents before being sent on to Ravensbrück, an experience she survived only because at war's end she was kept alive, although barely, as a potential hostage and plucked out of her cell by the camp commandant, who drove with her in his white limousine towards the American lines, hoping to trade this presumably important personage for his safety. After two years in the hands of the Germans she was a wreck, but she was able to tell the Americans who and what he really was, and his plan did not work as well as hers had. The Americans arrested him and freed Odette. Returning to England, she was able to fill in some pieces for Vera Atkins.

So were two of the other camp survivors. One was Brian Stonehouse, who was still alive and on his feet when the Americans drove into Dachau. Vera Atkins was waiting for him when he stepped onto English soil, his head shaved, hollow-cheeked, oddly dressed in bits of uniforms scrounged here and there, but willing and able to describe what he had seen that July day at Natzweiler. In an affidavit he described the arrival of the four women, accompanied by two SS men, and their progress down the terraced steps between the barracks until they disappeared from his view at the bottom of the hill, where the crematorium and the jail bunker stood.

Another was a prisoner known as Lieutenant Commander Pat O'Leary. He was actually Dr Albert Guérisse, a Belgian army physician who had fled to Gibraltar when the Belgian and French armies surrendered to the invading Germans in 1940 and joined a Royal Navy special unit operating in the Mediterranean. Arrested in the south of France, he managed to get away and helped put together an escape organization based in Marseille. When the head of the organization was betrayed and arrested, 'O'Leary', the cover name given him by the British, took over what came to be known as the Pat Line.

Hundreds of downed Allied airmen were found, hidden, and led to safety by men and women on the Pat Line at enormous risk to themselves and their families until Guérisse himself was betrayed and taken by the Gestapo. He was subjected to prolonged torture in one camp after another and ended the war in Dachau, working to save living skeletons in the infirmary, where typhoid was epidemic and medical supplies nonexistent.

On the afternoon of 6 July 1944 he had been a prisoner in Natzweiler. From the window of the infirmary he too had seen the women and had recognized one of them. She was a Frenchwoman who had worked on the Pat escape line. Ignoring the danger to himself if he were caught, he managed to work his way from one barracks to another until he came to the one nearest the bunker to which the women had been taken. A face appeared at one of the windows and he had a chance to exchange a few words with her in English before the face disappeared.

With Galitzine's help and the little she had to go on, Vera Atkins set out for Germany. All she had was the information provided by Galitzine's report and that of the SAS team, the camp records and the regional files left behind at Strasbourg by the retreating Germans, and what she had learned from the three people she knew who had travelled with, seen, or spoken to the women after they had left Paris and on their arrival at Natzweiler. Her self-defined mission was to find out what had become of all the F Section agents who had not returned, and her first step would be to establish the identities of the four women who had been seen at Natzweiler and determine what had happened to them.

In the following weeks, accompanying the head of the legal section of the War Crimes Investigation Unit, Atkins was present at the arrest and took part in the interrogation of several members of the SS who were in a unique position to tell her the answers. One had been the commandant of the Natzweiler camp, another had been in charge of executions and of the operation of the crematorium, and one had been the camp 'physician'. When she had heard what they had to say, she moved on to Ravensbrück, the next step in her bleak voyage of discovery. By then she knew the answers.

CHAPTER 5

Vera: A Parisienne Returns

In an affidavit presented to a military court in the spring of 1946, Brian Stonehouse described the four women he had seen being brought into Natzweiler almost two years earlier:

> There was one tall girl with very fair heavy hair. I could see that it was not its natural colour as the roots of her hair were dark. She was wearing a black coat, French wooden-soled shoes and was carrying a fur coat on her arm. Another girl had very black oily hair, and wore stockings, aged about twenty to twenty-five years, was short and was wearing a tweed coat and skirt. A third girl was middle height, rather stocky, with shortish fair hair tied with a multi-coloured ribbon, aged about twenty-eight. She was wearing a grey flannel short 'finger tip' length swagger coat with a grey skirt which I remember thinking looked very English. The fourth woman of the party was wearing a brownish tweed coat and skirt. She was more petite than the blonde in grey and older, having shortish brown hair. None of the four women were wearing make-up and all were looking pale and tired.

He added, 'As this was the first time that I had seen women at this camp the occurrence clearly stamped itself in my mind.'[1]

The fourth woman of the party, the 'more petite' and 'older' one, is the one who left the fewest traces. Some facts are known, but very little sense of her as an individual remains. No husband or parent, no close friend remembered her for the record. And

much of what record there might have been in the impressions of
those who interviewed her for SOE vanished along with so
much else as a result of the files having, according to the Foreign
Office, 'suffered at the end of the war from unsystematic weeding
and from an accidental fire'.[2] Almost everything thrown out,
burned up. Nothing left but a face in a photograph, a name on a
wall.

The name is Vera Leigh. On her birth certificate, her surname
was given as Glass. Born in Leeds on 17 March 1903, she had
been abandoned as a baby and adopted while still an infant by
Eugene Leigh, an American married to an Englishwoman. At
some point after her husband's death, the widow of Eugene
Leigh married Albert Clark, whose son V.A.D. Clark thus
became Vera's half-brother, although not a blood relative. He
became her friend and, when they were grown-ups, her confidant.
When it became necessary to name a next-of-kin, it was Clark
she chose.

Eugene Leigh was a well-known racehorse trainer, and Vera
grew up in and around the stables of Maisons Laffitte, the
fashionable racetrack near Paris. Clark later remembered that as
a child she had wanted to be a jockey when she grew up. In fact,
she moved from the world of racing to the equally fashionable
one of the *haute couture*. After gaining experience as a *vendeuse*
at the house of Caroline Reboux, she went into partnership with
two friends to found the '*grande maison*' Rose Valois in the
Place Vendôme in 1927, when she was only twenty-four. In the
prewar decade she moved in the sophisticated social scene of *le
tout* Paris. When Paris fell in June 1940 she left for Lyon to join
her fiancé of seven years, a M. Charles Sussaix, the managing
director of a Portuguese-owned film company. Her intention had
been to find a way, with his help, to get from there to England,
but she became involved with one of the underground escape
lines guiding fugitive Allied servicemen out of the country and it
was not until some time in 1942 that she herself took the route
over the Pyrenees into Spain. There, like most of those who
made the journey successfully – usually with the help of guides

who knew the route because they had been practised smugglers – she spent some months in the internment camp at Miranda de Ibro, some forty miles south of Bilbao, a place which was often described as nothing short of a concentration camp. Released through the efforts of a British embassy official, she was helped to make her way via Gibraltar to England.

She arrived in London at the end of the year with the intention of offering her services for the war effort and was soon identified by SOE. She struck her recruiter as 'a smart businesswoman'. The interviewer noted further, 'It is clear that commerce is her first allegiance'. But the authorities saw no reason to doubt her motives and her prewar life in Paris and her perfect French seemed to make her a natural for the job. She agreed to break off contact with Sussaix and was accepted for training.[3]

Her preliminary training report described Vera Leigh as supple, active and keen, confident and capable, 'a very satisfactory person to teach' and one with 'a very pleasant personality'. Her Commandant's report said she was 'full of guts', had kept up with the men and was 'about the best shot in the party'. He found her 'dead keen' and noted that she was greatly respected, had an 'equable nature', and according to him was a 'plumb woman for this work'. One of her instructors later remembered that she had a hard time dealing with maps and diagrams, but was 'extremely good with her fingers; she could do fiddling jobs with charges and wires and all that remarkably quickly and neatly'. He thought she might have been connected with the fashion business. 'She was very interested in clothes, and hated her hideous khaki uniform.'

She was forty years old when she returned to France as Ensign Vera Leigh of the FANY-ATS.

The FANYs had their beginnings around the turn of the century, at the height of the Edwardian era, which would prove to be the twilight of Empire. In 1898, during Britain's campaign in the Sudan, a wounded sergeant-major serving in one of Lord Kitchener's regiments had the idea of organizing a troop of mounted young women to supplement the existing field ambulance corps by riding out with the soldiers to tend to the wounded on the battlefield.

By 1907 he had succeeded in organizing the First Aid Nursing Yeomanry, the first women's voluntary corps in Great Britain. A contemporary newspaper reporter described its members, trained in riding and in first aid, as 'aristocratic amazons in arms'.[4]

Early recruits were drawn mainly from the upper-middle classes. They were women who could afford to volunteer their time and in many cases owned their own horses. In old photographs, standing erect in their long-skirted leather-belted quasi-military uniforms, their expressions and bearing suggest that many of them were anticipating feminist goals while still chafing under the restrictions on what were then considered proper roles for women in society. It would prove an ideal compromise, this opportunity to function in what had up to now been considered exclusively and unequivocally a male sphere.

During the First World War, FANYs broke the barrier that had kept women from serving in any capacity but nursing and began driving ambulances. By the end of what they were calling the Great War they were serving as drivers for government and press officials. During the years between the wars FANY training concentrated on the emergent field of signalling, including telephonic and wireless communications, and in the next national emergency, the general strike of 1926, FANYs participated in providing essential services in transport and communications, again demonstrating to a sceptical military establishment what women could do.

By the end of the decade they had won official recognition as an army volunteer transport unit. No longer confined to nursing and hardly yeomen, it was decided that their now obsolete acronym should be replaced by WTS, for Women's Transport Service. It didn't stick. Among themselves, and even in official documents, the name remained FANY, although when they served with Americans in the war still to come, the letters would have to be pronounced in full to avoid the unfortunate meaning of 'fanny' in US slang.

When Britain became mobilization-minded at the time of the Munich crisis in 1938, the 'Women's Transport Service (FANY)', as it was now known, became part of the Auxiliary Territorial Service, the ATS. They wore shorter skirts now in place of the voluminous ones in which their predecessors in the earlier war had sat astride their horses, but they were still called FANYs, they were still universally referred to as 'girls', and they still drove staff automobiles and jeeps as well as ambulances.

During the 1939–45 war years they were known as FANY-ATS and wore the four old traditional letters on their armbands. Their wartime headquarters was in the vicarage of St Paul's, Knightsbridge, in Wilton Place, where a plaque commemorating those who died in wartime service would later be placed on a wall in the churchyard. During those years they were a neighbourhood fixture. The local saddler managed to supply scarce leather for their uniform belts and the proprietress of the corner tobacco stand was somehow or other still able to produce their favourite brands of cigarettes. The local contractor would always turn up promptly to repair any damage when the bombs hit.

On the home front FANYs worked in canteens, hospitals, recreation centres, and military headquarters. They did office work, served tea and smiles, talked about home with lonely recruits. Overseas, they served in Italy, Greece, Finland, and as far afield as Africa. But their most dramatic wartime role was their connection with the country-sections – particularly F Section – of SOE.

It began with a kind of extension of the Old Boy to the Old Girl Network. In 1940 SOE's Colonel Colin Gubbins (who as General Gubbins would become chief of SOE in September 1943), from his headquarters in the 'Inter-Services Research Bureau' in Baker Street, made contact with the commandant of the FANYs through a former neighbour of his in Scotland now working as her assistant. He wanted to know if she could provide some personnel for highly secret work. In the beginning it would involve serving as escorting officers to agents in training, sometimes even making their practice parachute jumps with them; working on producing passports, ration cards, and other forged documents for use in occupied Europe; packing arms and sabotage equipment; and the typing, filing, and other routine jobs that kept the Baker Street offices running.

And eventually, the more than fifty training schools maintained by the various country-sections of SOE in mansions and estates throughout the English countryside were staffed by FANYs, who formed a kind of domestic service corps. There they did the cooking and cleaning that servants had done for them before the war, work they took on in the interests of security to avoid employing outsiders in the secret training schools of SOE. In addition to housekeeping, in the last hours before agents went across the Channel they provided companionship and comfort.

Lest they sound too much like geishas, it was understood that the job of these 'young ladies of good family', recruited, like members of a club, by invitation, was to provide sympathy but not intimacy. They were remembered by one veteran of the Norwegian Section's training school as 'always amiable – and unapproachable'. A paratrooper in the Polish Home Army remembered the FANYs at the waiting station where he spent his last days before leaving on a mission as 'likeable, cultured and friendly, hard-working and smiling,' and added that

> they created the relaxed happy atmosphere so necessary before the coming adventure . . . In the daytime they cooked, swept, put the place in order, or drove cars. In the evening, exquisite in their long gowns, they danced with us, tangos, fox-trots, waltzes and *obereks* and *kujawiaks* as well. Though they were young and attractive . . . we had no heart pangs over them. They remained in our memories as the pleasant and unaffected companions of our last days before the flight.[5]

By the end of the war over half of the FANYs were working for SOE and, no longer an exclusive province of the leisure classes, FANYs were being recruited at a rate of two hundred a month and were being paid for their services, like regular armed forces personnel.

The main operational work FANYs did during the Second World War was in signals, operating wireless sets, sending and transmitting, encoding and decoding messages to and from the field. By the summer of 1942 the coding section of SOE was entirely staffed by FANYs. It was tedious and exacting work, involving the not infrequent decoding of almost indecipherable messages, guessing at missing letters and garbled phrases, trying to figure out what an unclear word might mean from an equally ambiguous context, coping with the effects of interference, human and atmospheric. The average age of the signals FANYs was between nineteen and twenty.

It was in April 1942 that the War Cabinet made the decision to allow SOE to use women not just in auxiliary roles but in the field, since women would be able to move around more freely in an occupied country with forced conscription; it would be easier to find accommodations for them, since they would be less conspicuous, and easier to invent plausible cover stories for them.

It was an unprecedented decision, sending women – even volunteers – into places where they ran the risk of capture, brutal interrogation, torture, and death. It could probably not have been taken in full public view at the time, but SOE was a secret organization, and its decisions were made in secret. Afterwards, the accomplishments of the women agents would be considered a proof of what women could do. Then, nobody knew about these except the recruiters themselves and those they invited to become members of a little band of special operatives to be sent overseas to face danger and risk death.

Some of those who accepted the invitation were volunteers from the Women's Auxiliary Air Force. Others, like Vera Leigh, were civilians specially enlisted for a role in occupied territory because they spoke the language and knew the country. With no previous military affiliation, they were enlisted as FANYs, a convenience which provided them with a uniform as a cover for curious friends and relatives during their training in Britain. To anyone who asked what they were doing they could say they were being trained as staff drivers or for other support services.

Before going overseas, some were given, in addition to their FANY status, honorary commissions in the WAAF. It was hoped that rank as officers in the regular services would improve their chances to be treated as prisoners of war, and not as spies, if they were captured in the plain clothes they would be wearing in the field.

The moons of April to September 1943 were characterized by Hugh Verity of 161 Squadron as 'wonderful moons for the Lysanders'.[6] On the night of 13/14 May, Ensign Vera Leigh of the FANY was landed by Lysander on a moon-drenched field in the Cher valley, a few miles east of Tours. She was one of four agents landed that night in two planes received by Henri Déricourt, F Section's air movements officer in northern France. The others were Julienne Aisner (later Mme Besnard), an old friend of Déricourt's who had been sent to London to be trained and was returning to work as Déricourt's courier in his pick-up operation code-named FARRIER; Sidney Jones, an organizer and arms instructor who had been Elizabeth Arden's representative in France before the war; and Marcel Clech, a wireless operator who before the war had been a Breton taxi-driver. Vera Leigh was to be their courier and the three of them – Jones, Clech and Leigh – were to form a sub-circuit known as INVENTOR, to work with the Paris-based PROSPER circuit. When the two planes took off again a few minutes after landing, one of them was carrying a passenger. The agent on his way back to England for briefing was Francis Suttill, the head of PROSPER.

The instructions of the INVENTOR (most French Section circuits were code-named for occupations or professions) group were to sever contact with their reception committee as soon as possible and make their way to Paris to a safe house in Neuilly-sur-Seine, where they would receive further instructions.[7] Jones was given a password to use in contacting Henri Frager, the agent who headed another circuit in the PROSPER domain, this one known as DONKEYMAN to the British. It was '*Je viens de la part de Célestin*' (I've been sent by Célestin), to which the reply was, '*Ah, oui, le marchand de vin*' (Oh, yes, the wine merchant).

Each of them carried some francs and the necessary papers and had been briefed in the security measures to be observed and the wireless operator's orders stressed 'that you should only be on the air when necessary and your transmissions should be as short as possible. You will encode the messages yourself.' They were also given an address in Lisbon through which to contact London 'should you be in difficulties.' The instructions given to Clech, the wireless operator, reminded him that 'if, through any unforeseen circumstances, [Jones] should disappear, you will advise us and receive further instructions direct from us'.

Vera Leigh had chosen the name of Simone to be used among her fellow agents in the field, had been given the code name of Almoner to be used in communications with London, and the cover identity of Suzanne Chavanne, a milliner's assistant. With papers in her new name and under cover of her new job she moved around Paris and in and out of the city as far away as the Ardennes in the east, carrying messages from Jones to his various wireless operators and to Frager. The reports she sent to her superiors in London were described as 'extremely cheerful'. She moved into an apartment in the elegant Sixteenth Arrondissement, made rendezvous routinely at cafés frequented by other agents, and took up life as a Parisienne again.

The security measures that had been drummed into F Section agents during training were based on the expectation that they would be going to a strange and dangerous place. Instead, Vera Leigh found herself back in a city that, while changed in some ways by the occupation, seemed less unfamiliar than might have been expected. It may for that reason have seemed less dangerous to her than it really was. The familiarity was apparent. The dangers were not.

Paris was still unmistakably Paris, despite the German uniforms on the streets and in the shops and restaurants and cafés and the frequent identity checks in the Métro. The bicycle had replaced the automobile as the standard means of transportation, and *vélo-taxis* resembling the rickshaws of the Orient transported ladies and gentlemen who could afford to be pedalled around town by someone else. The few cars on the street were the *gazogènes*, which ran on natural gas, or the imposing front-wheel-drive Citroëns and occasional Mercedes saloons carrying Nazi officials. The Métro ran on schedule until curfew time, when anyone still out was liable to be picked up and taken to the police station. Those who minded their own business and got home by curfew time had nothing to worry about. The occasional glimpse of an unmarked black car disappearing around a corner or of a pair of leather-trenchcoated men entering a building had nothing to do with them. And most Parisians minded their own business.

There was food and clothing rationing, to be sure, and life was no picnic for the poor, but for those who could afford them, there were plenty of black-market restaurants, where a good meal could be had for ready cash, and there were plenty of customers. Elsewhere the good life went on where it always had. While the Germans on the whole preferred Maxim's, those who had the means could enjoy the famous duck, accompanied by *asperges au sauce hollandaise*, at the Tour d'Argent, or dine equally well at the Grand Véfour, Fouquet's, Lapérouse, the Pré Catalan, which Sartre and Simone de Beauvoir frequented, and any number of other such renowned establishments. Hermes, Cartier, and Bouchéron were doing a brisk business in jewellery and watches, and luxury goods of all kinds were available behind the façades of the Faubourg Saint-Honoré or on the auction block at the Salle Drouöt. For German officers who might not know their way around such possibilities, there were plenty of Frenchwomen willing to help them spend their money.

Huge fortunes were being made by the black marketeers, called BOF for *beurre, oeufs, fromage* (butter, eggs, cheese), and by the war-profiteers who operated as purchasing agents for the Germans, wheeling and dealing in materials and machinery needed on the eastern front. Some of the profits went back into the city's economy, through the doors of Balenciaga, Nina Ricci, and Dior, among others who carried on with the *haute couture* as usual. The wives and mistresses of prosperous citizens and of German officers needed the appropriate little something to wear to fashionable soirées, where they might find themselves seated next to Coco Chanel, who lived with a German officer at the Ritz throughout the occupation and could be heard at exclusive dinner parties inveighing against the Jews.

Other famous names were equally in evidence. Paul Valéry went on lecturing at the Collège de France. Colette and Jean Cocteau went on writing for the collaborationist press, which kept the newspaper kiosks full of papers and magazines, like the appropriately named ubiquitous weekly *Je Suis Partout*, whose common theme was a virulent antisemitism. Among the writers who remained active under the occupation were Simenon and Marcel Aymé. Sartre had no qualms about publishing with the German censor's official stamp of approval. Braque exhibited at the Salon d'Automne of 1943, while Picasso worked away in his studio on the Quai Saint-Augustin. If any of them were particularly troubled by any of the policies of the occupation, they took pains not to hurt the feelings of the occupiers by saying so publicly at the time.

Sometimes it seemed that only the Jews had left – and they had no choice.

The handsome façades of the city, which had seen no fighting, were unchanged in appearance. Only the occupants within had been replaced. The apartments belonging to Jews, as well as their contents, were up for grabs. The occupiers had taken over the best hotels in the best neighbourhoods, with the military headquartered in the Majestic and the Raphael near the Étoile and the intelligence staff in the Lutétia near the Luxembourg Gardens. Other branches of Reich officialdom were located in what had previously been French official buildings, such as the combined headquarters of the SS, its intelligence branch the SD, the Gestapo, and the military police, in what had once been the Sureté Nationale, the Ministry of the Interior, in the rue des Saussaies, or in what had once been luxurious private residences, like the Gestapo's impressive premises in adjoining mansions on the Avenue Foch.

Ordinary French men and women passed these places, as they did the directional signs in German all around the city, with a shrug. They were of interest primarily to those few *résistants* – and they were very few indeed until the invasion made liberation appear imminent – who, like SOE agents, had good reason to fear being brought there, and to that vast army of French informers who did business with the Germans there. Denouncing other Frenchmen – Jews, in particular those whose disappearance might release desirable property, as well as *résistants*, fugitives from the army or from forced labour in Germany, and those overheard criticizing the policies of the Nazis – became so popular a profession that it acquired its own name: *délation*. For those who did not become active *V-Männer*, anonymous letter-writing was the most favoured occupation.

Still, there were no overt signs of conflict. Not even the French-mandated yellow star was much in evidence, most of the Jews having been transported east by now, the French police having rounded them up and shipped them off. Paris was pretty much what the Germans had intended – a showpiece, the same city of light, illuminated by many of the same stars of fashion, society, the arts, publishing, and academia, only under new and enlightened management.

David Pryce-Jones summed it all up in his book *Paris in the Third Reich*: 'Paris under occupation remained more tranquil than it had ever been in the years of peace.' Until the eve of the liberation in August of 1944, there had been only one public demonstration of 'a French national spirit in distress'. It took place on the anniversary of the end of the First World War, when a few students placed wreaths on the Tomb of the Unknown Soldier at the Arc de Triomphe. There were no casualties, although a man who was probably a bystander was executed as an example. Except for that single instance, Parisians had accepted the occupation and adapted to it. 'Nothing had taken place', as Pryce-Jones noted, 'that can be called resistance.'[8]

Little wonder then that a Parisienne like Vera Leigh felt confident to move about the city in which she had spent so many years, seeing so much that seemed unchanged, almost *normale*. The world of fashion she had known before the war went on uninterruptedly. Parisiennes were still shopping for stylish hats to wear to the races at Auteuil, Longchamps and Maisons Laffitte. She installed herself in a series of apartments, first on the rue Lauriston, a few doors away from the headquarters of the notorious Bony-Lafont organization of gangster collabora-tors, then in the rue Pergolèse, round the corner from the Gestapo headquarters on Avenue Foch, and finally at 11 bis rue Marbeau, a stone's throw from the premises of both SD and Abwehr officials. She began to frequent the same hairdresser she had used before the war, who certainly knew that she was not a milliner's assistant named Suzanne Chavanne.

She had known many people in Paris; there were old friends and business acquaintances, even relatives. She was bound to run into some of them; it was inevitable that she would be recognized now and then. When she came face to face with her sister's husband in the Gare Saint-Lazare one day, she pretended at first not to know him, then suddenly threw her arms round him. The chance encounter led to the discovery that he too was involved in clandestine activity on behalf of the Allies. He had undertaken to hide fugitive Allied airmen in an apartment near the Madeleine and pass them on to an escape line that would try to get them over the Pyrenees across the frontier into Spain. In her spare time Vera began escorting some of these downed fliers, who spoke no French, through the streets from the safe house to their next point of contact on the line.

She spent time with Julienne Besnard, who was installed in an imposing building in a courtyard off the Place des Ternes from which she ran her husband's business, an effective cover for her activity as Déricourt's courier. Vera frequently met other agents at a café on the other side of the Place des Ternes, a short walk from the Place de l'Étoile in the Seventeenth. It was there in the Chez Mas, on 30 October, in the company of Jones' bodyguard, that she was arrested. Taken to the bleak prison at Fresnes a few miles outside Paris, she was registered as Suzanne Chavonne and placed in Cell 410 of the Troisième Section Femmes. She had been taught in training to hold out for forty-eight hours after capture in order to give fellow agents a chance to vacate any premises and destroy any records she might be forced to reveal, but it is almost certain she had no need to do so. There was nothing her captors didn't already know about her activities.

CHAPTER 6

Diana: An Expatriate Returns

The third girl, as Brian Stonehouse remembered her, 'was middle height, rather stocky, with shortish fair hair tied with a multi-coloured ribbon, aged about twenty-eight. She was wearing a grey flannel short "finger tip" length swagger coat with a grey skirt which I remember thinking looked very English.'

Diana Rowden was in fact the most typically English of the group, a girl who had grown up in France without becoming French. She was born on the 31 January 1915 to Christian Rowden, née Maitland-Makgill-Chrichton, and her husband, who 'pushed off', as Diana's cousin Mark Chetwynd-Stapylton put it many years later, leaving his wife to bring up Diana and her two brothers, Maurice and Kit.[1] Her cousin remembers being told to be nice to the three Rowden children when they came to visit. He remembers games of hide and seek in the garden, bicycle rides on Berkhamstead Common, and 'eyeing each other across the table at mealtimes, but without observing them closely with a view to the future.' Sixty years later he was left with a faint impression of Diana as 'a bit of a tomboy', reddish-haired, freckled, with slightly protruding teeth.[1]

Christian Rowden was one of many English people, unencumbered by the obligations of a regular job or profession, who found in the years between the two world wars that a small income went further in the France of those days than it did at home. In the early twenties she moved herself and her children to the south of France and took up residence on the Riviera, where Diana and her brothers spent much of their time on the beach, fishing and boating, swimming and gliding. A fellow expatriate remembers a wet Sunday in 1923 in Menton, when 'a nice looking young woman came into the row in front of me in St John's Church with three children in kilts' and recognized them as the inhabitants of a villa nearby, 'towards the Italian frontier close to the sea.'[2] The four of them lived for part of the year in rented quarters there and at St Jean Cap Ferrat and the rest of the time drifting along the French and Italian Mediterranean coast on a yacht named the *Sans Peur*, looked after by an Italian manservant named Vincenzo.

After the war one of Diana's brothers rescued Vincenzo and brought him to Hampshire, where he continued to garden and cook and clean for Mrs Rowden in a tall white building on a hill that had once been a semaphore station, what her nephew described as 'a rather weird house, Telegraph House, near Binstead, one of those somewhat gaunt edifices built in order to watch out for Napoleon's attack on the British coast'. There in her later years, overweight and with a weak heart, Mrs Rowden took to her bed, relying on Vincenzo to cope with daily life on her behalf. Some time after the war her younger son, Kit, had committed suicide. The elder, Maurice, blamed his mother for his brother's death and refused to have anything to do with her or with anyone else in the family from then on. Attempts to contact him through his solicitor when his mother lay dying came to nothing. Mark Chetwynd-Stapylton says, 'He simply didn't want to know'; and adds, 'a sad family, the Rowdens.'

Mrs Rowden seems to have been something of an eccentric, remembered by her nephew as 'amusing even if possessing a somewhat caustic – and biting – wit and not much worried over what she said and to whom.' When living in the South of France she was known to the locals, according to her sister, as 'the mad Englishwoman'. Still, she was mindful enough of her parental responsibilities, as Mark Chetwynd-Stapylton later put it, to decide that her daughter should receive a proper English education to finish off the rather haphazard schooling she had had at St Remo and Cannes, and in the late twenties brought her brood back to England and settled them at Hadlow Down, near May-field in Hampshire.

Diana was sent to The Manor House, a school set beneath a long low line of hills in Limpsfield, Surrey. A girl who shared a room with her there remembered the place later in terms of 'the smell of ink and chalk dust, the lazy droning of bees around the flower beds, goal posts pointing white and bleak towards a winter sky.'³ Diana hated it. In 1932 the school friend found her at seventeen 'one of the most diffident, most reticent people I had ever met.'⁴ She seemed 'shy, neat and urban.'⁵

The friend was Elizabeth Nicholas, who would write a book about her twenty-five years later. Despite, like Diana's cousin, not having observed her closely with a view to the future, her friend remembered how bitterly Diana had resented the restrictions of life at school. 'She was of it, but never part of it. She was,' she thought later, 'too mature for us. We were still schoolgirls in grubby white blouses concerned with games and feuds and ha-ha jokes. She was already adult, and withdrawn from our diversions; none of us, I think, ever knew her.'⁶ She was amazed to learn years later from Mrs Rowden about Diana's early years 'as a sea urchin', napping on the deck of the *Sans Peur* with a line tied around her big toe to wake her if a fish bit, gutting her catch 'with cheerful competence, marketing, carousing, sailing a small boat with reckless skill.' It seemed to Elizabeth Nicholas that the change in Diana's personality from spontaneity to reserve was explained by the change of scene. In her white bed in the low-ceilinged, wooden-beamed dormitory room they shared in a Surrey manor, Diana had longed for the life she had led in France, 'for the yacht and the sea and the warm sun of the Mediterranean and her raffish, careless, unpredictable companions.'⁷

When Diana was considered sufficiently educated, if not entirely finished, she and Mrs Rowden left the two boys at school in England and returned to France, where Diana enrolled at the Sorbonne and tried her hand at free-lance journalism. Then the war broke out and Diana volunteered to serve with the French Red Cross. She was assigned to the Anglo-American Ambulance Corps of the British Expeditionary Force, and in the confusion and panic of the early months of 1940 mother and daughter lost touch with each other. Mrs Rowden managed to reach England in a coalboat, but Diana chose to stay behind until mid-1941, when she crossed into Spain and made her way back to England through Portugal. Reunited, the two women took a small flat in Cornwall Mews in Kensington, off the Cromwell Road not far from the Natural History Museum, and Diana began to look for some kind of work that would make use of her knowledge of France, which included a familiarity with Normandy and Brittany in addition to the French and Italian Riviera, and her command of French, which was fluent if imperfect. No Frenchman hearing her speak would have taken her for French, but the years growing up in France and the subsequent drilling of a tyrannical French schoolmistress had certainly prepared her for any kind of translating or interpreting. In addition, she was fluent in Spanish and Italian.

Impatient and frustrated when nothing that seemed useful enough came her way, she enlisted in the WAAF in early September. A few days later she received an offer for just the kind of work she had been looking for. Harry Sporborg, a member of the SOE senior staff who became Gubbins' deputy when he was made head of SOE, had seen her file and put in a request for her as a secretary. But the opportunity had come too late and Diana went off to begin her military training. Three months later she was commissioned as Assistant Section Officer for Intelligence duties and went to work for the Department of the Chief of Air Staff. Her next posting, in July of 1942, was to Moreton-in-the-Marsh, where she was promoted to Section Officer.

Some time the following spring Diana was sent to the RAF convalescent home at Torquay to recuperate from a minor operation. There she met Squadron Leader William Simpson, OBE, DFC, who had been shot down over France in May 1940 and had been undergoing a series of operations in an attempt to repair his severe burns and multiple injuries. Bill Simpson seemed an embodiment of the spirit that made legends of the young pilots who fought the Battle of Britain. At the time, in between hospitalizations, he was working for the French Section of SOE. He and Diana, whom he later described as 'a girl of striking character', had time to talk during the long hours at Torquay, and she told him how devoted she was to France and how desperately she wanted to get back there and be part of a resistance effort to prepare for the eventual invasion. Back in London, he told some of his colleagues in Baker Street about her.

Early in March Diana received a letter inviting her to a meeting with an officer of F Section.[8] It was a preliminary interview, and the interviewer was favourably impressed. It was duly noted that she was 'very anxious to return to France and work against the Germans' and, after she had been seen by other members of the F Section staff, it was decided that she would have the chance she had been looking for. She was officially posted to Air Intelligence 10, actually seconded to SOE, on 18 March 1943, and immediately sent off for training.

Her training report described her as 'not very agile', but with 'plenty of courage', and 'physically quite fit'. One of her best subjects was fieldcraft, in which she 'did some excellent stalks'. She was 'a very good shot, not at all gun-shy. Grenade throwing, very good'. Her instructor found her 'very conscientious' and 'a pleasant student to instruct'. The Commandant's report described her as 'a strange mixture. Very intelligent in many ways but very slow in learning any new subject.' She had trouble with technical details and her signalling was described as 'a grief to herself and others, not worth while persevering with as it only discourages her. She hates being beaten by any subject, so must have got through a lot of hate down here.' He concluded, 'I think she has really enjoyed the course, and could be useful.'

On the 9 June 1943 Squadron Officer Diana Hope Rowden, WAAF received the orders for her mission and a week later, on the night of 16/17 June, she stepped out of a Lysander on a moonlit meadow in the Loire valley a few miles north-east of Angers. Within minutes two other new arrivals, Cecily Lefort and Noor Inayat Khan, had landed. The three women, who were being sent to operate as couriers for the organizers of various circuits in different parts of the country, were met by a reception committee organized by F Section's air movements officer, Henri Déricourt, and quickly spirited away towards their destinations.

Diana was bound for the area of the Jura mountains south-east of Dijon and just west of the Swiss border to work with the organizer of the ACROBAT circuit, John Starr, whose field name was Bob. She was given his circuit password, '*La pêche rend-elle* [*sic*] *par ici?*' (Is the fishing good around here?) to which the reply was, '*Oui, j'ai pris dix poissons la dernière fois que j'y suis allé*' (Yes, I caught ten fish last time I went). The number of fish would correspond to the time of the month, *une dizaine* from the first to the tenth etc. She was to make contact through an *épicerie* in St Amour. She was given a personal code to use if it should be necessary to communicate with London by means other than through Bob and his wireless operator and a Lisbon address as a contact should she be 'in difficulties' and unable to advise London directly. Her papers were in her cover name of Juliette Thérèse Rondeau. Her name in the field among fellow agents was Paulette and her code name for use in messages to London was Chaplain.

She arrived at the Hôtel du Commerce on the town square of St Amour, where the proprietress winked at the formalities and did not ask her to sign the register, and was given a small dark room in the back that had access to a roof should it be necessary to leave in a hurry without being seen. Then she was introduced by Starr to his 'pianist', wireless operator John Young, a blue-eyed black-haired young Scotsman who had met his French wife while travelling for an insurance company. Young, who was known as Gabriel, was ensconced with his set in an attic high up in the Château of Andelot-les-St-Amour, a tall medieval castle with circular stone towers on one of the hills overlooking the town. The only light in the old castle after dark was supplied by candles, and with no electricity Young had to transmit on batteries.

Young was a proficient W/T operator, but no one could have mistaken him for French. He spoke with a Northern accent so pronounced that, according to Starr, on the night they landed, a member of the reception committee heard Young speak a few words in French and said, '*Eh bien, mon vieux, il n'y a pas se tromper. Il vaudrait mieux que tu parles le moins possible*' (Look here, old fellow, let's not kid ourselves. It would be best for you to talk as little as possible).[9] His accent made it impossible for him to travel about unless he was with someone else who could do the talking for both of them. That became one of Diana's many responsibilities.

It was a hectic time in the area, and Diana travelled constantly, mostly by bicycle over the neighbouring mountain roads bordered by pines, but occasionally delivering instructions to agents as far afield as Marseille, Lyon, Besançon, Montbéliard, and even Paris, and bringing their messages back to Young for transmission. On one of her trips to Marseille the German police boarded the train and began inspecting papers. She locked herself in the WC until they had passed through her car. She got to know the local maquis, who later described her as without fear – *sans peur*. She went out at night to meet local members of the resistance in the moonlit fields, setting flares and shining flashlights to guide in the planes with parachute drops of arms and ammunition. Some of the explosives they received were used to sabotage the Peugeot factory at Sochaux, near the town of Montbéliard, which had been turning out tank turrets for the Wehrmacht and engine parts for the Luftwaffe.

This was a unique operation, the brainchild of Harry Rée, an agent known as César, who had worked with Starr, Young, and Diana Rowden in ACROBAT before taking charge of the nearby STOCKBROKER circuit to the north-east of them in the vicinity of Belfort and Montbéliard. The Peugeot works were located near the railway station in a heavily populated part of town. In mid-July an RAF attack had missed the target but caused hundreds of deaths among the civilian population.

Given the limits of precision bombing at the time, Rée thought local sabotage of the plant, while involving considerable risk for those directly involved, would be a more efficient and ultimately less risky way to put the factory out of production. And he added to this strategy a tactic that was pure inspiration. He got in touch with a member of the Peugeot family who was a director of the firm, and whom he had reason to think was sympathetic to the Allied cause, and put a proposition to him. He pointed out that the RAF could be expected to try again, in which case there was no way of estimating the damage a raid might do. On the other hand, if M. Peugeot would agree to cooperate in the sabotage effort, damage might be kept to a minimum and casualties eliminated.

To satisfy any doubt on M. Peugeot's part as to his authority to make such arrangements, Rée proposed that M. Peugeot give him a message of his own devising and promised that it would be read within a specified time on the BBC. When he heard his words among the *messages personnels* broadcast on the Foreign Programme a few nights later, he agreed to the plan. Rée was introduced to the machine-shop foreman and given a guided tour of the factory. Shortly afterwards a well-placed charge resulted in Rée's innovative arrangement putting an end to war production at Sochaux.

Then, barely a month after Diana's arrival, Starr was arrested, betrayed by a double agent who had infiltrated the circuit. The château was blown, the St Amour area was unsafe and suddenly Young and Diana were on the run. The British officers who had come to organize and give support to the resistance had found friends in the neighbourhood, and arrangements were made for Diana to hide in a little bistro and shop at Epy, a tiny hamlet in the hills three miles down the road from the château. While she was there she helped out in the shop. The owner later told Elizabeth Nicholas, 'I knew that she was not accustomed to do such things, *enfin*, she was a woman of refinement and education, but she was without vanity. She said it would help her not to be bored.'[10] After three weeks at Epy Diana joined Young in what would be their last hideout.

Among those who were willing to help the resistance was the family Janier-Dubry, which consisted of an elderly widow and her son and daughter-in-law of the family name, and her two daughters and their husbands, the Juifs and the Paulis. Together they ran a sawmill outside Clairvaux-les-Lacs, a village about ten miles from the town of Lons-le-Saunier.

At the outset of the Second World War France was still a rural nation. More than half the population still worked the land on family farms or lived in small towns and villages. Many of the country people, the men and women of the farms and villages, acted decently. Asked to hide an escaped prisoner, a downed flyer, a radio set, arms and ammunition, many of them said yes, and then found they were committed further and kept going. It was a matter of individual conscience. They knew the risks. Reprisals were savage. Many of them were caught, arrested, and many died in deportation.

Her son's family lived with the widow Janier-Dubry in one house near the mill and her two daughters with their families in another. In August Diana and Young were established in the house of the Juifs. Young was no stranger there. It was important, given the Germans' capabilities in radio detection, not to transmit from the same place regularly. The Juifs had been letting him transmit from their house since April, knowing what they risked if he was caught at it or his set was found there.

Since her description had undoubtedly been circulated, Diana dyed her hair and changed the way she wore it, got rid of the clothes she'd been seen wearing and borrowed some others. She also dropped the name of Paulette and assumed the name Marcelle. The family let it be known that their cousin Marcelle had come to recuperate in the country from a serious illness. It was a precaution they felt was not really necessary. Here in the countryside everyone was behind the resistance. People would mind their own business.

Still, Diana lay low at first, leaving the house only to walk in the woods surrounding the sawmill, where, to the chagrin of her hosts, she would occasionally smoke an unmistakably English cigarette in her holder. Given even a few seconds' warning and with any luck at all Young and Diana were confident that, if the Germans came, they could escape into the thick forest and hide there. Meanwhile, she helped around the house and in the kitchen, peeling vegetables for Madame Juif, who remarked to Elizabeth Nicholas afterward that 'one could see she was not accustomed to such work, but it was her wish to be one with us, not to add to my burdens, to be helpful.'[11] The children loved her. She joined in their games and went tobogganing with them down the log slide behind the house, and to Madame Juif she seemed as tough as a man and as tireless as a child.

Around the middle of November Young received a message from London informing him that a new agent was on his way to join them. His code name was Benoit. There was considerable interest in the prospect of news from home, perhaps letters from relatives, and word of what was going on in the world beyond Clairvaux. They would hear about London, the outfit, the progress of the war. And around 7.30 on the morning of the eighteenth, Diana, from behind a curtain at the window of the Juif house, saw a man walking down the road towards the house of the Paulis, who had been designated as his first contact. He was wearing the fur-trimmed flyer's jacket called a *canadienne*. He identified himself as Benoit, producing instructions hidden in a matchbox, and handed Young a letter from his wife, whose unmistakable handwriting provided the most impeccable of credentials.

Having established his bona fides, the new arrival announced his intention of returning to Lons-le-Saunier to retrieve a suitcase he had left there. M. Janier-Dubry offered to drive him there and Diana went with them. In Lons they met Henri Clerc, a *résistant* from St Amour, and had a drink with him at the Café

Strasbourg, one of the circuit's mail drops. They returned around six that evening and were chatting with Madame Juif, who was cooking dinner, when the door burst open and the room filled with Feldgendarmerie, the German military police, armed with machine guns. Outside, the house was surrounded by police cars.

Diana, Young and the newcomer were handcuffed and taken to Lons. Around midnight the false Benoit, as he later came to be known, returned to the Juif house with some of the Germans and confronted the family at gunpoint, demanding the wireless set and the precious crystals that made it operable. He fired into the walls and furniture while the Germans tore up the house searching, but nothing was found. Young had hidden the set, which was spirited away later by local members of the circuit still at large, and Madame Juif, when no one was looking, had taken the crystal out of Young's raincoat pocket hanging behind the door and managed to slip it under the mattress of her baby's crib.

In the end the family got off relatively easily. Everyone was interrogated repeatedly for a week and everything of any value – the family silver, trousseau linen, bits of jewellery – was carted off by the Germans when they left, taking only one member of the family with them. It was Madame Pauli, who, against all odds, was to return after the war from Ravensbrück.

When the war ended they expected Diana to come back to see them or at least to write. She liked to say that after the war she would return in her uniform and in a big American car and, instead of the laborious climb up to the château on foot, they would shoot up the hill like a rocket. They waited but they never heard from her again.

From Lons-le-Saunier Diana had been taken to Paris the next day. She remained at Gestapo headquarters in the Avenue Foch for two weeks and, on 5 December 1943, she was placed in a cell in the women's division of Fresnes, the grey fortress-like prison a few miles south of Paris.

Groups of political prisoners at Fresnes were occasionally

rounded up and taken to Paris for 'tribunal', interrogation at the looming dark building in the rue des Saussaies with its infamous cellars. On one of those occasions Peter Churchill, waiting under guard in a group of men and women, caught sight of Odette, who had been his courier and his lover when they were captured together at St Jorioz in the Haute-Savoie the previous April. She was to become SOE's most publicized heroine after the war and Churchill himself had an impressive postwar career writing and lecturing about his experiences in SOE.

Churchill later told how he had slipped up to Odette in the holding pen in order to exchange a few words when a girl he had never seen before but whom he described as 'patently English to her fingertips' placed herself between them and the guard so the guard would not see them in forbidden conversation. He was struck by 'the delicacy of feeling that made her turn about and face the German so as not to butt in on our privacy' and added, 'I could not imagine what this refined creature with reddish hair was doing in our midst.' He asked Odette who she was, and she told him, 'Diana Rowden, one of us.'[12]

CHAPTER 7

Andrée: A Working Girl Returns

Brian Stonehouse's description of the four women he had seen being brought into Natzweiler by two SS men on that July afternoon in 1944 had mentioned first a tall girl with very fair hair he remarked was not its natural colour; he noticed that the roots of her hair were dark. He remembered that she was wearing a black coat, French wooden-soled shoes, and was carrying what he remembered thinking at the time was 'a not very good fur coat' on her arm. The girl with the dyed hair and the cheap fur was Andrée Borrel, the first woman to be parachuted into occupied France and, in Elizabeth Nicholas' words, 'a towering figure in the history of the French resistance.'[1]

The only one of the four women who was born French – on 18 November 1919, just one week after the armistice that ended the First World War – she was the child of working-class parents who grew up on the outskirts of Paris and left school at fourteen to go to work for a *modiste* and learn the dressmaking trade.[2] After eighteen months she left and went to Paris, where she took a job as a shop assistant in a bakery, the Boulangerie Pujo in the Avenue Kléber, which runs through the fashionable Sixteenth from the Place de l'Étoile to the Trocadéro. Two years later she left to take another sales position in a shop called the Bazar d'Amsterdam in the rue Amsterdam, near the Gare St-Lazare. The new job gave her Sundays off so she could go bicycling, her favourite sport and one she was especially good at.

She was good at a number of sports. Her sister, Léone Borrel-Arend, described her as *un garçon manqué*. She had always wished to be a boy, had liked boys' games, and had boyish interests. She had a boy's physical strength and endurance. Her favourite pastimes besides bicycling were hiking and climbing, for which she liked to dress in trousers, not as common for women then as now, heavy sweaters and backpack.

When the war started Andrée Borrel was just twenty years old. She and her mother, a widow, left Paris like so many others and headed south to the unoccupied zone. They settled at Toulon on the Mediterranean coast, where they had friends, and at the end of October 1939 Andrée went to the local Red Cross to volunteer her services. She was enrolled in a crash course in nursing and, three weeks into the new year, she obtained the diploma that qualified her to serve as a nurse in the Association des Dames de France, first at a hospital at Nîmes, then at nearby Beaucaire, on the Rhône between Nîmes and Avignon, where she spent the spring months caring for wounded prisoners of war returning from Germany.

One of her fellow workers was a Lieutenant Maurice Dufour. When the hospital at Beaucaire was closed at the end of May, she and Dufour were both sent back to the Hôpital Complémentaire at Nîmes. Towards the end of July that hospital too was closed and Andrée was due to be transferred again when, at the request of Dufour, she was allowed to resign from what was in effect a quasi-military position. She immediately went to work for the underground organization with which he was involved, an escape line for evading British airmen shot down over France and escaped British prisoners of war.

Early in August she settled into a villa in Canet-Plage, on the Mediterranean just outside Perpignan, only a few miles from the Spanish border. Within a matter of weeks the villa had proved too small for the number of servicemen being hidden there until they could start on the journey back to England, and a larger one had to be found. It was known as the Villa Anita and Andrée kept busy organizing things there until, towards the end of December, word came that the line had been shattered. The section in the occupied zone had been betrayed by an informer. As a result the stream of men coming down from the north to be evacuated by sea or smuggled over the mountains could be expected to dry up and the Villa Anita would have to be abandoned, since it was highly probable that it was by now also *brulé* – burned.

Since the German invasion of Russia six months earlier and the United States' entrance into the war following the attack on Pearl Harbor earlier that month, two formidable powers had now joined forces with Britain, altering the prospects for eventual Allied victory considerably. Britain no longer stood alone against the Nazis. But to those like Andrée Borrel and Maurice Dufour who had been engaged in underground work from the beginning, England was still the fount of resistance. In the occupied north of France there was still little resistance to speak of, and in the capital itself Parisians were not finding it difficult to get along with their occupiers. In Vichy France things were even worse. The internment of Jews had begun and it was clear, to those who cared, that Vichy had become an active ally of Berlin. Some two thousand French men and women had followed de Gaulle to London, but he was still an unknown quantity, and anyone in France with any political sophistication knew that the game that was being played was as much about who would be in charge after the war as it was about winning it. Perhaps, cynics thought, even more so. And to anyone with working-class or even intellectually socialist leanings, de Gaulle was not at this point an obvious candidate to be the saviour of postwar France.

Andrée was taken in by the owner of the little Hôtel du Tennis, who had been using the cover of the hotel's restaurant to help her obtain food for the fugitives at the Villa Anita. She stayed there until mid-January 1942, when she travelled to Marseille to meet Dufour. She found a room in the modest Hôtel de Bruxelles on the rue Tapis Vert, not far from the old port, and spent two restless weeks waiting for Dufour to complete the arrangements for them to leave the country. On 1 February they left for Toulouse. They stayed at the Hôtel de Paris there for another two weeks and then, in mid-February, travelled back down to the Mediterranean coast to Banyuls-sur-Mer, a short distance south of their former headquarters at Canet-Plage and just a stone's throw from the frontier and the beginning of the rugged climb over the Pyrenees to Spain and from there to Portugal. When Dufour left for England at the end of March, Andrée went to work at the Free French Propaganda Office at the British Embassy. Finally, on 24 April 1942, she left from Lisbon by plane for England.

Soon after landing, like all arrivals from the Continent, she was taken to the Royal Patriotic School, the MI5 security clearance centre that had been established in what had once been known as the Royal Victoria Patriotic Asylum for the Orphan Daughters of Soldiers and Sailors Killed in the Crimean War. There she was interviewed by government officials whose job it was to vet the newcomers and identify any who seemed suspicious as well as any who seemed potentially useful. Their report concluded,

> Mlle Borrel's story seems perfectly straightforward. It is corroborated by Dufour who, on arriving in England, vouched for her. She is an excellent type of country girl, who has intelligence and seems a keen patriot. From a security point of view, I can find nothing against Mlle Borrel and recommend her release to the FFF.

The Free French Forces, however, were not enthusiastic about people who had worked for the British unless they were willing to make what amounted to an act of contrition, starting by confessing everything they had learned in their underground capacities – including such particulars as names and places as well as operational details. They would establish their loyalty to de Gaulle's organization by such an act of trust, but there remained the matter of their loyalty to those they had left behind and who trusted them. Dufour and Borrel had their reservations and refused. This did not endear them to the FFF staff at Duke Street, who bitterly resented the prerogative of British Intelligence to process refugees from France before they themselves had a chance to interrogate them, even though there was an agreement – not always scrupulously followed in the field – whereby F Section would not recruit from among French citizens.

What happened to Dufour as a result has, like so many events of those years, been in dispute for half a century. What is certain is that internecine rivalry between various branches of both Allied and German intelligence was so intense that it sometimes seemed unclear just who the enemy was – the other country or the other agency. While in occupied France the Abwehr, the old military intelligence organization, battled with the Sicherheitsdienst (SD), the Nazi Party intelligence service, for supremacy, a similar scenario was played out in London between MI6 and SOE and between the Free French and their British hosts. Reluctant to be placed in any role subordinate to British authority, the de Gaulle staff had succeeded in having a second French section created within SOE alongside F. It was known as RF and worked, through its British liaison officers, in cooperation with de Gaulle's lieutenant André Dewavrin, known as Colonel Passy (an appellation taken, like those of all his original senior staff, from the names of Paris Métro stations).

RF was mainly concerned with unifying resistance activities inside France, an objective with more political ramifications than that of F Section, which was concerned simply with starting up, training, and arming local resistance groups to perform acts of sabotage and be at the ready to support an eventual invasion. According to SOE's official historian, M.R.D. Foot, 'Inter-section jealousies within SOE were endemic; between F and RF sections they often raged with virulence.'[3] While this was true of the staff officers in London, F and RF Sections' agents worked together in the field with no such problems, cooperating rather than competing.

Dufour later maintained that when he refused to reveal what he considered confidential information about British-assisted underground activities in France, he was kidnapped and imprisoned in the basement of the Free French headquarters in Duke Street and brutally beaten, an account of events which was denied by Passy's men, who on their side maintained that Dufour was an MI6 agent attempting to infiltrate their organization. After claiming to have escaped from a French detention centre in the countryside just outside London with the help of a friend at Scotland Yard, Dufour filed suit against the Gaullists. In early June 1944, with D Day imminent, he agreed to an out-of-court settlement which granted him compensation and an opportunity to enlist in the Royal Canadian Air Force in time to participate in the liberation, all parties to the suit having agreed that it was hardly the kind of public relations France and de Gaulle needed at the moment.

Andrée had no such problems and no such adventures. To the staff of F Section she appeared to be just the ticket – a bona fide Frenchwoman who would be able to move around in France without arousing suspicion – and they grabbed her. She was happy enough to be grabbed, preferring the British to the Gaullists and straining to get back to underground work. In fact, as her sister saw it, she had found her *métier*, to be accepted in a man's world to do a man's work.

Her SOE interviewer commented:

Since arriving in London, she attempted to join the Corps Feminin of the Free French movement but they have made it a condition that she would give them all the intelligence concerning the organization for which she was working in France. This she refuses to do and apparently they refuse to employ her unless she does. I think that she would make an excellent addition to our own Corps Feminin and it should not be difficult to get her . . . She said that she was perfectly willing to let us have the information she refuses to give to the Free French.

She joined SOE on 15 May 1942, and a few days later began her training with the first group of women to be trained by SOE.

During the months of training she had a mentor in one of the older women in the group, Adèle le Chène, who felt that Andrée seemed to need guidance in certain things. 'She came *des petits gens*,' she said. 'She knew little of the world . . . She was not of great education.' So Madame le Chène undertook to educate her in such ways of the world as what behaviour was and was not considered becoming to an officer. Smoking in the street when in uniform, for example, was not *comme il faut*. Andrée was a quick learner. She was 'cool and calm and brave' and, according to her mentor and guide, 'a good comrade for men, an excellent friend, but nothing more, you understand?'[4]

Her training report proved how difficult it is to predict the character men and women will reveal in extreme situations. It assessed her as intelligent but lacking in imagination and judged that 'she has little organizing ability'. Wrong on that score, it was right on others: 'She is thoroughly tough and self-reliant with no nerves. Has plenty of common sense and is well able to look after herself in any circumstances . . . absolutely reliable . . . she should eventually develop into a first class agent.'

When the last obstacle course had been cleared and the decision made to send the newly trained agent into the field, she was sent to Ringway for parachute training. That course completed, she was ordered to report to the flat in Orchard Court. It was autumn of 1942.

Lieutenant Andrée Borrel of the FANY was to be the first woman dropped by parachute into occupied France. She was followed in a matter of seconds by another new trainee named Lise de Baissac, whose brother Claude was running the SCIEN-TIST circuit in the crucial Bordeaux area. The de Baissacs were ideally suited to operate as F Section agents in France. They were Mauritians, which meant that as residents of the island in the Indian Ocean they held British citizenship, while they had been brought up by French parents, educated in Paris and thus steeped in the language and culture of France.

Years later Lise de Baissac, now Madame Villameur, would remember the events surrounding that drop, on the night of September 24/25.[5] 'I was trained with the second group that consisted only of women and I only knew the five or six other women I trained with. At Beaulieu, where we went for security training, and in the apartment in London, where we had to go for the information about getting sent out, we were always kept apart from the others. So I had never met Andrée Borrel until the evening we were to go over.

'As it happens, we went twice. The pilot wouldn't drop us the first time because the lights on the landing field were not quite accurate, so we had to come all the way back, which was very trying. You were squashed in that little plane with a parachute on your back and your legs drawn up, and, of course, there was the danger too. Back in England they told us the reception committee had a man missing and so they couldn't place the lights for the signal the way they were supposed to.

'We went back again the next night. We sat on the floor in the airplane [a Whitley bomber], much too tense for conversation, which in any case was not possible because of the noise. I don't remember how long it was until the dispatcher opened the hole, which meant we were arriving. We crept nearer, getting our legs into position. We had drawn straws and luck gave Andrée the first jump. I went immediately after her. You had to jump very quickly, one right after the other, because the plane is going on and you might be dropped very far from each other.'

They landed safely in a field at a tiny village called Boisrenard, across the Loire from the town of Mer, about a hundred miles from Paris in the château country near Blois and Chambord. The field belonged to the father-in-law of one of the three men who received them, a local recruit to the cause named Pierre Culioli. 'We didn't have to bury our parachutes or carry things or do anything,' recalls Lise Villameur. 'They did it all for us. There was very little talk, only what was essential. They took us in the moonlight to a shed in the woods nearby and we spent the rest of the night there. When the curfew ended in the morning they brought round a horse and cart and we climbed onto it and Culioli took us to the the place it had been arranged for us to stay for the next few days.'

This was the house of the Bossards, an elderly couple who lived on a farm outside the little village of Avaray, a few kilometres from Mer, and who had been persuaded by Culioli to let their place be used as a safe house for parachuted agents on the first stage of their journey to join their circuits. It was their horse and cart he was using to transport the agents and remove parachuted containers collected on the dropping zones to hiding places. It was a tremendous risk for them to take. Lise Villameur remembers the Bossards as warm and hospitable and as particularly helpful in preparing the two agents, whom they knew only as Odile (Lise) and Denise (Andrée), for life in the occupied zone.

'Denise had been in France after the occupation started, but to me it was all new. I had never seen a German uniform, only the pictures they had shown us. The old people told us a lot of little things about everyday life, the regulations about identity cards, how to use ration tickets for food and clothes, which days different things were allowed or forbidden. We went out to look at the people, the different German uniforms. We went to the station to see the crowded trains and how they worked.

'We talked about the war. We were not supposed to ask questions about our lives, past or present, and we kept to orders. I don't remember how it cropped up that Denise had worked in a baker's shop on the Avenue Kléber and I realized it was the same bakery I used to go to every day to buy my bread. That was the only thing I knew about her life before. She never mentioned her sister or her parents. I only knew her by her code name of Denise. But during those few days I appreciated her manner, her character. She was quick, determined, ready to face any situation. I liked her.'

When they left Avaray, Lise de Baissac went south to Poitiers to start a new group, to locate suitable dropping zones and find people who would help her. Andrée, as Denise, went north, to Paris. Her job was to prepare for the arrival of two agents, an organizer and a radio operator, for whom she had been assigned as courier in a threesome that was the typical pattern of an SOE team. As it turned out, she would be much more than a messenger, becoming an indispensable partner of the new chief being sent to reactivate circuits in the Paris area, where things had been falling apart since the demise of the AUTOGIRO circuit. He was known as Prosper, and the vast network they would soon establish came to be known by that name too.

His real name was Francis Suttill and his real identity was that of an English barrister at Lincoln's Inn. Born in 1910 in Lille to an English father and a French mother, he was educated in both France and England. He spoke French fluently but with an accent that, while not recognizably English, was certainly not that of a native Frenchman; it was said that he could have passed for Belgian. When war broke out he enlisted, was commissioned, and shortly afterwards was recruited for F Section. He was immediately recognized as someone special, even in that crowd of talented, idiosyncratic, sometimes brilliant, sometimes raffish, not always quite respectable individuals who made up F Section's roster of agents. M.R.D. Foot would call him 'a brave, ambitious man of strong character, with marked gifts of leadership and charm.'[6] A Frenchwoman who belonged to his circuit described him as 'exactly one's idea of an English gentleman, refined, responsible and always considerate.'[7]

He was understood to be above local politics, a decided advantage in being taken seriously by the various politically fragmented local resistance organizations whose obsessions often seemed to run more to who would be in charge when the Germans were finally got rid of than to the immediate business of getting rid of them, while the British would work with anyone who would make common cause with them in the singleminded aim of defeating the Nazis. F Section agents were also perceived as a nuisance by the staff of MI6, whose agents preferred quiet in the vicinity of their intelligence-gathering activities to the commotion caused by acts of sabotage or even the attention insecure circuits had a way of calling to themselves.

Suttill was thought to be a man who could manoeuvre his way through these hazards. He was also a man who had all the

qualifications for becoming a tragic hero of mythic proportions
– beauty of person, nobility of purpose, and a kind of pride, an
inflexible sense of integrity, that could undo him. Fifteen years
later, a man under a cloud of suspicion for his role in F Section's
operations said of him, 'Prosper was magnificent, strong, young,
courageous and decisive, a kind of Ivanhoe; but he should have
been a cavalry officer, not a spy [sic]. He was not sufficiently
trained in these things.'[8]

Suttill was jumping, quite literally, into a volatile situation.
There was increasing pressure for a second front to relieve the
Soviets sooner rather than later. To support the invasion that
would put the Allied forces back on the Continent would require
mustering all the available forces of resistance and preparing
them to rise up and strike at the right moment. Suttill was one of
the people sent to lead that effort and Andrée Borrel, now
Denise, was sent to prepare for his arrival.

Andrée's operational instructions were to

> go by train to Paris and call on les Tambour (ask for
> Monsieur or Madame Tambour) at 38 Avenue Suffren,
> Paris 15e, and say you come *de la part de Charlot*. You
> will tell them to expect two friends of yours, who should be
> arriving a few days after you. Les Tambour will advise you
> regarding the present conditions in Paris, where to lodge
> and where your two friends should lodge.

'Les Tambour', it is worth mentioning, were among those listed
by CARTE's André Girard in his voluminous records of prospective
agents' names and addresses which had already fallen into the
hands of the Germans.

Andrée was to contact Prosper – who was to be dropped
'blind', that is, with no reception committee – at a café she had
described to him, in the rue Caumartin where her sister lived. He
was to wait for her from midday until about five minutes past
every day during the current moon period until she turned up.
She had been given detailed instructions about security and a

system for disguising addresses by using the Bottin business directory, a listing of commercial and industrial firms throughout France, and the 1939 Paris telephone directory; she had learned how to use the grid system of references to Michelin road maps for designating landing fields; she had been taught the Playfair and Benn codes; and she had been given the circuit passwords for use only with her chief and his principal lieutenants. They were, '*Ou peut-on trouver de l'essence à briquet?*' (Where can one get lighter fuel?), to which the reply was, '*Du carburant, vous voulez dire?*' (You mean gasoline?).

She had been given the address of a postbox in which to deposit detailed reports from her circuit for transmission by courier to Baker Street. Such messages, too long to be transmitted in the limited time a wireless operator had to be on the air in order to escape detection, would be carried back by the Lysanders bringing agents over. And she had the address of a safe house 'if you ever need to make a getaway'. She carried with her 300,000 francs for the circuit's use. Her own salary, three hundred pounds a year, would be paid into her Lloyd's bank account during her absence from the country.

She was also instructed that, in case Prosper was unable to leave by the scheduled moon period, she should listen to the BBC Foreign Programme on the evenings of the 1st and 2nd October for the agreed message alerting her to stand by for his reception and then, when the signal was repeated, to carry out the arrangements. In case Prosper would not be coming over as scheduled, Andrée would hear the message, '*Carmen envoie ses amitiés à Eugénie*' (Carmen sends her regards to Eugenie).

As M.R.D. Foot would say of Prosper, 'He was not particular about where he made his contacts.' A friend and fellow agent, Armel Guerne, later reported having first met Prosper and his courier a couple of months after the chief's arrival 'at a night club in Montmartre where', according to Foot's account of the report, '[they] were demonstrating sten guns to an interested mixed audience.'[9] The starting point for his contacts was the list of names provided by CARTE. It proved an unfortunate source.

What he was lacking when he arrived was a sense of how things worked in the day-to-day world of occupied France. Given as well his somewhat suspect French, it seemed prudent for Andrée to accompany him everywhere he went, and so they travelled together building up circuits all over the north. His papers identified him as a salesman of agricultural products; hers made her out to be his sister. It was assumed that it would cause no comment if she did most of the talking in what F Section's chief, Colonel Buckmaster, characterized as 'a society where the women have generally done all the bargaining.'

All this activity generated the need for a good deal of coded-message traffic, and a month after Prosper's arrival a wireless operator was dropped to complete the triad of chief, an assistant/courier, and a 'pianist', the slang for the W/T man. His name was Gilbert Norman – he arrived on the same field in Boisrenard where Andrée Borrel had landed, and he too carried papers that identified him as a travelling salesman. Like Prosper the son of an English father and a French mother, he had been born at St Cloud on the outskirts of Paris in 1915. John Goldsmith, who trained with him at Wanborough Manor, described Norman as a superb athlete, 'absolutely bursting with self-assurance. Whatever we did in physical training he could always do that little bit better,' and added that his French was excellent.[10] Norman's code name was Archambaud, but in the informality that resulted from the rather relaxed habits of the group around Suttill, who was himself called Francis or François, Norman was most often addressed as Gilbert, a fact which made it easy to confuse references to him with those meant to apply to the air movements officer Henri Déricourt, whose code name was Gilbert.

By the beginning of 1943 the PROSPER network was thriving. In March Suttill told Baker Street that Andrée, who at twenty-three was ten years his junior, had been acting as his lieutenant. 'Shared every danger. Took part in a December reception committee with myself and some others. Has a perfect understanding of security and an imperturbable calmness.' He told them that 'everyone who has come into contact with her in her work agrees with myself that she is the best of us all,' and added, 'Thank you very much for having sent her to me.'[11] That month, having been officially appointed second in command of the network, she took part in a sabotage operation at the Chevilly power station. It was followed by others.

Sabotage was increasing, and with it reprisals, more and more vicious. Shortly after the agents known as Denise, Prosper and Archambaud established themselves in the Paris area, the North African landings provided the pretext for the Germans to cross the line of demarcation into the Vichy zone and occupy the rest of France.

The German presence in the south was followed over the next few months by mass arrests of resistance leaders throughout the area, including many on the CARTE list. One of its former leaders, Henri Frager, a Nice architect, would be sent to build the DONKEYMAN network, with sub-circuits reaching far over the countryside, north to the Jura and beyond to the area of the Yonne River just south of Paris, where he made contact with PROSPER. And new agents had begun arriving towards the end of 1942 to start new circuits in the occupied zone. As they set about recruiting, establishing letter drops and safe houses, and setting up lines of communication, they were in contact with Prosper and his group as the centre of a vast network they had every reason to believe would be called on to support an invasion as early as the coming spring.

But by now the stakes had been raised. The German Military Command had decreed that men helping or hiding Allied servicemen on the run would be executed; women would be deported to the camps. The reward for denouncing them was ten thousand francs. And those who were sent east for aiding the resistance, although they could not know it at the time, were not likely to come back. The NN decrees specified *Rückkehr Unerwünscht* – return not required. On the streets of towns all over France through that bitterly cold winter the Germans' direction-finding vans closed in on more and more radio transmitter signals. By the end of the year, young men of military age might be stopped on the street at any time and conscripted for forced labour in Germany.

And by now Suttill, Andrée, and Norman had become a triumvirate united in more than their official duties. They regularly ate together in restaurants, met to play poker almost every evening at a café near the Porte de Clignancourt, and in general ignored the security measures that would have kept them apart. Foot suggests that in this they were following the lead of Andrée, the only one of them who had previous experience in the resistance. 'In the PAT escape line,' he would write, 'she had belonged to a splendid and daring fellowship of resisters, who would have scorned to steer clear of their personal friends lest seeing them should endanger the circuit.'[12] She had made contact with her sister when she arrived, and sometimes arranged for Suttill or Norman to meet her in her sister's apartment in the rue Caumartin near the Opéra.

By the end of May 1943 they had drop zones on fields all over the farms of the Ile de France and had received over two hundred containers of arms and explosives, an indeterminate but reputedly significant share of which were passed on to communist groups in the area for use in various attacks on Germans carried out in the streets of Paris.

By this time members of PROSPER's sub-circuits included the director of the École Nationale d'Agriculture at Grignon, near Versailles, which became a meeting place for the members of the réseaux, and many of his associates, including Professor Alfred Balachowsky of the Institut Pasteur.

Another sub-circuit was the Jewish-led one known at Baker Street as JUGGLER, with headquarters at Châlons-sur-Marne in the Champagne country east of Paris. Its leader, Jean Worms, code-named Robin, was one of the early résistants in the Paris area, a Parisian businessman who had made himself useful to British intelligence and had been brought out to London in the autumn of 1942 and sent through the SOE special training schools, returning at the beginning of 1943 to organize and carry out railway sabotage actions.

Worms was parachuted with another of F Section's newly trained recruits, Henri Déricourt, a French pilot who had escaped to England, been passed through the Patriotic School's vetting process for new arrivals from the Continent and quickly trained to undertake the job of air movements officer for F Section. He was to find suitable landing grounds and organize receptions for agents flown in by Lysanders, the small planes that could land on a tiny field and take off again within minutes carrying returning agents and messages for Baker Street. Déricourt's operation would serve the entire PROSPER network, which by now was in communication with connecting *réseaux* in practically every strategic corner of France.

There were also a number of smaller groups of local resisters throughout the area, especially in the Normandy countryside, where large out-of-the-way estates with outbuildings provided good hiding places for stores of arms and ammunition. To the north-west, between Paris and Rouen, a friend of Suttill's named George Darling, a Frenchman of English background, headed one of many such groups. In the Sologne, to the south of Paris, Yvonne Rudellat, who had been infiltrated into France by F Section the previous summer, had teamed up with Pierre Culioli, organizing receptions and carrying out sabotage operations.

By early summer 1943 the PROSPER network radiated out from Paris to spread throughout the north of France, from Nantes on the south-west near the Atlantic coast to the borders of Belgium and Luxembourg at the Ardennes on the north-east. The circuits were snowballing, and overlapping with others to the east and west and south of them. And PROSPER's many sub-circuits, despite the requirements of a more perfect security than the realities of the situation seemed to allow, had increasing contact with each other, as some of the same meeting places, couriers and wireless operators came to be used by many of them.

Throughout the spring and early summer months the pace of

activity gathered momentum. Déricourt's operation was in full swing, receiving agents and seeing off returning ones along with the circuits' mail for London, some of it coded, much of it consisting in long reports written in clear. At the same time other PROSPER dropping grounds were receiving hundreds of containers of arms and explosives on moonlit fields all around Paris and throughout the north. On clear nights the countryside buzzed with the sound of planes, the fields were dotted with the glow of the signal lights guiding them in, the curfew was broken by the rushing around of men and women gathering up containers, loading them onto carts and carrying them off to be stored under the hay in barns on the surrounding farms and whatever other hiding places could be improvised.

The atmosphere that spring and summer of 1943 was one of frantic anticipation. There were heavy Allied bombing raids that seemed like a harbinger of things to come. There was increasing talk of a second front, to engage the Germans in the west and relieve the pressure on the Soviets in the east. Invasion of the Continent was expected, it was thought to be imminent, and the task ahead seemed to be a matter of holding out for another few weeks, until the end of summer, or, at the most, until into autumn. No one was predicting that 1943 would have come and gone – and half of the following year as well – before the invasion. No one was thinking of ways to avoid being drawn into the Germans' tightening nets while carrying out the dangerous work of the resistance, with all of its inevitable risks and pitfalls, for another whole year. No one thought they would have to.

In April of 1943 the Tambour sisters were arrested, undoubtedly as a result of the trail provided by the Marsac/Bardet/Bleicher connection. Among those whose names were on the purloined CARTE list, they were now living in Paris, where they had been Prosper's first contact on arrival and where they served as a letter box for numerous members of the PROSPER network.

Hearing that the Tambour sisters had been picked up and were being held in Fresnes, Suttill undertook an attempt to rescue them. Learning that the two women were being taken to the Avenue Foch in a prison van every day to be interrogated by the SD, he had an intermediary enter into negotiations with prison officials to have them released on the way. A sum of a million francs was agreed on as a ransom and half of the money was turned over in exchange for two female prisoners. What the would-be rescuers got for their money, however, were two faded prostitutes turned over to them in a confused scene at the agreed time and place. The real sisters were deported and never came back.

After the first abortive attempt to rescue them, Suttill, more in the spirit of chivalry than of security, persisted. Defying everything he had been taught at Beaulieu and should have known from experience by now, he arranged this time to have the two women delivered to him and Gilbert Norman personally. They were waiting at a café table when a large black car pulled up and discharged a number of tough-looking men in raincoats. They got away that time, but not before one of the men – even before they had a chance to move – had photographed them both.

In mid-May Suttill was recalled to London for consultations. He left on the Lysander that had brought in Vera Leigh among others, one of Déricourt's operations. In London, he was summoned to a private interview with Winston Churchill, whose interest in SOE, his brainchild, had led to other occasional meetings with individual agents back from the field. No record of the meeting remains.

When Suttill returned to the field he insisted on being received by Culioli rather than on one of Déricourt's fields. He came back either believing that the invasion and the opening of the long-awaited second front was planned for that autumn in the north of France, or having been persuaded to act on that belief, although aware the invasion would not take place that summer or even that year.

Madame Guépin, George Darling's fiancée, at whose house near Gisors Suttill often stayed, said later that he had returned from London a changed man. 'He looked ten years older, so grey and strained I thought he must be ill.'[13] In answer to her questioning, he said he didn't have the right to tell her what was weighing on his mind. Of Andrée, Madame Guépin said the work she had done as a pioneer in the field before Suttill and Norman arrived had been a heavy charge for a twenty-two-year-old. 'But she was capable. She had a head on her shoulders and a will of iron.' They were very different, the educated upper-class English barrister and the somewhat rough-mannered French girl with her socialist ideas, but Andrée, Madame Guépin said, was 'utterly loyal and devoted to Prosper, as her chief, and to Archambaud.'[14]

On 21 June, Suttill, Andrée, and Norman, along with some of their friends in the circuit, met at an outdoor café alongside the Gare d'Austerlitz to wait for the arrival of the two agents from the ADOLPHE sub-circuit in the Sologne, Pierre Culioli, who had received Andrée on her arrival nine months earlier and Suttill himself only days before, and Yvonne Rudellat, known as Jacqueline. She had trained with Andrée in the first group of women agents and had been the first woman sent over to France by F Section, landing on the Riviera from a fishing boat in July, two months before Andrée's parachute drop. At forty-seven, she was also the oldest of the women agents trained by SOE and had been doing very effective team work with Culioli in the château country of the Loire valley. They were bringing with them two new arrivals, Canadians named Pickersgill and Macalister, who were supposed to be carrying some new quartz crystals intended to enable Gilbert Norman to change transmitting frequencies. The foursome never showed up.

That night Suttill and Andrée took part in receiving a parachute drop. Suttill slept late the next day after the exertions of the night before and lunched with the Guernes, friends and fellow agents, at their apartment in Montparnasse before going off to Gisors on circuit business. It was 22 June.

On the night of 23 June, after dining at the Guernes' in Montparnasse, Andrée Borrel and Gilbert Norman left separately and went to the apartment where he was staying, near the Porte de la Muette at the edge of the Sixteenth Arrondissement near the Bois de Boulogne. They had some coding to do and were both still there when, a little after midnight, a knock at the door was followed by the command, '*Ouvrez! Police allemande!*'

Three hours later the Feldgendarmerie arrived at the little hotel in the rue de Mazagran near the old arch of the Porte St Denis where Suttill had registered, before leaving town, as an engineer by the name of François Desprée. When he returned from Gisors at ten in the morning they were still there.

At the Avenue Foch, where they were all taken, Andrée exhibited what Foot later described as a fearless contempt for her captors, maintaining 'a silence so disdainful that the Germans did not attempt to break it.'[15] As it turned out, they had no need to.

Later, from her damp cell behind the massive grey walls of Fresnes, she found a way to get messages out to her sister. She wrote in tiny characters on bits of cigarette paper hidden in the hems of the lingerie she was allowed to send home to be laundered. To her sister, her imprisonment brought a sense of relief. It was her expectation that Andrée would remain there, uncomfortable but out of harm's way, until the war ended. She was totally unprepared to hear, in May 1944, almost a year after her capture and with invasion already in the air, that Andrée had been taken to Germany.

CHAPTER 8

The Journey

The journey began on the morning of 13 May 1944, when Andrée, Diana, Vera and a fourth young woman were brought from Fresnes to the Avenue Foch with four other women whose names were Yolande Beekman, Madeleine Damerment, Eliane Plewman and Odette Sansom (now Mrs Hallowes). All of them were F Section agents.

In the once elegant mansion they were installed in a former drawing room to wait for whatever would come next. Odette remembers, 'We travelled from Paris to Germany together. We did not know each other before. We all did our training at different times, we all went to France at different times. I had never seen the others at Fresnes, although I heard the voice of one of them once. They were not in a solitary cell like mine and they were able to communicate a little with people outside through the top of their windows. We met for the first time in the Avenue Foch.'[1]

Almost half a century after the event, Odette is talking in her still heavily French-accented English over the tea she has ordered for a visitor at the Army and Navy Club, known to habitués as the In and Out Club because of the signs on either side of the driveway that fronts on Pall Mall. She is remembering another tea.

'It was a lovely hot day, a beautiful day. And the Avenue Foch is beautiful, and the house where we were was a beautiful house. And I thought, What do I risk? I might as well ask for something while we are waiting. So I said to the German guarding us there, "You've got a lot of English tea, I know" – they used to get all kinds of contraband, tea and cigarettes – "Why don't you make us some tea?" And we had it, in proper cups, china cups. None of us had seen anything like that in a long time.' She laughs at the thought of her boldness and at what she describes as the automatic response of the German to the imperious tone of her request, almost a command. She is frail now, and looks almost lost in one of the large leather armchairs that line the room, but her voice still suggests the robust young woman in the official photographs of the wartime years.

'I remember little things. One of the girls had a lipstick and we all used it, passed it around and put it on. It was quite a treat. We were young women, after all . . .

'And we talked and talked and talked, of course. We talked about when we were captured, and what this one thought about it, what that other one had to say about it. I remember what one of them said because I had the same feelings. She and I, we had a feeling that something had been wrong. The others thought they had been captured because of the work they were doing or the people they were with. She had the feeling, because she had been arrested as soon as she arrived in France, that there was an informant. And I did too.

'We were all young, we were all different, but we all had the feeling in the beginning that we were going to be – helpful. That was why we went into it. And to have impressed the people around them as they did is almost enough. They impressed everyone – the Germans, their guards. They behaved extremely well, those women.

'Everybody tried to be a little braver than they felt. All of us had a moment of weakness, we did all cry together at one moment, there were a few tears, but after all it was a lovely spring day in Paris. Riding in the van from the Avenue Foch to the station we could get a glimpse of what was going on in Paris, people sitting on the terraces of cafés drinking their ersatz coffee or whatever . . .' She stops for a moment, then goes on, 'I was looking forward to the trip. I had spent a year alone in my cell and I thought, Now I am going to be with these other women.

We will be together in the same camp. I will be with them. Well, that never did happen. Because I never saw them again after we got to Karlsruhe . . .

'On the train we were handcuffed, each one of us handcuffed to somebody else, so we were not free to move around or anything, but we did not look absolutely miserable. No, we made the best of it. I remember one of them even asked a guard for a cigarette, and he gave her one.'

A paper in Vera Leigh's file, apparently the draft of a recommendation for an award, and written in the public-relations tone of such, says that 'throughout the journey, during which the prisoners were handcuffed together and which lasted for several days [sic], Miss Leigh's own courage never failed, and she was continually cheering her companions by her implicit faith in an Allied victory.'

Odette says, 'We were frightened deep down, all of us. We were wondering what was the next thing, a normal thing to ask yourself in those circumstances. Were we going straight to our death, were we going to a camp, were we going to a prison, were we going to – what? We couldn't not think of those things. Our only hope was maybe to be together somewhere.

'We were starting on this journey together in fear, but all of us hoping for something, above all that we would remain together. We had all had a taste already of what things could be like, none of us did expect for anything very much, we all knew that they could put us to death. I was the only one officially condemned to death. The others were not. But there is always a fugitive ray of hope that some miracle will take place.'

They crossed the Rhine, which had been the prewar frontier, and were placed in the civil prison at Karlsruhe. There they were separated from each other and placed in small dark cells with two or three German inmates. Some of their cellmates were ordinary criminals but most of them were political prisoners, in one case a woman who was picked up by the Gestapo and imprisoned because she had been overheard telling an anti-Nazi joke.

'When we got to Germany and we were parted to be put into separate cells we didn't feel too good about that,' Odette says. 'We didn't know what to expect, and I remember saying, "With luck, we may see each other again, we may go somewhere else together," or something like that. It was never to happen, of course . . .

'I was put in a cell with some German women. One of them had been there for three years. She had been denounced by her own daughter. For listening to the BBC. The daughter was a member of the Hitler Jugend. They were fanatics. To give away your own parents made you like a little god. And some of the others belonged to the Bible people [Jehovah's Witnesses]. They had been in prison for a long time because of their faith.'

In Karlsruhe the British agents were treated no differently from the other inmates, given the same food, meagre but certainly not the near-starvation rations they had subsisted on at Fresnes, and taken out for exercise in the prison yard. There was a daily inspection during which they stood in the corridor where, despite the regulations, they managed to exchange a few words and pass messages to those in adjoining cells. They made friends with some of the other women prisoners, who shared the food parcels they received from outside and added their clothes to the laundry they were allowed to send out to be washed. During the day they were given manual work to do, peeling potatoes, sewing. It helped the time pass. Despite the hardships and restrictions of prison life, they were certainly better off than if they had been in concentration camps.

Occasionally through the small high-barred windows of the cells they could hear the sound of bombers overhead. They were British and American planes, on their way to cities and industrial targets deep within Germany. There was always the possibility that they would die in an Allied air raid, but on the whole things looked good for the seven women agents. The end of the war was unmistakably near and they could reasonably expect to be released by the liberating forces of the Allies before too long.

Then, some time between four and five on the morning of 6

July, not quite two months after they had arrived at Karlsruhe, four of the women were awakened and told to get themselves ready for a journey. They were taken to the reception room where their personal possessions – parcels, a small suitcase, a fur coat – were returned to them and they were handed over to two Gestapo men. It was noted in the meticulously maintained prison records that they were taken away to a concentration camp (*einem ZZ-Lager zugeführt*).

The Gestapo ordered them into a closed truck and they were driven some sixty miles south-west by the road through Strasbourg to the camp at Struthof, where they arrived around three in the afternoon.

There the four women were ordered out of the truck and taken into the Politische Leitung, the office of the political department of the camp. The camp dentist later remembered seeing them there, 'three or four women who were busy unpacking their kit – one was brushing her hair.' An SS officer asked him for a cigarette 'which I offered to him, and I did the same to one woman with blonde hair who was standing near me.' It might have been Diana, who had dyed her hair at Clairvaux. He noticed that all four of the women were very quiet.

From there they were marched between the SS men down the steps in the middle of the camp between the two sets of blocks, long single-storey wood and concrete barracks-like buildings on either side of the steps. Their progress was observed by a number of the prisoners, who saw them taken into the Zellenbau, a block of cells that constituted a prison within the camp, at the bottom of the hill, next to the crematorium. They were locked in together at first but during the course of the afternoon were split up, first into two cells, then into separate ones. Through the windows, which faced those of the infirmary, they managed to communicate with several prisoners, including Dr Guérisse, whose PAT escape line Andrée Borrel had been part of. Another Belgian, a Dr Boogaerts, who had known her on the PAT line, passed her some cigarettes through the window. She threw him a little tobacco pouch containing some money. Vera Leigh asked if someone could get her a pillow.

As evening approached the cell-block leaders spread the command throughout the camp that all prisoners were to be in their huts by eight o'clock with blackout covers in place over the windows. It was forbidden to look out.

Nevertheless, there were those who did, and they would remember what they saw that night.

CHAPTER 9

The Trial

The 'politicals' in Natzweiler would not have been there if they were the kind of men who automatically did as they were told. Among those prisoners was Albert Guérisse, the Belgian doctor known as Pat O'Leary. Despite the threat that anyone seen at the window that night would be shot, he did manage to look out of a window of the infirmary, and later he was able to tell a military court what he had seen. First, however, he had told Vera Atkins.

Following the trail of the missing F Section agents, she had interrogated a number of former functionaries of the SS's highly efficient concentration-camp system. The trail that had taken her to French jails and German prisons led finally to the camps themselves. It was there that the missing agents had ended up, in Mauthausen, in Dachau, in Buchenwald, in Natzweiler, in Ravensbrück . . .

The lucky ones were shot. Some of the others were hung from meat hooks with piano wire, to make their death as slow and as painful and humiliating as possible. And some just died of starvation, disease, and hopelessness, the concentration-camp syndrome.

It was not clear why the F Section SOE agents had been sent from Fresnes to the women's prison at Karlsruhe, although it later appeared that the transfer had been a convenience enabling the official in charge of them in Paris to be closer to his home and family in the German city. In any case, the Karlsruhe Gestapo was instructed by the Reichssicherheitshauptamt or RSHA, Gestapo headquarters in Berlin, to take delivery of the eight British military prisoners and hold them 'in protective custody' in separate cells. This was somewhat irregular, since the prison was a civilian one, and after several weeks had passed, the warden, in the interests of efficiency and wishing to operate strictly according to regulations, asked the prison governor for further instructions to clarify the position of the anomalous prisoners. He, in turn, requested further instructions from the local Gestapo and from there a letter was duly sent to RSHA asking what was to be done about these women. In reply, a teleprint message came back with orders in consequence of which four of the women were to be taken to Natzweiler. About a week later another of the women was sent to Ravensbrück and two months later the remaining three were sent to Dachau. One of the Gestapo men who brought the women to Natzweiler later said he had told them they were on their way to a camp where they would do agricultural work.

It was 6 July 1944, exactly a month after D Day. On the journey, the women chattered in English. They had reason to suspect the end of the war was near, reason to expect it meant liberation for them. They welcomed the prospect of going to the country, to work on farms until they could be repatriated.

Among the officials of the concentration-camp system Vera Atkins had occasion to interrogate was Rudolf Hoess, the commandant of Auschwitz, who insisted with a certain pride on correcting upwards by a few million her estimate of how many millions of people had been gassed there, like a businessman insisting on correct production figures. Another was Peter Straub, who had been in charge of the crematorium at Natzweiler.

Natzweiler had been the first concentration camp entered by Allied troops. It was Yurka Galitzine, who had been among them, and whose report on what he found there had been suppressed by Allied Headquarters, who later took advantage of the administrative confusion at the end of the war to keep the war crimes investigation team going even after the orders to close down the special services. He had not forgotten what had gone on there: slave labour, death by torture, live prisoners used as guinea pigs for 'medical' experiments. He had not been able to forget the human skeletons with empty eyes, in filthy striped rags, staggering or crawling, dazed, in a landscape of slaughter, piles of human bones, of human ashes, of what had been people's clothes, shoes, eyeglasses. 'The thing that really one remembers most of all', he said years later, 'was the smell. I didn't realize what it was at the time – human flesh that had been burned in the crematorium.'

It dismayed him that in the euphoria of VE day, 'People were beginning to say, Well, it's peacetime, let's forget what's past. The senior people in the War Office, the politicians, they were ready to settle down to the quiet life.' Given the opportunity to support the investigation by special forces officers into the fate of their missing men and women, he established them in a house in the town of Gaggenau in the French-occupied zone of Germany, put them in direct radio communication with his office in London, and kept them on the payroll while they searched the towns and countryside, woods and villages for evidence of atrocities and for the men who had committed them, now on the run or in hiding.[1]

And so there were the trials. At Nuremberg the surviving major architects of the systematic terror that had engulfed Europe and of the holocaust that had destroyed millions of innocent men, women and children were put in the dock to answer to the charge of war crimes – violations of the laws or customs of war, including the murder of prisoners of war – and crimes against humanity – murder and other inhumane acts committed against civilian populations. And in a series of more specific trials, individuals were charged with the crimes that had been routine procedure of the SS. One of them was the trial of the men who had run the Natzweiler camp at the time that the four women SOE agents were brought there.

The Natzweiler trial took place at the Zoological Gardens in Wuppertal, not because of any dark sense of humour that might have chosen a zoo as the appropriate place for the consideration of the inhuman behaviour under investigation, but because it was the only structure in the vicinity large enough to accommodate the proceedings. The evidence for the prosecution had been gathered by Squadron Officer Vera Atkins and Major Bill Barkworth of the SAS War Crimes Investigation Team, well after the organizations to which they and the missing men and women had belonged had officially ceased to exist. It was a kind of personal vendetta of principle. Years afterwards Vera Atkins said, 'You owe people something, after all, who fought for you and risked their life for you.' She added, 'One knew them . . .' and the phrase was left hanging. She may have been remembering filling them in on details about life in occupied France, helping them check for telltale signs of Englishness in their apparel or manners as they got ready to leave, seeing them off at the airfield, wishing them luck, reading their messages from the field, keeping in touch with their children during their absence . . .

'One knew them . . .'

Among the inmates at Natzweiler were the criminals transferred from German prisons who could be relied on by the SS staff to run the day-to-day operations of the camp. One of these, a man named Franz Berg, had the job of stoker of the crematorium furnace.[2] When his services were required, he would light the oven in which bodies of inmates who had been executed or who had died more gradually and even more miserably were disposed of by being burned up. A pot of ashes was usually forwarded to the next of kin, accompanied by the required paperwork. The ashes may or may not have actually been those of the deceased in question, but the forms were always in order. They usually stated that the deceased had been shot while trying to escape or specified some other cause of death exculpating the camp authorities. In the case of NN prisoners, of course, there were no remains forwarded and no forms filled out. They were, like the prisoner's return, not required.

At the Natzweiler trial, Berg testified as to what had happened on the evening of 6 July 1944. His testimony neatly complemented, like an adjacent piece of a jigsaw puzzle, what Vera

Atkins had heard from Dr Guérisse, who had recognized Andrée Borrel and had managed to exchange a few words with another one of the women before she disappeared. She had told him she was English. That was all there had been time for.

Then, after dark, looking out of a window of the infirmary, he had seen the SS camp doctor going down the steps in the centre of the camp towards the crematorium. A few minutes later, he saw the figure of a woman being escorted from the Zellenbau, the building where the four had been placed in cells. She was taken to the crematorium building a few yards away. And then, a short time later, he saw the flames, the gust of flames from the chimney that all the prisoners recognized as the sign that the door of the oven had been opened and shut. He saw this sequence again, and again, and again, four times in all. He told the court,

> I saw the four women going to the crematorium, one after another. One went, and two or three minutes later another went. The next morning the German prisoner in charge of the crematorium explained to me that each time the door of the oven was opened the flames came out of the chimney and that meant a body had been put in the oven. I saw the flames four times.

The prisoner Guérisse referred to was Franz Berg, who was able to describe what had gone on inside the crematorium building during the time that Guérisse was watching out of the infirmary window. He told the court that he took his orders from Peter Straub, the SS political officer in charge of the crematorium, who was present at all executions that took place in the camp. 'He counted the bodies, filled in the death certificates and so on . . . we used to burn bodies about three times a week.'

About six o'clock on the evening of the day the four women (whom he refers to as 'four Jewesses') arrived at the camp, Berg said Straub told him to have the crematorium oven heated to its maximum by nine-thirty and then to disappear. He told me also that the doctor was going to come down and give some injections. I knew what this meant. At nine-thirty that night I was still stoking the fire of the crematorium oven when Peter Straub came in, followed by the SS doctor, who had come with Hartjenstein [the camp commandant] from Auschwitz.

In addition to Obersturmbannführer Fritz Hartjenstein and Untersturmführer Dr Werner Röhde, the group described by Berg included the former SS doctor of the camp, who that night was already wearing civilian clothes, and such other officials as Obersturmführer Johannes Otto, an adjutant in training at Natzweiler for his subsequent career at Dachau, Schutzhaftlagerführer Wolfgang Zeuss, staff sergeant in charge of keeping order in the camp, Arbeitdienstführer Robert Nietsch, in charge of the work parties, and Oberscharführer Emil Bruttel, a medical orderly. Although later they would all deny their complicity, there seems to have been no lack of *Führers* – SS officers – present at the occasion.

'The doctor in uniform chased me out of the furnace room,' Berg testified. He went to the room in the crematorium which he shared with two other prisoners, and a few minutes later the commandant and his adjutant 'looked into the room to see if we were all asleep. I pretended to be asleep.' Then the door was locked from the outside. There was a small window over the door from which it was possible to see the corridor outside. The prisoner who occupied the highest bunk was able to look through it and kept up a running commentary on what he saw. He whispered to Berg that

> they were bringing a woman along the corridor. We heard low voices in the next room and then the noise of a body being dragged along the floor, and he whispered to me that he could see people dragging something on the floor which was below his angle of vision through the fanlight.

1. Andrée Borrel, Denise

2. Vera Leigh, Simone

3. Diana Rowden, Paulette/Marcelle

4. Sonya Olschanezky

5. Francis Suttill, Prosper

6. Vera Atkins

7. Gilbert Norman, Archambaud

8. Eliane Plewman

9. Noor Inayat Khan, Madeleine

10. A Mark III Westland Lysander adapted for agent pick-up duties.
Note the ladder and the long-range fuel tank

11. Nicholas Bodington

12. Colonel Maurice Buckmaster

13. Odette Churchill

14. Francis Cammaerts

15. Madeleine Damerment

16. Maurice Buckmaster and Francis Cammaerts, some time in the 1960s

17. 84 Avenue Foch

18. Lise de Baissac

19. Yolande Beekman

20. Hugo Bleicher

21. Jean Overton Fuller

At the same time that this body was brought past we heard the noise of heavy breathing and low groaning combined.

The next two women were also seen through the window by the prisoner in the top bunk,

and again we heard the same noises and regular groans as the insensible women were dragged away.

The fourth, however, resisted in the corridor. I heard her say '*Pourquoi?*' and I heard a voice which I recognized as that of the doctor who was in civilian clothes say '*Pour typhus.*' We then heard the noise of a struggle and the muffled cries of the woman. I assumed that someone held a hand over her mouth. I heard this woman being dragged away too. She was groaning louder than the others.

From the noise of the crematorium oven doors which I heard, I can state definitely that in each case the groaning women were placed immediately in the crematorium oven.

When [the officials] had gone, we went to the crematorium oven, opened the door and saw that there were four blackened bodies within. Next morning in the course of my duties I had to clear the ashes out of the crematorium oven. I found a pink woman's stocking garter on the floor near the oven.

Some time later Brian Stonehouse saw the Rapportführer, one of the SS men who had taken the four women down the camp steps when they arrived. The prisoners called him Fernandel because he looked like the French comic actor of that name. He was walking up the steps in the middle of the camp from the crematorium carrying the fur coat Stonehouse had seen on the arm of one of the women.

There were other witnesses whose testimony provided pieces of the story of what had gone on that night.

Dr Georges Boogaerts, a Belgian prisoner, had spoken to one

of the women through the window of the block nearest to the Zellenbau where they were being held that afternoon. She was a Frenchwoman who had told him her name was Denise. When he was shown photographs of the four women he recognized Andrée Borrel.

The most dramatic testimony came from Walter Schultz, who had been an interpreter in the camp's Political Department. It was here the orders came regarding prisoners transferred to the camp by the Gestapo for 'special treatment', a euphemism the meaning of which was clearly understood by all. It was not necessary for files to be made for new arrivals accompanied, like the four women, by requests for special treatment.

Schultz claimed to have learned about the events of that night a day or two later from Peter Straub, who was known as the camp executioner:

> He was very drunk on that day, and I put a direct question to him as to what had happened to the women, because on the next morning it was talked about in the camp that they were dead, and Straub told me that he had been for a long time in Auschwitz but had never seen such a thing before; he just said, 'I am finished'.

Schultz testified that, according to Straub,

> The women were told to undress in front of the doctor. They refused. Then it was said that they were going to be inoculated and they asked why, and then it was said it was against typhus, and then they laid bare their arms and were inoculated. They were taken singly into the room where they were inoculated, and they were taken back singly to where they had come from. As the second was taken back to the place, the first one was already in a kind of stupor.

Asked whether Straub said they were dead as a result of the injection, Schultz replied,

He said they were finished. They were stiff, but the word 'dead' was not mentioned ... The fourth woman as she was being put into the oven regained consciousness ... He showed me a few scratches on his face and said, 'There, you can see how she scratched me ... Look how she defended herself.'

It has never been explained why Straub, who had put four million people up the chimney, as he himself put it, is said to have found this occasion particularly affecting. Perhaps it was because he had no reason to think any of the women involved were Jewish and hence might still have seen them as human beings. When he was finally tracked down and arrested by the war-crimes team, it was Vera Atkins who was given the job of interrogating him. He still had scars on his face.

Straub was not the only one who claimed to have been upset by the unpleasant necessity of administering 'special treatment' to the four women. Werner Alfred Julius Röhde was forty years old when he came to Natzweiler in early July 1944 as Standort-arzt, to replace the former doctor, one Heinrich Plaza. He was resting on his bed after the midday meal when Plaza and the adjutant came to his room 'and told me that four French spies had been condemned to death, and were to be hanged. They told me that Peter Straub had said that to hang them would involve a great to do [*würde ein grosses Theater geben*], and they went on to suggest that these women should be killed painlessly by injections.' Röhde says he refused at first – after all, he was a medical man, was he not? – but when Otto 'insisted that it must be done in this way ... as Otto was my superior in rank I had to agree.'

Röhde gave the injection to the first woman who was brought in and he later claimed her death was instantaneous. Straub took the body away and at that point, Röhde testified, he was so upset that he was unable to administer the injection to the second woman who was brought in and Plaza, presumably less easily shaken, had to take over from him and inject all three of the others. Plaza was not there to contradict his colleague's account of events. In extenuation of his complicity, Röhde added that he considered that 'it was more humane to kill them with painless injections than to let Peter Straub hang them'. The question remained as to how instantaneous, how painless a death it had been, since it appeared that what was injected was not a drug with anaesthetic properties but an extremely strong caustic which was in liberal supply as a disinfectant in Germany in the summer of 1944. It was recognizable as the odour of hospital corridors – the smell of carbolic acid.

Emil Bruttel, formerly a grocer in civilian life, was employed as a medical orderly at Natzweiler. He testified that Dr Plaza had phoned him from the officers' mess that evening to ask him to check the medical supplies and see how many capsules of a narcotic called Evipan were on hand. Bruttel told him and about ten minutes later Dr Plaza called again. 'See if we have any phenol, and if so, how much,' Bruttel remembered him asking. He reported that there was about 80 cc. The third time Dr Plaza called he ordered Bruttel to report for work and to bring along the phenol and a 10 cc syringe as well as one or two strong needles.

Bruttel and another orderly, described with no apparent irony as an SS First Aid man, met the doctors, the adjutant and other officers of the camp and it was only as they walked together towards the crematorium by the light of an oil lantern that he learned that four women were about to be killed on orders from the RSHA, which had requested 'special treatment' for them. He also remembered hearing that the women had been arrested in Paris.

According to Bruttel, he and the other orderly had no choice but to go on and remain with the others.

There was no way back for us as we did not carry security lanterns, and to go through the blacked-out camp without one was certain suicide as the guards would shoot instantly.

We went into a little room where there were several beds. It was here that we learnt from the explanations given by the doctors the details of the plan. The two block leaders were dispatched to fetch the women separately from the cells. Before each injection, the doctors told the woman that she was being vaccinated against typhus. The woman about to be executed had to lie down on a bed [and was given an] intravenous injection into the arm. In each case 10 cc of liquid phenol were used. According to the doctors, it was pure phenol ... One doctor gave the injection while the other controlled the pulse and announced the death with the words: 'Death has taken place.'

At the trial, Röhde described exactly how death had taken place:

A sudden cramp spread over the whole body. The breathing stopped, the pupils of the eyes rolled upwards, the muscles of the face were paralysed ... [followed by] complete muscular collapse ... the face took on a waxen colour, the lips lost colour, the body became limp, the pupils of the eyes again returned to their normal state and the eyes were half closed ... the air escaped out of the lungs, caused by the paralysis. The pulse could not be felt any more, and breathing entirely stopped.

According to Röhde, it was impossible for any of the women to have regained consciousness and thus have been burned alive. If Straub had made a statement to that effect 'he can only have said this whilst in an unbalanced state of mind.' He added, 'In concentration camps the most impossible rumours about the most impossible things are current.'
Berg again:

After the execution was over and the women had been undressed, they laid the corpses on the conveyor apparatus for the crematorium oven. Apparently some mistake was made as the last corpse was being put into the oven, as it almost fell out again.

Next morning I heard that the officers and doctors had celebrated in the mess until the early hours. But this may well have been connected with Dr Plaza's departure.

The case of the three British agents and their unidentified companion was not unique. At the end of 1944 and the beginning of 1945 most of the officers of British special services who had been captured and put in concentration camps were exterminated. More than thirty were hanged at Buchenwald alone.

At the Natzweiler trial, as elsewhere, the two main defences were 'I was only carrying out orders' and 'I wasn't there.' The defendants said, 'I did nothing, I only stood . . . I was there as a spectator . . . I was ordered to do it . . . I did not kill anybody, I did nothing . . . I did not take part in it and do not know what happened . . . I myself did not do this; it was all carried out by [someone else] . . . I cannot agree that I should be held responsible' (this from the camp commandant) 'for things which may actually have taken place during my absence.' What was the explanation for the evidence, the sworn statements that he had been present at the execution? 'I presume it is a case of mistaken identity.' The commandant firmly maintained that all responsibility belonged with his adjutant, who was unable to dispute the charge, having committed suicide at the end of the war.

During the period of their detention together at Recklinghausen awaiting trial, several of the defendants had second thoughts about the statements they had made to Barkworth and sworn to earlier. At the trial they expressed the wish to revise some of the evidence they had given in their affidavits implicating each other. Some lost their memories, others refreshed theirs. This led to some retractions having to do with just exactly who was present in the crematorium that night. But it didn't matter. There was ample evidence to convince the court of the guilt of those in the dock.

The trial testimony provided a glimpse into some aspects of the concentration-camp culture. There was the ordinariness of the working day's routine to those who looked at the misery and pain of other men all day long and then went home at night to join their families. The SS staff sergeant whose job was to see to it that the requisite number of slave labourers went off to the quarries every morning said he was not there when the women were killed. He was occupied visiting the various factories in the area in order to 'ask them whether they wanted working parties who were available to be employed in the armaments industries.' He said his wife would know when he came back from this business trip because 'at that time I went for walks with my wife and children to collect berries and mushrooms.'

The adjutant, described as 'a family man with eight children,' who had been a schoolteacher before the war, and the camp dentist, whose wife was visiting him at the time, were guests at the commandant's birthday party. The dentist remembered that was in early July, 'mainly because my own birthday is on 10 July and we held another party.'

One of the party guests was the 'SS doctor', surely an oxymoron in an atmosphere purposely designed to inflict overwork, starvation, suffering, and death. He recalls that he took up medical studies 'because of my pleasure at the profession of healing and in helping mankind.' It was his 'medical experiments' which provided corpses for the use of Professor Hirt of the Department of Anatomy in Strasbourg.

To these men, it was all just a business, pretty much like any other. There was on-the-job training. ('Otto came to Natzweiler in order to learn how to carry out the duties of adjutant of a concentration camp before being posted to Dachau. For this purpose,' says the camp commandant, who describes the said Otto as 'an apprentice', he 'worked out a timetable which put him through all departments to get a knowledge of every department.' Another SS man is described as being 'trained to be able to handle the oven,' as though he were working in a bakery.)

Apprentices who demonstrated an aptitude for the profession might be sent for further education ('Zeuss was destined to go to the Führer School') and there were conferences at which commandants of various camps compared notes on management techniques. There were also work incentives. (Straub testified, 'For cremating each day I received sausage. Alcohol was issued after an execution.') It was even, in some cases, a family business. The post of Schutzhaftlagerführer, held by Zeuss at Natzweiler, was held at a different time by his brother Josef, who was later put in charge of an adjacent camp.

And there is the contrast between the meticulous care taken over paperwork and records and the total disregard for living human beings. Endless forms, files, and detailed reports were continuously made out and scrupulously maintained by men keeping careful track of the comings and goings of other men – suffering, doomed. 'I had to deal with the formalities in cases of deaths,' says one, eager to explain his duties. 'Inform relatives, make the necessary entries on the register and see to cremations.'

There is a certain irony in the fact that the manner in which these four women died can in a sense, as the defence contended, be seen as more humane, as easier – involving at the very least less time in which to anticipate and feel pain and dread – than those of the wrecked corpses strewing the grounds of Ravensbrück, or those millions of others who disappeared into the flames at Auschwitz or wasted slowly of starvation and disease at Belsen. Yet only in their case was there clear evidence and a specific body of law applicable to their killing and suitable for the prosecution of their killers. Only in their case were there advocates to appear and plead on their behalf.

There is a seeming disingenuousness in the prosecution of the charge that there was no trial, no sentence, no legal warrant for the death of these four, as though there had been for any of the millions of others. We have it from no less an authority than Thucydides that killing the enemy's agents without trial in wartime is at least as old as the Peloponnesian War. There are even accounts of interviews with prospective F Section agents which make it clear what could be expected. Selwyn Jepson told the biographer of the agent known as 'Madeleine': 'As usual, I stressed immediately . . . that in the event of capture . . . since she would not be in uniform she would have no protection

under the international laws of warfare . . .' And there were so
many crimes, so much human suffering in Natzweiler that the
attention given to these four makes no sense unless it is understood as symbolic.

Something that we call humanity is instinctively repelled by
the systematic hunting down of the weak and helpless and the
bestiality practised on them by the Nazis. That this proved not
to be the case for so many Germans and so many others in so
much of the supposedly civilized world was the great shock that
at the end of the war so many wanted to look away from.

For others, there was a perceived need to mourn the dead, to
celebrate their deeds, and to caution. It was impossible to focus
the world's attention on millions. They could only be perceived
as an abstraction. But four – four could capture the public's
attention, the reader's sympathy.

'Human memory is short,' Sir Hartley (later Lord) Shawcross,
the attorney general at the time, observed in his foreword to the
published proceedings of the trial.[3] He thought the horror and
revulsion at what had been done in the name of the New Order
should not be allowed to fade and disappear,

> not to encourage a morbid interest, not to keep alive
> feelings of ill will against our late enemies. But because the
> horror through which the world passed in those dark years
> was not just a nightmare which cannot recur . . . The
> fearful cremations at Natzweiler had their counterpart a
> thousand times at Auschwitz. Hoess told us, 'The foul and
> nauseating stench from the continuous burning of bodies
> permeated the entire area and all the people living in the
> surrounding communities knew that exterminations were
> going on at Auschwitz.'

> I do not recall these grim matters of the past for mere
> morbidity. I mention them as a reminder that the men
> convicted of the murder of Miss Denise [sic] Borrell,
> F.A.N.Y.; Section Officer Diana Rowden, W.A.A.F.; Miss
> Vera Leigh, F.A.N.Y., and another gallant woman, were

not isolated, exceptional killings. These crimes were not sporadic or isolated, depending on the brutality of some individual sadist. They were a part of that system which arises when the totalitarian state submerges the fundamental right and destroys the dignity of man. Month by month, day after day, killings like these went on by the thousand all over Europe . . .

But the mind which is lastingly impressed and shocked by a single crime staggers and reels at the contemplation of mass criminality: becomes almost impervious to horror, conditioned against shock. And as events recede into the past, those who did not themselves experience them . . . begin to question whether these things could indeed have happened and wonder whether the stories about them are really more than the propaganda of enemies.

To such questions, Shawcross felt, the publication of the war crimes trial records would give 'a grimly positive answer.'

As he noted at the time, the Natzweiler defendants were 'the minor henchmen' of those in the dock at Nuremberg. Yet he found the record of what they did a more poignant illustration of the consequences of the Nazi system than the massive Nuremberg record. It was after all a doctor, who had presumably sworn the Hippocratic oath, who stood most directly accused here, an example of the extent to which professional and moral standards can be debased, as they were in totalitarian Germany, 'when ruthless dictatorship and the omnipotent state takes the place of the individual judgment and personal integrity.'

He might have added that a sense of having acted on their individual judgement and maintained some measure of personal integrity was the only comfort left to those who lived and died at places like Natzweiler.

In the end, like all of the war crimes trials, the Natzweiler trial was not about justice, it was about law. Law may be a step on the way to justice — without it there can be no justice — but it does not always seem like enough.

Vera Atkins never claimed that justice had been done, or even to know whether in such circumstances any kind of justice was possible. When she was asked decades later about the final fate of the Natzweiler defendants, she said she had been finished with them after her interrogations; she had never been interested in the sentences handed out.

But the trial did gain a certain amount of public attention. The manner in which the four women had died at Natzweiler was widely reported in the British and French press. However, their names were not published, in deference, according to statements by the authorities at the time, to the feelings of their surviving relatives.

The names of the three of the four whom Vera Atkins had been able to identify became a matter of public record two years after the trial. Their publication in May of 1948 would begin a new chapter in the history of F Section's legacy.

PART TWO

Fanning the Flames

A nondescript express in from the South;
Crowds round the ticket barrier, a face
To welcome which the mayor has not contrived
Bugles or braid: something about the mouth
Distracts the stray look with alarm and pity.
Snow is falling. Clutching a little case,
He walks out briskly to infect a city
Whose terrible future may have just arrived.

December 1938, from W.H. Auden, 'Gare du Midi'

CHAPTER 10

Gold in the Furnace

On a Saturday early in May 1948, readers of *The Times* of London saw a column headed BRAVE WOMEN HONOURED/ TABLET UNVEILED/SECRET AGENTS WHO GAVE THEIR LIVES. The article below began,

> Some of the bravest figures of the war are commemorated among the names of 52 women to whose memory a modest tablet was unveiled yesterday by Princess Alice, Countess of Athlone, Commandant-in-Chief of the Women's Transport Service, at St Paul's Church, Knightsbridge.
>
> The 52 are those members of the W.T.S. (which began in 1907 as the First Aid Nursing Yeomanry) who fell in different theatres of the war ... Of these women and girls 13 met death in German prison camps, after having been parachuted into enemy-occupied territory as secret agents to serve the allies by aiding the resistance movements ... There is no formula by which to calculate how much of cold courage was embodied in these 13 women, or what they endured in dying for their countries.

The list of names that followed included those of Andrée Borrel, Vera Leigh, and Diana Rowden. The fourth woman killed at Natzweiler had never been identified, but the names of three of the others who had travelled together from France into Germany in the spring of 1944 were given. They were Yolande Beekman, Madeleine Damerment, and Eliane Plewman.

The account described the tablet, 'on an outside wall of the church in a quiet corner of Wilton Place, away from the bustle of Knightsbridge. The vicarage, the next building, served as the F.A.N.Y. headquarters during the war.' It went on to describe the service held in the church before the unveiling of the memorial. Those present included Major-General Sir Colin Gubbins, 'who controlled the special force to which the 13 secret agents belonged' and added that

of the survivors of that group of 40 brave women about a dozen were at yesterday's ceremony, among them Mrs Odette Churchill, G.C., M.B.E. The congregation that almost filled the church included parents, husbands, and children of the women who were being remembered; many Frenchwomen; not many men; a young officer of the Parachute Regiment; parishioners of St Paul's, Knightsbridge; past and serving members of F.A.N.Y. and of the other women's services.

There were passages in the service which seemed more than usually applicable to the particular occasion – sentences that awakened far but clear echoes of adventures and exploits among the most desperate of the war. The lesson was from the Book of Wisdom: 'But the souls of the righteous are in the hand of God, and there shall no torment touch them . . . For God proved them, and found them worthy for Himself. As gold in the furnace hath he tried them.'

Blake's 'Jerusalem' was sung. Prayers were offered, and the congregation knelt as the choir sang the Contakion of the Faithful Departed – 'Give rest, O Christ, to thy servants with thy saints, where sorrow and pain are no more.' The vicar spoke from the text, 'Their name liveth for evermore', and quoted the words that one of the dead women was remembered to have used: 'I would do anything for England.' When the stone had been unveiled by the Princess and dedicated by the vicar, a wreath of poppies was laid by the commanding officer of the FANY corps and a drummer of the Coldstream Guards sounded

Last Post and Reveille. *The Times* noted that 'Among the wreaths laid after the ceremony was one from Mrs Odette Churchill, inscribed in her handwriting: "To those who failed to return; with love and homage." '[1]

Among the readers of *The Times* that May morning, three years after the end of the war in Europe, was a woman who recognized the name of one of the dead – Diana Rowden. She had been at school with her, and she was astonished to find her name in this context. She could not reconcile her memory of a diffident and reticent girl with the account of a woman who had been sent into occupied France and gone to a martyr's death at the hands of the Germans. It disturbed her that she had never suspected the capacity for risk-taking, what she called the 'stubborn fibre' such acceptance of danger had called for. She wrote later that she had thrown the paper down, annoyed at the discrepancy between what she had read and what she remembered. But by that time, ten years later, she had made it her business, her mission, to find out everything she could about her old schoolfriend and the other women who had accompanied her on the journey into Germany. And in so doing, she had found out quite a lot about what had happened to them – and how it had come about – that went beyond the official record.

It was 1955 when Elizabeth Nicholas turned her attention full-time to picking up the threads where Vera Atkins had left off. By the time she finished her book two years later, she had provided a partial solution to a puzzle, pieces of which were still being put in place half a century later.

Meanwhile, in 1952, another writer had published a book dealing with the life and death of one of the women she had known and whose name she too had recognized in *The Times*'s account of the memorial in Knightsbridge. The book was called *Madeleine* and it told the story of Noor Inayat Khan, an agent Vera Atkins had thought, at the beginning of her investigations, to have been the fourth woman killed at Natzweiler.

Noor was one of the most romantic of the SOE agents and one whose suitability to be sent into the field has often been questioned. The great-great-great-granddaughter of the legendary Tipu Sultan, the eighteenth-century Muslim ruler who died in the struggle to stem the British conquest of South India, Noor can thus be said to be a descendant of resistance fighters. Her father was the leader of the Sufi mystic community. Her mother was an American related to Mary Baker Eddy, the founder of Christian Science. Inayat Khan, Noor's father, took his family to pre-revolutionary Moscow, where they were taken up by members of the Imperial Court and where a daughter was born in the Kremlin on New Year's Day of 1914. She was given the name Noor, meaning 'light of womanhood', and would be known by her father's name, the patronymic Inayat, and the title Khan, an honorific denoting aristocratic birth.

Inayat Khan moved his family to London shortly before the outbreak of the First World War but poverty and prejudice led to another move, this time across the Channel, where they settled on the outskirts of Paris. Gentle, shy, sensitive, musical, dreamy, poetic Noor lived by what her biographer called 'a different rhythm' from the other children in the village of Suresnes, where a follower of her father had established them in a house with a walled garden overlooking the capital with all its landmarks – the Eiffel Tower, Notre Dame, Sacré Coeur. When Noor was thirteen her father died, leaving her, as the oldest child, the mainstay of her grieving mother, who withdrew into seclusion, and her younger siblings. At the Lycée Saint Cloud she struck her classmates as 'being elsewhere'. She loved tales of chivalry and sacrifice and took up the harp in imitation of the women and angels in pre-Raphaelite paintings.

At seventeen she graduated from the *lycée* and enrolled in the École Normale de Musique in Paris, where she was a student of the noted pianist Nadia Boulanger. She continued her musical studies for the next six years, composing for the harp and the piano, and little by little becoming more European and less Oriental in her habits and dress. She moved about more independently than the veiled women of the tradition out of which she had come. She wore makeup that made her skin lighter. She took a degree at the Sorbonne in child psychology, studied several modern languages, travelled on the Continent with her brother Vilayat, and began a career as a free-lance writer. She became a frequent contributor of articles and stories to newspapers and magazines and her children's fairy tales were broadcast by Radiodiffusion Française. A book of her stories was published in England in 1939 and she was about to bring out a children's newspaper in Paris when the war broke out.

During the early months of the war, before the tanks began to roll westward over Europe, Noor and her sister took a Red Cross nursing course, intending to join the war against the Nazis in the only way that seemed practical. With the Germans approaching Paris, the family joined the exodus from the city. They made their way to Bordeaux and, because Vilayat had been born in England, they managed to get on the last boat evacuating British subjects. It was two days after Marshal Pétain had asked Hitler for an armistice.

It was when they arrived in England that Jean Overton Fuller met them. Noor was twenty-six years old and living with her family in Oxford when the Battle of Britain began at the end of August 1940. Nursing didn't seem to her like enough. Her brother had joined the RAF and in November Noor enlisted in the Women's Auxiliary Air Force. As Aircraftwoman 2nd Class Nora Inayat Khan she was posted to Harrogate with the first group of WAAF to be sent for training as wireless operators. In June 1941 she was posted to a bomber training school station, where she found the work dull. She applied for a commission and was selected for an intensive course of more specialized and highly technical signals training. That month a fairy tale she had written was broadcast on the Children's Hour of the BBC.

Noor told her brother and her friend Jean that she thought she would not get her commission; she felt she had made an unfortunate impression on the officers interviewing her by becoming too emotional on the then problematic subject of Indian independence. To Jean her brother expressed the concern that what he called Noor's unworldliness would be her undoing – that she was 'born for sacrifice'.

And then, 'out of the blue', as these summonses were always characterized, Noor was asked by the War Office to present herself at a room in the Hotel Victoria in Northumberland Avenue for an interview with a Captain Jepson. He told her about the need for W/T operators to work with other British officers organizing resistance groups in occupied France, and made clear the risk of capture, torture, and death at the hands of the Gestapo. More than that, he told Jean Overton Fuller later, he agreed then and there 'to take her on'. He had 'no misgivings' about Noor, found her 'sure and confident', and 'had not the slightest doubt that she could make it.'[2]

While she waited for her special training to begin, Noor spent much of her spare time with Jean Overton Fuller, with whom she shared an interest in mysticism, in reincarnation and clairvoyance. Then, early in February 1943, with all of Europe occupied by the Germans and talk of opening a second front beginning to be heard, Noor was posted to the Air Ministry, Directorate of Air Intelligence, seconded to the FANY, and sent to Wanborough Manor to begin her SOE training. From there she was sent to Aylesbury, in Buckinghamshire, for special training as a wireless operator in occupied territory. She would be the first woman to be sent over in that capacity, all of the women agents before her having been sent as couriers. Having had previous W/T training, she had an edge on those who were just beginning their radio training. She was fast, and she was accurate.

From Aylesbury she went on to Beaulieu, where the security training was capped with a practice mission – in the case of wireless operators, to find a place in a strange city from which they could transmit back to their instructors without being detected by an agent unknown to them who would be shadowing them. The ultimate exercise was the mock Gestapo interrogation, intended to give agents a taste of what might be in store for them if they were captured and some practice in maintaining their cover story. Noor's escorting officer found her interrogation 'almost unbearable' and reported that 'she seemed absolutely terrified . . . so overwhelmed she nearly lost her voice' and that afterwards, 'she was trembling and quite blanched.'[3] Her finishing report, which the official historian of F Section found in her personal file long after the war, read: 'Not overburdened with brains but has worked hard and shown keenness, apart from some dislike of the security side of the course. She has an unstable and temperamental personality and it is very doubtful whether she is really suited to work in the field.' Next to this comment Buckmaster had written in the margin 'Nonsense'.[4]

Meanwhile, events in the Paris region were rushing to a head and Baker Street was desperate for another radio operator to deal with the stepped-up message traffic. Noor had not finished the security course, but she was the best prepared operator on hand, and it was decided to send her. She was given the cover name and identity of Jeanne-Marie Regnier, a children's nursemaid, and the code-name Madeleine. She left from Tangmere by the May moon, but the reception committee was not on the ground to meet the plane, and it had to return. After the buildup of tension and anxiety, the anticlimax was a distinct letdown.

Two other women agents waiting with Noor for the next moon period and favourable weather for crossing the channel wrote to Baker Street about her; they didn't think that she should be sent. Before she left, she asked Jean Overton Fuller to cast her horoscope and read her palm. She said she thought it would be useful to her in her work to know 'what were the traits in her character through which she was most likely to come to grief.'[5]

Then it was the next moon period. When the time came for her flight, Vera Atkins accompanied her to the airfield. They travelled in an open car through the flowering countryside of the south-east coast to Tangmere, where they had supper in the ivy-covered cottage that was operational headquarters for 161 Squadron. In the party were an agent bound for Marseille to do sabotage and another on her way to the south-east countryside as a courier, as well as Diana Rowden, on her way to the Jura.

Hugh Verity remembered that supper just before take-off. They were all cheerful and the only sign of nerves was someone's slightly unsteady hand holding a cigarette. After supper they went upstairs to use the bathroom, and while waiting Vera Atkins saw a paperback book beside one of the pilots' beds. Its title was *Remarkable Women*. She remembers saying that the book would have to be rewritten 'after these girls have done their stuff.'⁶ The date was 16 June 1943.

Early the next morning, Noor climbed out of a Lysander in a moonlit meadow a few miles north-east of Angers, near where the Loire meets the Sarthe, in a double operation that had been organized by air movements officer Henri Déricourt. As the two planes came in, one agent climbed out of each while another handed out the baggage before following down the ladder. Within minutes the planes had taken on five returning passengers for England, who included three French political figures and F Section agents Jack Agazarian and his wife Francine. He was a wireless operator for Prosper; she was a courier.

By that evening Noor had made her way to Paris to present herself at the apartment of Émile Henri Garry, to whom his chief, Prosper, had given the code name Cinema, presumably because of his resemblance in form as well as name to film star Gary Cooper. Garry was a Frenchman, not trained in England, who was working for Prosper in the Eure-et-Loire and the Sarthe *départements* south-west of Paris, with headquarters at Le Mans. Baker Street, not amused by Prosper's little joke, had changed Garry's code name to Phono and sent him a badly needed wireless operator.

When she arrived, however, Noor was under the impression that the password with which she had been provided was intended for an old lady. Garry, who was anything but an old lady, found himself in turn bewildered by his visitor, who had arrived carrying a bunch of flowers for her contact, until finally one of them broke the ice and passwords were exchanged to their mutual satisfaction. What happened from then on was pieced together by Jean Overton Fuller after the war from the accounts of those who had known and worked with Noor during the months between her confused arrival and her arrest in the autumn.

They included Garry's fiancée, with whom Noor would stand up at their wedding at the end of the month, as well as his sister Renée and another F Section agent named France Antelme, an imposingly tall and tanned Mauritian major codenamed Antoine, all of whom were living at Garry's. When Noor arrived they found she had had nothing to eat since leaving England, twenty-four hours earlier. She had been given a forged ration book, but she didn't understand how to use it and was waiting until someone could explain the procedure to her.

Noor was introduced to the PROSPER team and Gilbert Norman, her fellow wireless operator, took her out to Grignon, north-west of Versailles, to meet the members of the network working out of the agricultural institute there. The Balachowskys were dismayed to see her casually leaving a briefcase containing her codes out on a table in the entrance hall, where, as they pointed out to her, anyone might have come along and found it. But, although they may have been more security-minded than Noor, their caution had its limitations too, and the following weekend the whole crowd – including the Balachowskys, Suttill, Norman, Andrée Borrel, Noor, and a few others – lunched together in Paris, waiting for the agents from the Sologne who never arrived. It was the last such get-together. Barely a week after Noor's arrival on the scene, Suttill, Norman and Andrée Borrel were arrested. The Prosper debacle had begun.

The agents who survived were those who scrupulously obeyed the laws of caution. In cities, they took care that even their associates did not know where they lived or what their cover name and identity was. In the country they moved from one house to another every few days. If they were radio operators, they did not stay on the air for more than a few minutes at a time and transmitted from different places whenever possible.

Those who eluded capture were seldom those who were seen dining together in black-market restaurants, talking things over in English. And even those had to have luck.

With the wave of arrests washing over the circuits, Noor's was one of the few radios still operating. With a sense of the importance of her unique position which amounted to a sense of mission, she refused an offer to bring her back to England. And from then on, she was on the run, transmitting from a series of different houses and apartments, trying to avoid the direction-finding trucks, several times just managing to elude the Gestapo, once sensing she was being followed on the street, another time stopping at the Étoile beside the Arc de Triomphe and noticing the men in trench coats lounging around the corner of the Avenue Mac-Mahon and the rue Tilsit where she had an appointment to meet a fellow agent.

At the beginning of July the Germans came to Grignon. Noor had gone there to transmit to London but saw the uniforms and managed to beat a retreat. By now the ranks were decimated as the arrests of Prosper's agents and sub-agents rolled on, and Buckmaster, informed of the extent of the disaster, sent a message suggesting that Noor return to England at the next moon period. She refused. She felt her Poste Madeleine had become an indispensable link to London in the crisis and she wanted to carry on. Baker Street agreed.

For the rest of the summer Noor moved around looking for places she could transmit from safely. Either in that search or out of loneliness, she went back to Suresnes, where she had grown up and was still vividly remembered, and called on her old harp teacher, her old schoolfriends, the family doctor, her one-time next-door neighbours. She took a tiny room in an apartment complex in Neuilly-sur-Seine almost entirely inhabited by German officers and the story has come down that one of them courteously offered her a hand when she was having difficulty hanging her aerial out on the branch of a tree.

In the August moon period Noor's radio handled the arrangements for an operation that took several agents back to England. Among them was Nicholas Bodington, who as Buckmaster's deputy had been sent to appraise the wreckage of the Prosper disaster and had managed to move about Paris without falling into the hands of the Gestapo. Bodington had given Noor instructions to lie low until she could be brought out.

The courier, the written mail in both code and clear that passed between London and agents in the field, went on board the August flight as usual. In one of the bags was a note from Noor to Vera Atkins in which she said, 'I remember you so often cheered me up so sweetly before I left. Lots of things have happened,' she went on with truly British understatement, adding, 'I'm awfully happy. The news is marvellous, and I hope we shall soon be celebrating.'

The news that sweltering European summer of 1943 did suggest celebration was round the corner. Since Montgomery had defeated Rommel in North Africa, Allied airborne troops had landed in Sicily and were working their way up the Italian boot. Italy was all but out of the war. Meanwhile the RAF was pummelling Germany, and on the eastern front the Russians were counterattacking, driving the Germans back on a Continent that increasingly seemed ripe for invasion.

While she waited for it to happen, Noor worked with those who were left in the Paris area. One of them, a Frenchman recruited in the field without benefit of the security training course at Beaulieu, had his own misgivings about Noor's habits and appearance. He convinced her to visit a skilful hair colourist and bought her a less English-looking set of clothes, but he couldn't convince her not to carry her notebook with her wherever she went. It was an ordinary school copy book and in it she kept a record of all the messages she had sent and received since arriving in France, in code and in clear. It was a stunning breach of the most elementary security precautions and it seems to have been the result of a misunderstanding on her part of the phrase in her operational orders instructing her to 'be extremely careful with the filing of your messages.' Evidently she was unfamiliar with the use of 'filing' in the sense in which a journalist 'files' – that is 'sends' – a story, and thought she was meant to keep them in some sort of filing system.

The telltale messages were on the table beside her bed when she was arrested in her room, along with her codes and her security checks. They would prove invaluable to her captors.

It was from them that Jean Overton Fuller learned the story of Noor's arrest and captivity. After the war, embarked on her own quest for the story of Madeleine, she tracked down some of the same SD officials from whom Vera Atkins had taken depositions and interviewed them herself. She also followed the trail that led her to some of the other players in the drama – and eventually beyond the story of Madeleine to the larger one of which it was only a part.

Noor had eluded the Gestapo all through the summer and early autumn and at the end of September told some of her friends that she expected to be going back to England very soon. It was early in October when the SD was contacted by someone who called herself Renée with an offer to sell them Madeleine – a name they knew well as that of an F Section radio operator they had so far been unable to run down. The woman seemed to know a great deal about F Section, including that Madeleine worked for Phono, a name they also recognized, as well as the piece of information she was offering them for a small fraction of what they were prepared to pay for it – the address in the rue de la Faisandérie where Madeleine was living. Like so many others of the apartments inhabited by F Section agents, it was only a few minutes away from Gestapo headquarters on the Avenue Foch.

The three handsome buildings at 82, 84, and 86 Avenue Foch had been taken over by various departments of the SD, the counterintelligence branch of the Gestapo, and it was here, at number 84, that important foreign agents who were caught were brought for interrogation. From the outside it looked – and still looks – like the epitome of Parisian elegance, a Belle Époque façade in keeping with the grandeur of the wide avenue itself, the most imposing of the broad boulevards radiating from the Place de l'Étoile, now the Place Charles de Gaulle.

Behind the ornamental black iron gate and inside the impressive premises, a wide marble staircase led from the elaborate entrance foyer of what before the war had been a private mansion to the floors above, now used as offices by the various departments housed there. On the second floor was the wireless section run by a former schoolmaster, Dr Josef Goetz, whose French was as perfect as his German. The marble staircase ended at the last of the high-ceilinged floors, the fourth. A carpeted anteroom furnished with Louis XV chairs, where Odette would order tea for the eight women on their way from Fresnes to Karlsruhe in the spring of 1944, gave on to two spacious rooms facing the avenue. The largest, dominated by a crystal chandelier hung from the high decorative plaster ceiling, was used as his office by SS Sturmbannführer Josef Kieffer, a former police inspector from Karlsruhe who was in charge at number 84 and who reported to Boemelburg, the Gestapo chief ensconced at number 82.

The rest of the floor served as office space for Kieffer's assistant and for his private quarters. From outside his bedroom a narrow white wooden staircase went the rest of the way up to the top storey of the house, where seven tiny dark maids' rooms at the back of the house had once held some of the domestics who kept the prewar life of the affluent running smoothly. Now they held prisoners it was considered desirable to keep incommunicado while they were being interrogated.

At the front of the top floor were two larger, lighter rooms which must have once belonged to the senior members of the housekeeping staff. One of them was now the guardroom, the other the office of the interpreter, a civilian who was given the responsibility of interrogating the most important prisoners himself, presumably because of his skill at getting them to relax as he talked with them as much as because of his knowledge of English and French.

It was sometime in the second week of October when Noor

found an agent of the Gestapo waiting for her when she let herself in to the apartment in the rue de la Faisandérie. She put up such a struggle, biting and clawing at him, that he had to keep her covered with his gun while he phoned headquarters for help in order to bring her in. They also brought in her transmitter and the notebook containing all her messages, codes, and security checks.

They took her up to the fifth floor at number 84 and within an hour she made an escape attempt, climbing out of the bathroom window onto a ledge where she was spotted and brought back in. She was beside herself with frustration and furious. Gilbert Norman was brought out of his cell to try to calm her down. Later, she was shown copies of reports she had sent to Baker Street in the Lysander courier mail, and given enough details about people and procedures at Baker Street to infer that someone, either in London or in France, had been talking. She saw too that her codes had already been mastered.

For the next five weeks she was interrogated daily by the personable interpreter, who never mistreated her, although he kept up a constant pressure for her to cooperate. She refused, and never told him anything of an official nature beyond that her name was 'Nora Baker' and that she was a WAAF officer. She did talk to him a little about her family, though, about the children's stories she had written, and about other apparently innocent matters it may have comforted her to be able to reminisce about. And she continued to make trouble for her captors in whatever little ways she could. At one point she asked to have someone bring her some clothes and other personal items from the rue de la Faisandérie and wrote a note asking that they be given to 'bearer'. The bearer represented himself as a member of the resistance and when he returned a second time for some cosmetics and eau de cologne he found Garry there and recognized him as the long-sought agent Phono. Noor's note requesting her things gave no indication that she was not at liberty somewhere, in hiding, and her things were packed up and given to the messenger, who left with them to return a short time later with three fellow Gestapo men. Garry did not come back from Buchenwald. (One remembers the words on Noor's finishing report, suggesting that despite her eagerness she was 'not overburdened with brains . . .')

Meanwhile Noor had made contact with two other prisoners being held on the fifth floor at the Avenue Foch. One was a French colonel named Léon Faye, a leader of ALLIANCE, an early French intelligence network with connections to MI6, and the other was John Starr, code-named Bob, the organizer of the ACROBAT circuit to which Diana Rowden had been sent as courier shortly before his arrest in July. She saw him again face to face when she was brought here to the Avenue Foch herself in November along with John Young, who had been arrested with Diana Rowden.

After his arrest, when Starr was brought to the Avenue Foch from Fresnes for interrogation, Kieffer had asked him to draw in the area of his circuit on a map of France on which the circuits of other captured agents had already been marked. Starr, who had been a commercial artist before the war, did so with such style that Kieffer asked him to do other jobs of mapping, lettering, and copying and eventually had him installed in one of the cell-like rooms on the fifth floor so that he would be available on a regular basis. He worked in the guardroom, fulfilling such requests as making greeting cards for the staff, editing their translations and correcting their English spelling, and executing a portrait of Kieffer for the Sturmbannführer to present to his wife at the approaching Christmas holidays. The work was certainly preferable to that being performed by Brian Stonehouse and the other captured agents in the camps and quarries, and, although his room was small, the food was excellent compared with wartime rations elsewhere.

From his vantage point in the guardroom Starr was able to observe the prisoners who came and went, and he was seen by many of them as soon as they arrived, just before it was revealed to them how much was known at the Avenue Foch about what went on in Baker Street. Those who, like him, returned to

England after the war, but from less pleasant circumstances, were never quite able to shake off a decidedly negative view of his arrangement, although he maintained afterwards that he had had his ear to the ground all the time, hoping to collect information to bring back to London if he could manage an escape.

Starr almost did manage to get away and both he and Colonel Faye might have made it if it had not been for Noor and for that chivalry that would not permit them to abandon her. It was the same code of honour that made a promise, once given, binding, and that doomed Noor and Faye.

Starr managed one day, on his way to the lavatory, to slip a note under Noor's door suggesting a place where they could leave messages for each other. She was already communicating with Faye by means of Morse signals tapped out on the wall between them. Together they hatched an escape plan. Starr was able to squirrel away a screwdriver he got hold of when he offered to repair a carpet sweeper for the cleaning woman. Taking turns using it, the three worked away at night loosening the bars of the skylights in the ceiling of each of their rooms. They made ropes of blankets to enable them to lower themselves from the roofs once they had climbed out of the skylights and, as soon as Noor gave the signal that she was ready, they agreed to go that night.

Starr and Faye had no trouble getting out onto the roof, but when they made their way over to Noor's skylight, they found that she was still working away at her bar, which she had not yet completely loosened. More than an hour went by before she could be extricated. They had begun the precarious journey to the ground along the sloping rooftops and were almost free when they heard the air raid sirens go off. They knew a guard always made the rounds of the prisoners' cells during a raid and that they would be missed within minutes.

They tried to make a run for it across the rooftops but the block had already been cordoned off and they were surrounded. Faye, in the lead, was grabbed first by the SS guards, and a few minutes later Noor and Starr were seized inside one of the houses where they had tried to take refuge. Kieffer was livid and threatened to have the returned fugitives shot on the spot but in the end settled for asking for their 'parole' – a written promise not to try to escape again. He was asking for their word of honour, and, while Starr agreed to give his, both Faye and Noor refused.

Instead of their word of honour they gave their lives. But they must have known that was the risk they were taking. Kieffer had them each shipped off to Germany immediately, Faye to be executed in a prison there and Noor to be locked up in the women's section of a civil prison at Pforzheim where, as a 'very dangerous' prisoner,[7] she was kept in chains, her hands and her feet chained together, with another chain connecting hands to feet, unable to feed or clean herself. She was kept in solitary confinement in a cell separated by two sets of iron gates from the rest of the prison. The governor of the prison, interviewed years later by Jean Overton Fuller, 'said he thought the tranquillity did her good.'[8]

Some Frenchwomen sent there as political prisoners at the beginning of 1944, about two months after Noor's arrival late in November, managed to exchange some furtive messages with 'Nora Baker', as she was calling herself, probably to protect her relatives still in France. By this time it was summer and Noor's scratchy messages noted the Fourth of July and Bastille Day, with little sketches of the appropriate flags. The last words from her, in a shaky hand, were, 'I am leaving.'[9] It was 11 September.

Two men from the Karlsruhe Gestapo came to Pforzheim that night, almost ten months after she had been locked up and chained there, to collect 'Nora Baker'. They took her to Karlsruhe and from there, along with three other women, to Dachau, about 200 miles away. The two men, named Wassmer and Ott, were the same two who had brought four other women from Karlsruhe to the camp at Natzweiler the previous July.

Wassmer later described the September trip to Dachau for the English writer who was so interested. They had gone by express train and he told her he had given the four women the window seats. They had passed around some English cigarettes one of them still had in her possession and he had given them some of his German ones when they ran out. Their conversation was lively; he didn't think they were frightened, but of course he didn't understand what they were saying. They spoke English.

They got to Dachau around midnight. The other three were also F Section agents, their names carved on the memorial plaque in Knightsbridge, along with those of A. Borrel, V.E. Leigh, D.H. Rowden C de G, and N. Inayat Khan GC, as Y.E.K. Beekman C de G, E.S. Plewman C de G, and M. Damerment L d'H, C de G.

The four walked up the hill from the station to the camp, where they were locked up separately overnight, and in the early morning they were taken to a spot strewn with sand stained with blood and told to kneel down there. They knelt in pairs, holding hands, as an SS man came up and shot them from behind.

From the Shadows

By the time Elizabeth Nicholas was at work full-time on the book which began with her interest in Diana Rowden's fate, Jean Overton Fuller had published a second book dealing with the affairs of SOE's French Section.[1] Overton Fuller had started by reason of her attachment to Noor. By the time she had finished her researches for *Madeleine*, she had become attached to one of Noor's companions in the ill-fated escape attempt from the Avenue Foch and determined to write his story as well. What she found out researching this second book would lead her to another character, another attachment, and still other volumes over the coming years.

The Starr Affair, published two years after her earlier book, in 1954, was an apologia for Starr's conduct in captivity and a criticism – the first such explicit one to be published – of the organization that had sent him.

John Starr had been sent to the Riviera in the summer of 1942, while Peter Churchill was still feeling his way through the CARTE confusion, and left in November on a fishing boat that brought in Odette and his own brother, George Starr, who was to become one of the outstanding SOE organizers. George Starr, known in the field as Hilaire, was on his way to Gascony, where he would build up a circuit called WHEELWRIGHT in the area of Toulouse and eventually lead it in effectively holding back the Germans in the south-west after D Day. In that unexpected momentary encounter there was no way to predict that one of the brothers would return a hero and the other under a cloud.

On John Starr's arrest, following his betrayal by a double

agent who had infiltrated the circuit, he made it a point to hold out for the forty-eight hours required to give fellow agents time to learn of his arrest and make arrangements for their own safety. Then, beaten up repeatedly at Gestapo headquarters in Dijon, where his interrogators took to punching the untreated wound he had suffered in an escape attempt, he gave them some information, but only, he insisted, information he knew Martin, the double agent, already had. Left alone one day when his interrogator was called out of the room in which he was being questioned, Starr took the opportunity to take a quick look at the papers lying on the table in front of him.

What he saw, according to his later account, was a complete and correct list of all the F Section training schools and their teaching staffs. There were no gaps he could see and no omissions he was aware of. The list did not look like something that had been assembled piecemeal but like a copy of an original document. But copied how, and by whom? And how had it come to be in the possession of the SD? Starr's shock gave way to amazement when the questioning later turned to the subject of the training schools and he was asked only about the ones he himself had actually attended. How did they know? And what else did they know about F Section? It was something to think about in solitary confinement, his wound continuing to fester and given little in the way of nourishment and nothing with which to clean himself, until he was removed to Fresnes.

There he was put into a cell with three other *résistants*, one of whom had belonged to a group connected with the PROSPER network. This man told Starr that when the Germans came to arrest him they demanded to be taken to where the arms and ammunition dropped by parachute in the area had been hidden. They were in possession of a map, he told Starr, on which the exact spot was marked. He told him further that when he was brought to Paris he was shown copies of the written communications that had passed by plane between the PROSPER agents and London. The Germans seemed to know a great deal of what was passing between London and those in the field and, he had also learned, there had been a large number of arrests around the time he had been taken, late in June.

When Starr had left England in May he had been given to understand that invasion was only two or three months away. The course of the war in Europe since that springtime prophecy made it seem more than likely that it was about to be realized, and Starr was not the only one who acted on that belief. He had held out well over the prescribed forty-eight hours, but after that he made judgements about security that he might not have made if he had known that another winter and another spring would pass before the Allies landed on the Continent.

Taken to the Avenue Foch for further interrogation, when he was asked by Kieffer to fill in the areas controlled by F Section circuits on a map of France, he talked it over with his cellmates. They agreed that it might be an opportunity to learn things that could prove useful to Baker Street if he were able to escape and make his way back to London. So he agreed, and was brought to 84 Avenue Foch and established in one of the little servants' rooms that had become cells for prisoners in whom the Gestapo took a special interest. By day he worked at his drawing and lettering in the guardroom, where he saw and was seen by many if not all of the captured agents who were brought there. One of them was his childhood friend and fellow agent Maurice Southgate. Southgate, known as Hector, was the highly respected leader of the STATIONER circuit, active from the area around Châteauroux, almost in the centre of France, all the way south to the foothills of the Pyrenees. He was one of the four British agents of the more than forty sent to Buchenwald who was still alive when the camp was liberated. When he returned and was debriefed, he said Starr had greeted him by his real name when he saw him at the Avenue Foch.

Among the other agents Starr saw when they were brought in were Diana Rowden, who had been his courier, and John Young, his former radio operator. What they and the others who passed through Avenue Foch on their way to Natzweiler, Mauthausen, Buchenwald or Ravensbrück made of his presence in that place in such obviously comfortable circumstances has been an object of some speculation. He had never, he insisted, been the source of what the Germans knew about F Section. And the Germans backed him up on that long afterwards.

When he was being questioned, Starr told Jean Overton Fuller, Kieffer produced copies of the messages that had passed between agents in the field and Baker Street via Lysander flights. He found this as troubling as his cellmate at Fresnes had found it mysterious. He also saw another British officer in the guard-room, reading a book and listening to music on the radio, obviously at his ease. He later learned that this man, whom he had never met, was Gilbert Norman, Archambaud. It was Norman who delivered the bombshell, the information that shocked Jean Overton Fuller as it had shocked Starr, and made her feel she must write his story, revealing what he had told her as much in order to expose the problematic facts as to rescue his reputation.

From Norman, Starr told Overton Fuller,

he learned that not only had the Germans been able to make copies of the messages in transit between France and London; they were also operating the radio sets of some of the captured wireless operators. London was con-tinuing to make deliveries in response to the messages sent, but of course straight into the hands of the Sicher-heits Dienst.[2]

Norman also told Starr that he had given the Germans his own code, but not his security check, relying on the fact that any messages presumably from him but received without it would be understood not to be genuine. That, after all, was the purpose of the security check. Dr Goetz, the head of the wireless section at number 84, then said to Norman, 'You haven't given me your security check.' Norman then gave it to him, this time relying on the assumption that while Goetz might have learned there was a security check, what he wouldn't know was that there was a double check – a second part he hadn't been given. He was right. Goetz was satisfied with the incomplete check and promptly sent a message off to Baker Street via one of his operators, presumably doing his best to imitate the 'fist', or characteristic touch, of Norman's style of transmission as it had been overheard while he was still at large. And what came back, to Norman's horror, was an answer from London including the admonition, rather like that of a nanny reproaching a child who forgot his manners at the tea table, 'You have forgotten your double security check. Be more careful.'[3]

There was more. What Norman told Starr and what Overton Fuller was the first to reveal was the immediate cause of the wave of mass arrests that had taken place in the Paris area and beyond in late June and early July following the arrest of the PROSPER leaders.

Francis Suttill had made a deal with Kieffer. He had given him the names and addresses of all of the men and women who worked in the *réseaux* of the PROSPER network in exchange for Kieffer's promise that their lives would be spared. It was a promise given and received by two individuals still living by an obsolete code but it would not be honoured by those in command. It could hardly have been expected by any hard-headed realist that such a promise would carry any weight with members of the master race, the shapers of the new order. But Suttill was something of a romantic, and a man made desperate by disillusion. After his summons back to London for top-level meetings in May he had returned to Paris demoralized, having learned something that made him bitter and weary. And when the trap was sprung on him and he was shown photostats of the Lysander mail and copies of the deciphered wireless messages and realized how much the Germans already knew, he had tried the one thing he thought might possibly salvage something from the destruction he realized was inevitable. There is no evidence that Kieffer did not enter into the pact in good faith. But once rounded up, the British agents and their French accomplices in resistance would face a fate decided on by others, who had made no such promise and to whom it would not have been binding even if they had.

Among the agents brought in while Starr did his lettering and drawing in the guardroom was France Antelme. Overton Fuller was told by the German who had interrogated him at the Avenue Foch that Antelme, who had been dropped straight into the arms of an SD reception committee, 'spoke in great anger of those in London who had sent him, and seemed to think that they had sacrificed him deliberately, for he called them "murderers".'[4] He added that all of the agents who had been met on the field in this way 'were very bitter against London.'

According to Starr, his sole purpose in accepting the position at the Avenue Foch was to collect information to bring to London if he managed to escape. He had come into possession of information that could not have been more vital – that it was the Germans on the other end of the wireless transmissions to and from London, and that F Section, in response to messages exchanged with captured radio sets being played back to them by the Germans, was sending agents out to be met on the field by the Gestapo. And he did attempt to escape with it, only to be brought down by his and Faye's reluctance to abandon Noor and by the unfortunate timing of the air raid that revealed their absence. Afterwards, only he had given his word of honour not to attempt escape again, and only he had returned from the captivity at Sachsenhausen and Mauthausen that in the end even he did not manage to avoid. In the meantime, the ambiguity of his position at the Avenue Foch did not go unnoticed or uninterpreted during the winter and spring of 1943/44.

To Francis Cammaerts, the leader of the JOCKEY circuit, looking back at these events almost a half century later, 'those who tried to play games with the Germans were bound to lose. We were amateurs, they were professionals, and there was no hope of outsmarting them. They were skilful manipulators of information and made it appear they knew more than they did.' As for 'the parole nonsense', the reluctance to break a promise given under such circumstances, it was, he thinks, 'unspeakably stupid'.

Cammaerts' own circuit in the south-east remained one of the most secure right up to the end. The agents he worked with agreed that, if arrested, they would give only their name and rank and say only that they were British officers. Anyone might give way under torture, but it was agreed that they would hold out for forty-eight hours in order to give other members of the group a chance to bury their traces and get away. Cammaerts says,

> It seemed to me then and it seems to me now that you had to have a clear and simple agreement of this kind, backed up by a deep sense of trust. But there were some who responded to the Germans' offers to bargain. To do so was a betrayal of what had been agreed on.[5]

In May a group of eight women were brought into the room next to the one in which Starr worked. While they were waiting there for whatever would happen next, Starr went in to see them and gave them some chocolate. Then they were taken away, to proceed on the next leg of the journey that would end for four of them at Natzweiler and for three of them at Dachau, with only one survivor of the little group to return from Ravensbrück to England.

When Starr finally returned to London after the war, it was with the impression, he told Overton Fuller,

> that men had continued to be sent from London solely in order to keep the Germans occupied while something more important was going on, and that some, if not all, of those sent straight into the hands of the Sicherheits Dienst had been sent knowingly, to keep the game going – that is, to make the Germans believe that the French Section still had confidence that it was their own men who were transmitting to them. If this were not so, he could not understand how

London could have carried on, with all the warnings they had received.

And his impression was duly recorded in the detailed report he made on his return. After that, he told her, he heard little more from other members of the outfit. They were polite, but distant, and Starr returned to take up his life with his family in France.

It was Overton Fuller who learned, in pursuing the matter with Vera Atkins and other F Section alumni, that it was believed that Starr had, as Vera Atkins put it, 'let the side down.'⁶ Not that he had been a traitor, but a man who had inadvertently harmed his own side by thinking he could outfox the Gestapo while in actuality being led to assist them. Once the escape had failed, she felt, he should have accepted the same terms of detention as the others. Instead, he had put himself in an invidious position, keeping his privileges when there was no longer any justification. At the very least he became 'a most demoralizing spectacle'⁷ for other prisoners who saw him at his ease at the Avenue Foch.

But Jean Overton Fuller felt differently. Starr had got under her skin, as she put it. It was a susceptibility of hers, this obsession with lifting the clouds of ambiguity that hung over some of the actors in the drama that had been played out in those few months of the war years. And she had come to feel, by the time she published her book on Starr in 1954, that he had been politely but coldly received on his return because he knew too much, because there were things done in the heat of battle that London would not like to become public knowledge, especially in France, where so many had suffered and died as a result of their complicity with the British effort to set Europe ablaze.

By the time the book came out Starr had been investigated by a French tribunal and cleared of the charge of having had 'intelligence with the enemy'.

And by that time other revelations had begun to appear.

Early in 1953 something of a sensation resulted from the publication in England of a book by the former head of German military intelligence in Holland during the war. In *London Calling North Pole*, Colonel Hermann J. Giskes of the Abwehr told the story of the *Funkspiel*, or radio game, he had played and won against England starting in the spring of 1942. The game was set in motion when a Dutch informer, one of those the Germans in occupied countries called *V-Männer*, infiltrated an SOE circuit in Holland pretending to be a resister. One of those he betrayed was an SOE wireless operator, who was captured with his wireless set and with his ciphered messages in his pocket.

In due course the agent, Hubert Lauwers, agreed to the Germans' demand that he continue to transmit under their instructions, confident that Baker Street would spot a failure to include his correct security check. Instead, London's reply was the news that another agent would be sent in by parachute, and for over a year N (for Netherlands) Section continued to send more agents, each of whom was met on the ground by a German reception committee.

The signals staff at Bletchley Park, where the messages were received and deciphered, had sent them on to N Section's operational staff with the notation that both the agent's bluff check and his true check were missing, but N Section heads had chosen to ignore the fact, seemingly attaching no significance to the omission. When the absence of his security checks failed to rouse London, Lauwers tried inserting the letters C-A-U-G-H-T in his messages. N Section still went on sending information about arriving agents and parachuted drops to his set. When another captured radio operator refused to transmit any messages for the Germans, and insisted that he had never been given a security check, they had one of their men transmit a message to London on the agent's set. The signals that came back read INSTRUCT NEW OPERATOR IN USE OF SECURITY CHECK, thus exposing the agent, who was then forced to reveal it. Meanwhile, several MI6 agents in Holland joined SOE agents in captivity after attempting to contact them.

Eventually the Germans were transmitting to London on seventeen different wireless sets in the radio game the SD referred to as the *Englandspiel* and the Abwehr code-named *Nordpol*. (When Giskes was first informed that the British were about to make a parachute drop arranged on the captured radio he found it so unbelievable his response was, *Gehen Sie zum Nordpol mit Ihren Geschichten* – 'Go to the North Pole with your stories.' Thus 'Operation North Pole'.) Before it was over the Germans received a stream of over fifty agents and repeated drops of containers of munitions, including the new secret plastic explosive, and valuable currency and gold in what David Kahn's authoritative postwar history of wartime cryptography would call 'the worst Allied defeat in the espionage war.'[8] Eventually two of the agents who had been captured on arrival managed to escape and make their way through occupied Europe to tell their story. It was not believed in London, where word had been received from one of the captured sets that they had not really escaped but had been 'turned', and were operating as double agents.

By the time the game was over, fourteen months after it had begun, it was the spring of 1944. On April Fool's Day of that year the Germans who had run the *Englandspiel* sent a message to SOE in London. It read: YOU ARE TRYING TO MAKE BUSINESS IN THE NETHERLANDS WITHOUT OUR ASSISTANCE STOP WE THINK THIS RATHER UNFAIR IN VIEW OUR LONG AND SUCCESSFUL COOPERATION AS YOUR SOLE AGENT STOP BUT NEVER MIND WHENEVER YOU WILL COME TO PAY A VISIT TO THE CONTINENT YOU MAY BE ASSURED THAT YOU WILL BE RECEIVED WITH SAME CARE AND RESULT AS ALL THOSE YOU SENT US BEFORE STOP SO LONG.

The care referred to had meant concentration camps for all of those who had been sent and particularly horrible execution at Mauthausen and Gross-Rosen for all but five of them, the total number to survive the *Englandspiel* catastrophe. The other results of the more than a thousand messages exchanged in the game were the arrest of some 150 Dutch resisters and the liquidation of several intelligence and sabotage groups as well as the lives of some fifty British airmen shot down in bombers transporting the arms and ammunition, radio and radar equipment, supplies and money which fell into German hands.

North Pole was a disaster for SOE, and it led to others. The head of N Section supplied one of the captured wireless sets in Holland with a contact address in Paris, thus enabling Giskes to send one of his assistants, purporting to be the Dutch agent, into the very heart of the PROSPER network, one of the circumstances that led to the disaster of summer 1943. After that, of course, F Section too had its *Fünkspiele*, run by Dr Josef Goetz, the former schoolmaster whose French was as perfect as his German, from his second floor offices at 84 Avenue Foch for the better part of a year, until April 1944. To the results of the radio games must be added the arrest, deportation and many deaths of the French *resistants* – estimates of whose numbers range from 400 to 1,500 – who were taken in the roundups following the arrests of Francis Suttill and Gilbert Norman as a result of the pact they negotiated with the Germans.

Yet the ultimate goal of the wireless deceptions was not attained by Giskes and his colleagues in the SD, who never did succeed in learning from any of the messages exchanged with London what the Germans most needed to know – where and when the Allied invasion of western Europe would take place.

Not all of the details of the *Englandspiel* later revealed by Dutch government investigators were presented in the Giskes book, but enough was there to reveal colossal ineptitude, inexcusable poor judgement and, to some, to suggest even worse possibilities. Despite the fact that weak signals from the field and agents' haste operating under pressure meant that most messages were at best imperfect and often so garbled that, according to David Kahn, 'the decipherers were happy if they could just read the text,' there seems no arguing with his conclusion that the negligence of SOE in ignoring the absence of the crucial security check noted on the majority of the messages handed on to them from the decoders 'bordered on the criminal'.[9]

And meanwhile other sources shed some glimmerings of light on the murky muddle of errors and betrayals that were beginning to be perceived in the postwar sorting out of events in occupied France.[10] On the Continent, not only participants in the events in question but scholars and journalists were unearthing rather less savoury aspects of the past than the British were prepared to acknowledge. Not frustrated by the destruction of records and the lack of cooperation from government officials that plagued British writers, French historians were able to start earlier and delve deeper into the recent past.[11]

What the French chose to remember was not always the same as what the British recorded – and vice versa. For the French, the shame was the extent of their enthusiastic collusion with the Nazis under the occupation; they were willing enough to expose whatever sins could be attributed to the British. And stereotypical British reticence did nothing to dispel the impression that where there was a smokescreen, there must be something to hide. Exactly what it could be remained a mystery.

CHAPTER 12

Cat and Mouse

Early in 1954 a memoir appeared, first in German and then in English, that provided some of the clues to the mystery. It was the account of the exploits of Hugo Bleicher, the sergeant in the Abwehr who, as Colonel Henri, had insinuated himself into the very heart of the French resistance.

In addition to his fluency in French, his success appears to have been due at least in part to his charm. Although not particularly handsome, Bleicher was attractive to women. In fact, he seems to have had the ability to seduce them with little effort, as well as the ability to gain the confidence of men and convince them of his sympathy. His attractions are not discernible in anything he wrote, nor are they obvious in his photographs, but the record of his accomplishments is the record of a series of encounters in which he was able to persuade men and women under duress that he was their friend and their ally. In truth, he was neither, but the ease with which he was able to turn men and women round to his purposes set into motion a train of events which ended in cataclysm. Where it began was in CARTE, the early but ineffective resistance organization in the south of France.

By the end of 1942 things had come to a head among the rival would-be organizers of resistance on the Riviera. André Girard, who used the name of the phantom organization, Carte, as his own code name, and his second-in-command, Henri Frager, known as Paul, were no longer on speaking terms. It would be necessary for Baker Street to make a choice – Girard or Frager as leader of the resistance in the south. By the new year the split had become irrevocable and, forced to choose, Peter Churchill decided on Frager as the more practical of the two prima donnas. Baker Street was so informed and in the spring of 1943 Frager became F Section's man. In March he accompanied Churchill on a Lysander flight to London for briefing.

The plane that took them out brought in Francis Cammaerts, the eventual organizer of the outstandingly successful JOCKEY circuit in the south-east. Cammaerts' mission was to look over the CARTE situation and use his own judgement as to whether to work with them or move on and start afresh somewhere else. A far more perspicacious judge of men and means than either Churchill or Buckmaster, Cammaerts saw the essential frivolity of Carte and his claims and the dangerous insecurity of the group around Odette, some of whom told him, 'We are negotiating with the Germans', and he made the right decision.

Meanwhile in Paris, the very day after Cammaerts' arrival, Bleicher had arrested the luckless CARTE agent Marsac in a café off the Champs Élysées and deposited him in Fresnes. There, with his usual sympathetic manner, he had convinced Marsac that he was an anti-Nazi German army officer who deplored the tactics of the Gestapo, and cooked up a deal with him whereby the credulous Marsac would be released with Bleicher's help. It would be necessary, he explained, for Marsac to produce a fellow agent to plan the next move with them. Bleicher promised that no harm would come to anyone as a result of the scheme and Marsac sat down and wrote a letter to his assistant, one Roger Bardet, asking him to come to Fresnes to visit him and discuss his escape. It was Marsac who dubbed Bleicher 'Colonel Henri', the name of a German officer he had known before the war.

Armed with Marsac's letter to Bardet and another to Marsac's wife, 'Colonel Henri' set off that evening for the beautiful mountain lake country of the Jura, where he had been directed in order to contact Bardet at a villa called Les Tilleuils, the Lime Trees, in the tiny village of St Jorioz near Annecy in the Haute Savoie. There Bleicher made contact with Mme Marsac and

Bardet, who agreed to come to Paris. Before he left, Bleicher had a chance to appraise the rest of the group. He noted the squabbling that went on and the resentment some of the sloppier old-time agents felt towards the newcomer in their midst, the somewhat imperious agent they called Lise, whom he would come to know as Odette Churchill. Most important, he noted the inadequate security measures that had made it possible for him to eat his lunch within arm's length of the group of British-led agents at their local hangout, the quaint chalet-like Hôtel de la Poste.

Back at Fresnes, it was easy for Bleicher to persuade the impressionable Marsac, with what Bleicher called 'his unlimited confidence in me'[1] to send Bardet back to St Jorioz to make arrangements for a flight to London for the two of them, Marsac and 'Colonel Henri', who would presumably try to broker peace negotiations there on behalf of a group of anti-Nazi Germans. Arrangements were also to be made for a transmitter to fall into Bleicher's hands, supposedly to allay any suspicions on the Germans' part about Marsac being released in order to work for Bleicher.

The Byzantine complications of all of this plotting become dizzying. Foolish and dramatic, chaotic and unrealistic, the behaviour of everyone involved played into Bleicher's hands. Marsac even agreed to give Bleicher, as an earnest token of his intentions, a list of about twenty addresses of circuits in Bordeaux, Marseille, Strasbourg and elsewhere. They were groups up to then completely unknown to the Germans. 'My success', admitted Bleicher, 'surprised me'.[2]

He continued to visit Marsac in Fresnes every day, exploiting the other man's loneliness and fear by means of his gentleness and sympathy, which proved more effective than violence. After a series of casual daily talks in Marsac's cell Bleicher knew just about all there was to know about what was going on in St Jorioz. Marsac only misled him on one point – he evidently believed, and told Bleicher, that Peter Churchill was the great man's nephew. Which made him all the more interesting to an ambitious operator in a field in which he not only had to watch out for his enemies on the other side but for the enemies on his own side – the SD. The competition between the two services dealing with spies and saboteurs was intense and often bitter. It would be an undoubted coup for a lowly sergeant, and one which would earn him the gratitude of his superiors, if the Abwehr were to bring in the St Jorioz group.

In a move that should have spelled failure for Bleicher's purposes, Baker Street's response to Bardet's request for air transport for Marsac and his 'Colonel Henri' was to refuse unequivocally and to insist that all contact be broken off immediately with both Marsac and his colonel, who was described as 'highly dangerous'. Instead, ignoring London's orders, Bardet returned to Paris, where he was arrested with a group of other agents at a meeting Bleicher had set up in Mme Marsac's apartment. Bleicher immediately set off for St Jorioz. He found Les Tilleuls empty, but not, as might have been expected, because Churchill and Odette had left the area, as they should have after receiving London's reply.

Another hiding place had already been arranged for them across the lake, but they had decided to put off leaving until the following day. They were spending the night at the Hôtel de la Poste, and it was there that Bleicher, accompanied by the arresting Italian officer, found them. It was now mid-April of 1943. They were handed over on 8 May to the German military authorities in France and sent to Fresnes, where they joined so many other of their fellow agents betrayed by luck or by opportunists or by their own carelessness. Odette would spend a year there before joining the seven doomed women on their journey from the Avenue Foch to Karlsruhe.

Bleicher did not win a medal for the capture of the two agents the Germans considered at the time to be more dangerous than they really were. He did not even get a promotion. What he did get was Roger Bardet.

According to Bleicher, prison opened Bardet's eyes as it had those of La Chatte. Rotting away in a cell was not his idea of how to pass the remainder of the war; life was too short for that, and he did not intend to shorten it further by getting himself shot, or worse. What he offered was inside information about F Section and in particular about hidden weapons the organization had parachuted to its agents in the Savoie. What he asked in return, in addition to his freedom, was Bleicher's assurance that no harm would come to Henri Frager, his chief and his intimate friend. It was Frager whom London sent to become the organizer and leader of DONKEYMAN, a successor to the AUTOGIRO circuits, with subgroups all over France.

Bardet finally allowed himself to be persuaded that he must deliver Frager into Bleicher's hands and was allowed to escape and make his way back to Frager, who evidently accepted the story concocted to explain Bardet's escape and welcomed him with open arms. His fondness for the younger man seems to have outweighed the strictures against trusting anyone who had lately been in German hands. It was always to be understood that what looked like an escape might really have been an arrangement purchased at the price of being turned round to work for the other side. In the case of Roger Bardet it was exactly what had happened. And his mentor, blinded by affection, fell into the trap.

Sooner or later, all those who worked closely with him were bound to follow. Bardet offered to provide some really good new identity papers, for which purpose photographs of the British members of the organization, including Vera Leigh, were turned over to him. The forgeries turned out to be remarkably good indeed, having been issued by the German intelligence staff at the Hôtel Lutétia. 'It was not going to be difficult', observed Bleicher, 'to locate these agents and arrest them when we pleased.'[3]

In his own account of the arrest of Vera Leigh, whom he describes as 'the British woman agent, Simone, who had been acting as liaison officer to Paul [Frager]', Bleicher says, 'she lived hardly more than twenty paces from me, in a single room in the next street'.[4]

It was the beginning of 1944 and everyone with a finger to the wind knew what was about to blow across the channel. 'Everybody in France', Bleicher mused, 'was beginning to realize that the Germans had lost the war. Even the most reliable agents we had were going over to the Maquis, to rehabilitate themselves.'[5] One of them was Roger Bardet, who would manage to switch sides again and join the resistance, but not before performing a last service for the Germans.

Things were tough for the Germans all over France, and the 'colonel' was about to see all of his good work go for nothing. In February the military intelligence organization had been absorbed by the RSHA and his orders were as clear as was his peril if he should disobey them. He did what he had to, and arranged through Bardet for a rendezvous with Frager on 2 July 1944. Bardet made himself scarce and Frager found himself suddenly placed under arrest by the supposedly sympathetic anti-Nazi German colonel, who met his proffered hand with a pair of cuffs. 'I will never forget Paul's expression,' wrote Bleicher later, 'as he glanced at me in that instant'.[6] Hatred? Surprise? Utter disbelief at his own gullibility? No one will ever know. Frager was one of those hung from a meathook in Buchenwald in October 1944.

To anyone reading Bleicher's memoirs not just as another of the multitude of war adventures pouring off the British presses in the early 1950s but as part of a puzzle crying to be solved, the most interesting passage was contained in two paragraphs:

Strict orders came to Paris from Berlin that no longer were captured wireless operators to 'play back' their own sets to London. Wehrmacht wireless operators were to take over from them, and the agents were to be arrested immediately.

For the British were now turning the tables on us. They were perhaps placing their agents intentionally in reach of us, knowing that in due time these men would be decidedly useful.[7]

CHAPTER 13

Entanglements

Death Be Not Proud, the book that had grown out of Elizabeth Nicholas' interest in the fate of Diana Rowden, tied together many previously loose ends in a plot that had become so complex, so far-reaching, and so surprising to a public used to tales of heroic accomplishments by romanticized figures that it caused a sensation.

Nicholas was a journalist, a travel writer for the *Sunday Times*, who knew her way around France, spoke French well, and on a number of visits to the places where Diana and the others had been sent, met and talked at length with those who had known them in the field.

In doing so, she learned a good many details about how Diana and her travelling companions to Natzweiler had been caught, and about the other three women on the train from Paris to Karlsruhe who had not come back.

The oldest of the three, Yolande Marie Beekman, had been born in Paris in 1911. She went to school in London and liked to draw. She expected to be a designer or illustrator. Like Noor, she had a gentle disposition and an interest in the world of children. And like Noor, she did not seem the type to become involved in the world of secret military operations. Like so many other young women of all types, she joined the services, and somehow found – or was found by – the scouts for SOE. She was perfectly bilingual.

She was a WAAF officer just short of her thirty-second birthday when she climbed out of a Lysander on a field near Tours in the last autumn before the invasion of France. She travelled alone from there through Paris to Lille with her wireless set. It was a dangerous journey, especially with the luggage she was carrying, but she had an advantage over some of the other women agents who, like Diana Rowden, may have spoken French, but could hardly have been mistaken for Frenchwomen. Yolande Beekman, who was known in the field as both Mariette and Yvonne, actually was French. At St Quentin, north-east of Paris in the Aisne, she went to work as his radio operator for Gustave Bieler, a Canadian known in the field as Guy. Contemporary reports described him as 'very conscientious, keen and intelligent . . . sound judge of character . . . absolutely reliable' and a 'born organizer' and the official history of SOE in France describes his wireless operator as 'as steady, as reliable and as unforgettable as himself'.[1] They were by all accounts both outstanding agents of integrity.

As organizer of the MUSICIAN circuit in eastern Picardy, where significant numbers of railway sabotage actions were carried out under his direction, Guy was in contact with Prosper as well as with a number of other members of his group. As many as ten of them, including Gilbert Norman and Andrée Borrel, used the same house as a meeting place. This staggeringly insecure arrangement was on the premises of Germaine Tambour, whose name was on the list of CARTE, itself the weakest link in the chain of security forged in the early days of clandestine activity.

Four months after her arrival, in January 1944, Yolande and Bieler were arrested together in the Café Moulin Brulé. Guy Bieler was shot by the SS at Flossenburg, where his demeanour so impressed his captors that they provided a guard of honour to escort him to his death.

Yolande Beekman was remembered in St Quentin as laughing, pretty, unafraid. A photograph taken of her before the war shows a young woman in a checked summer dress, a wide-brimmed straw hat on her lap, her graceful hands holding a parasol over her shoulder. She is smiling into the camera. The sun is in her eyes. She looks nothing like a candidate for the

Croix de Guerre. Like Diana Rowden, she had talked of coming back after the war, in her officer's uniform, to celebrate the liberation with the people there who had taken her in and given her a place from which she could transmit to London.

They never saw her after her arrest. She was taken to Fresnes and four months later to Germany, handcuffed to Odette, in the same compartment with Andrée Borrel and Vera Leigh. She was killed at Dachau in September, three months after the long-awaited invasion, with three of her fellow agents.

One of them was named Eliane Browne-Bartroli Plewman. Her fellow agent Pierre Raynaud remembered her decades later as 'of all the "girls", the most remarkable, beautiful, extra-ordinary'.[2] She was the child of a Spanish mother and a British father who had lived for most of his life in Marseille, where she was born in 1917 and where she spent most of her childhood. For a while she had been sent to school in England, and later to be 'finished' in Spain. After finishing school she returned to England and went to work for an importing firm in Leicester, where she handled business correspondence in Spanish, French, German, and English. Because she was born in France to an English father, she had had the option of choosing French or British nationality. She and her brothers had chosen to be British; one of them, Albert Browne-Bartroli, was also an F Section agent. He capped an impressive record in the Lyon area by surviving to the end.

In Leicester Eliane met and fell in love with a young man named Tom Plewman. They planned to marry but when the war broke out she went back to the Continent to work for the British Embassy in the neutral countries, first in Madrid and then in Lisbon. Tom Plewman had joined the army and in the spring of 1942, when Eliane returned to England to work for the Spanish Section of the Ministry of Information and Tom had received his commission, they decided to marry. The wedding took place that summer in Kensington. Eliane was twenty-four. A year later she would be dropped by parachute into occupied France. Tom Plewman said later he had never even tried to talk her out of going, knowing it would be useless, and in the end she had gone only after a first failed attempt had sent her back to Tempsford with shattered nerves but determined to try again.

She was dropped in mid-August 1943, twenty miles from where she was supposed to land, and made her own dangerous way to her destination. She was to work as Gaby with an agent named Charles Skepper, known in the field as Monk, as his courier in the Marseille area. Skepper had already been in France for two months; he had landed in the double Lysander operation that also brought in Diana Rowden and Noor Inayat Khan.

Like Vera Leigh in Paris, Eliane Plewman had been sent to an area where she was well known and risked chance encounters every day with someone who might recognize her. She would have been easy to recognize, a handsome young woman. In a formal photographic portrait she looks out with a straight gaze under arched brows, almost an icon of what we have come to think of as the forties look, her dark hair in an upsweep, her mouth defined by dark lipstick. She travelled back and forth between Marseille and Roquebrune and St Raphael on the Riviera, sometimes by train, sometimes in a *gazo*, a charcoal-fuelled old Ford truck driven by another agent, carrying messages and arranging for parachute drops and sabotage actions. The people who worked with her described her as pretty and gay, with a lively intelligence, the kind of woman who lit up a room when she entered it.

In March of 1944 Skepper was betrayed through information provided by a Frenchwoman who was the mistress of two men, one a member of the MONK circuit and one an employee of the Gestapo. He was arrested after a struggle in his apartment in the rue Mérentié and it was there that Eliane Plewman was caught the next day, having walked into a Gestapo trap along with the circuit's radio operator. Unlike most of the other women agents, she was subjected to a physically rough interrogation, perhaps because the Germans did not already know – or could not be sure they already knew – whatever she might have to tell. She never cracked, and told them nothing. After three weeks in the prison of Les Baumettes near Marseille she was sent to Fresnes. She left there in May of 1944 with the seven other women sent to Germany. Only three of them were left in Karlsruhe in September, when they were taken, along with Noor, to Dachau.

The third was Madeleine Damerment. Unlike the other two, she never worked in the field, never put any of her training into practice, and left no record behind other than of her captivity. She was dropped by parachute, on the night of 29 February 1944, straight into the waiting arms of the Germans.

She was dropped with her organizer, France Antelme, whose courier she was intended to be, and his radio operator, Lionel Lee, about twenty miles east of Chartres, an hour's drive for the reception committee that had set out from the Avenue Foch to meet them on the landing field. They put up a futile struggle and the tall, imposing Antelme was brought into Gestapo headquarters still in a towering rage. The Germans knew who he was. On his previous mission he had been seen often in Paris wining and dining with the PROSPER circle. And they had made the arrangements for his return on one of the captured radio sets they were playing back to London – the one belonging to Noor, the one on which she had transmitted for her organizer Garry, and it had been operated by enemy hands since her capture four months earlier.

At that time the Germans had also come into possession of her codes and security checks and the batch of her past messages she had kept under the misapprehension about filing instructions. These enabled the Germans to study her Morse signalling style. In addition, they had been monitoring her transmissions on their direction-finding equipment for some time before pouncing on her, and one of their operators was able to imitate her touch. Still, Baker Street had reason to distrust the messages it was presumably receiving from her. There had certainly been reports of the spreading disasters in the Paris area.

Around Christmas time some messages were sent to her radio concerning her family, on the assumption that only she herself would be able to answer appropriately. Answers did come back, and they were the right ones, although she was already in chains in a German prison. Like other prisoners, she occasionally talked to a sympathetic listener among her jailers, simply for what pleasure could be derived from reminiscing about what was dear to her, thinking what she talked about could not have any importance to anyone . . .

The F Section staff then turned to Antelme, who had got to know her in Paris, and who, after looking over the messages that had been received recently from Poste Madeleine, concluded that in all probability it was Noor herself who was transmitting them. It would follow that the PHONO circuit was still secure enough to arrange his reception.

It was a terrible error. And it sealed the terrible fate of his courier, Madeleine Damerment.

She was twenty-six, the same age as Eliane Plewman, with whom she would leave Karlsruhe to go to her death along with Yolande Beekman. She had been born in Lille, near the Belgian border, during the First World War. Her father was a postal official there and her upbringing was traditional French Catholic. In the early days of the occupation the entire Damerment family became involved in the resistance. It began with providing food for French prisoners of war working for the Germans in local factories and ended in organizing escapes. Like Andrée Borrel, Madeleine Damerment first took part in clandestine work on the PAT escape line established by the Belgian army doctor Albert Guérisse.

After two years of helping to shepherd downed Allied airmen along the way back through neutral territory, she found the Gestapo on her trail and had to escape herself. Like all of those who made it over the mountains and across the Spanish frontier to be caught on the other side, she was interned in the notorious concentration camp at Miranda de Ibro, south of Bilbao. The British Consulate in Madrid negotiated the release of British subjects as well as other prisoners who had worked for the Allies, and Madeleine was eventually freed and sent via Gibraltar to England, where army doctors and the care of a family with whom she stayed near Oxford made up for the months of internment with its meagre bad food and inadequate sanitation. She made friends with some of the members of the Free French Forces she met in England and for a while lived among the nuns at a convent. Fresh-faced, round-cheeked and dimpled, her head framed by a cloud of curly dark hair, she looks in a somewhat blurry photograph like a smiling teenager. A brooch on the collar of her dark blouse suggests a pair of wings.

In October of 1943 she volunteered, as a War Office document put it, 'for work as a courier with a British controlled Resistance Circuit in France'.[3] By the middle of February she was an ensign in the FANY and ready to take off on the mission that would land her in France and the waiting arms of the Germans.

For the four months they spent in Karlsruhe Eliane and Madeleine, who had shared a train compartment on the way there with Diana Rowden, were in adjoining cells. They were able to communicate through other prisoners, and knew when Odette Churchill and four of the other women they had travelled with from Paris disappeared. They had no idea where they had gone or what had happened to them. Towards the end, in the late summer and early autumn of 1944, they heard the loud droning of British and American bombers overhead and the wail of the air raid sirens.

Three months after the assault on the beaches of western France the Allies had achieved supremacy in the air over Germany. The French had retaken Paris, with the British and the Americans stepping aside to let them take the bows. De Gaulle had returned and French men and women followed him down the Champs Élysées. That summer had seen furious resistance activity. There were tragic maquis defeats like the one on the Vercors plateau in the south-east, and there was a steady succession of sabotage actions, particularly of railway lines, that held up the German divisions and made it difficult for them either to reach Normandy in the crucial early days following the invasion or to retreat eastwards later. By autumn, SOE operations in France were over and Baker Street was winding up its affairs.

During the heavy raids on Karlsruhe, Madeleine clasped her rosary beads and prayed. And sometimes sang, to keep her spirits up. She had made friends with a German woman in her cell with whom she traded memories of home and family as well as bits of food. They told each other the stories of books they had read and plays they had seen. It was this woman, who had been denounced and imprisoned for telling a joke about Hitler on the street, who told Elizabeth Nicholas years afterwards about those days and nights in early September.

They ended on the morning of the twelfth, when Madeleine and Eliane Plewman and Yolande Beekman were brought together in the grim reception room of the prison with Noor Inayat Khan, who had been transported from the prison at Pforzheim the previous evening. They were given their few remaining personal possessions and handed over to the same two Gestapo officers who had escorted the four other women agents from there to Natzweiler two months earlier. The four women and their Gestapo guards boarded an early train for Munich, where they arrived in the late afternoon and changed for the last train to Dachau.

No one would ever have known what had become of these women if not for Vera Atkins and the quest she undertook out of her personal determination. But she never did discover the identity of the fourth woman killed at Natzweiler, the eighth passenger who made the journey on the train from France into Germany in May of 1943. It remained for Elizabeth Nicholas to make that discovery.

In the course of the travels and interviews she began in the effort to find out what had happened to her friend Diana Rowden, she made a number of surprising – even to her – discoveries, and from them she drew a number of conclusions, some of them bitter ones.

Crisscrossing France on the trail of Diana and the other women who made the journey into Germany with her and did not come back, starting in the summer of 1955 Elizabeth Nicholas visited towns and hamlets where she talked with the ordinary men and women who more than ten years earlier had sheltered them and worked with them and, in some cases, been deported like them. She learned about those who, like them, had not come back. She also met and talked with some of those who had been involved in their betrayals and arrests, and read the depositions provided by others. And putting together everything she had learned about the seven women whose friends and hosts, enemies and stalkers she had listened to, as well as those of Noor, who had joined them at the end, Nicholas concluded that all eight had been betrayed through the radio game 'or through Bleicher and his band of traitors'. She asked how it had been possible 'that so many groups, involving so many people, that should have been entirely watertight were in fact integrated to a degree where penetration of one meant penetration of all'.[4] And she accused F Section of a negligence she stopped just short of characterizing as criminal in matters of proper security.

She was the first, although she would not be the last, to suggest the possibility – she called it 'a truly dreadful theory' – that:

> London was engaged in a game of double bluff: that is to say, it had known very well that the Poste Madeleine had been taken over by the Germans, and was busily feeding to it false information to deceive the enemy. More than this, in order to convince the Germans that London believed the Poste Madeleine was still in British hands, London was prepared to send agents deliberately to a reception committee organized by the Germans, so as to maintain the deception.

She was also neither the first nor the last to point out that 'such action would demand a logical and cruel ruthlessness such as the British never employ, even in war'.[5] Still, how was it possible to explain that London had continued to exchange signals with agents whose arrests and imprisonment had been reliably reported? That question would go on occupying historians, journalists, and other interested parties for the next half century.

A second accusation that grew out of the contacts Elizabeth Nicholas made in the course of her research was that F Section had neglected the families left behind by the murdered agents and in fact treated their next of kin rather shabbily. All of them had gone on receiving 'good news' letters – routine communications intended to allay the anxiety of relatives of agents in the field, reading something like, 'We continue to receive excellent news of X' – long after the agents who were their wives, daughters, or sisters were known to have been captured. Vera Leigh's half-brother had learned of her arrest from relatives of theirs in France, while the War Office was still pretending ignorance of her whereabouts.

When their deaths had finally been revealed to their families, it was in identical form letters on which only the names and dates were different. And on the letter informing Tom Plewman that his wife was dead – sent almost two years after she had been shot at Dachau – her name was misspelled throughout. Diana Rowden's mother had thought for ten years that Diana must have ended her career in some kind of disgrace, she had been told so little about her service. And she was never informed that Diana had been awarded a posthumous Croix de Guerre until Elizabeth Nicholas discovered the fact and arranged for it to be sent to her.

Andrée Borrel never received a decoration of any kind – not even the Médaille de la Résistance. From the postwar French government's point of view, she had worked for the British, not for France. And, although she was recommended for a Military Cross, it turned out that it could only be awarded to men. The official explanation given for London's refusal of Diana Rowden's Croix de Guerre was that the British government had a policy of not accepting posthumous decorations conferred on British service personnel by foreign governments because some countries issued such awards more liberally than the British, who would therefore have been unable to reciprocate in kind. In fact, it seemed to Elizabeth Nicholas more like part of a pattern to assure that as little as possible would be known about the failures, as distinct from the successes, of the agents SOE had sent into the field in France.

It was a policy consistent with the final charge in the indictment drawn up in her book, in which she accused SOE of playing favourites among the authors who sought help in writing books about the organization. Those whose subjects were agents who had returned and were portrayed in the most favourable light as heroes and heroines in an extraordinary adventure were given War Office permission to publish and even some information from the closely guarded files and whatever other records remained. Those who wanted to write about the agents who did not return and question what had happened to them were rebuffed. SOE matters, it was claimed, had to be kept secret, but some, Nicholas maintained, were being kept more secret than others.

She also showed how the postwar governments of both France and Britain had managed to ignore the earliest and truest resistance fighters – the simple people who had no politics and were without influence, who got no medals or any recognition at all for having, long before it became prudent to do so, helped to hide a downed flyer or a cache of arms in their barn, brought food to the maquis in the hills or let a British agent throw an aerial out of an attic window in order to transmit wireless signals from inside their house. Many of them had been deported. Those who returned were given no fanfare, no parades. To the de Gaulle government, their position was ambiguous. Not exactly traitors, they had been working in aid of a foreign power. That power was Britain, and consorting with the English would sometimes seem to have been a worse offence than to have consorted with the Germans, like so many of those who roused themselves to action against the occupiers only when it was clear that they were on the run and who did end up with medals. Timing was all. Or perhaps not quite all. Elizabeth Nicholas thought that in the places where resistance had sprung up early it was because 'a few good people' of character had taken the first decisive step and others had followed their lead, forming a growing network around this original hard core wherever it existed.

In St Quentin Elizabeth Nicholas talked with the woman who had provided attic space in her simple house for Yolande Beekman to transmit signals from and with the woman who ran the little café in which Yolande and her organizer had been arrested. The café owner had been sent to Ravensbrück; her husband had died in Buchenwald. Ten years later she said;

> All the honours went to the resisters of the last hour, who were still alive and free at the liberation. Most of us, who had resisted at once when it was most dangerous, were dead or in concentration camps. When we, the survivors, came home in 1945 it was all over. No one was interested in us.[6]

Although the words read bitterly on the page, Elizabeth Nicholas described them at the time as simply spoken matter-of-factly. All of the ordinary people, working-class or from rural areas, who had helped the British agents when there was the greatest risk involved and who were forgotten or ignored afterwards, made similar comments. 'What we did is something we know ourselves . . . For me, there could have been no other choice; now I am at peace . . . It is enough for me to know that I need not reproach myself . . . I can live on good terms with myself and that is all that matters.'[7]

In April 1956 Nicholas went to the little town of Tettnang near the West German shore of Lake Constance to interview Hugo Bleicher, whom she found 'a chubby, amiable, cosy little man, busy selling tobacco'. She had expected Genghis Khan or Sherlock Holmes. What she got instead was more like Pickwick. Once again, his charm was put into operation. It still worked. And this on a woman who knew everything he had set in motion and where it had ended. In spite of herself, Nicholas found him,

as he retold his exploits with his children on his lap, seeming like
the kindly father figure he had seemed to all those agents, men
and women, he had once beguiled in their prison cells.

To Bleicher the women agents were 'poor little things' who
'did no harm'. He waved a dismissive hand as he told her how
he 'let them go their innocent little ways, unless they had the
misfortune to cross my path, to get in my light'. Then, of course,
he was forced to 'take action'. And he told how Vera Leigh,
'Simone' to him, had crossed his path, tangled in the web he had
spun with Roger Bardet in which so many of Frager's and
Suttill's agents had been caught. 'As a matter of fact', he told
Nicholas, 'for months I would watch her tripping along the
pavement in the morning, so busy, so *affairée*. She was of no
interest to me; so long as she kept out of my way, she could play
at spies.'[8]

Bleicher agreeably provided a good deal of material – not all
of it necessarily trustworthy – that would bear on future attempts
to untangle the various threads of the F Section disasters. He
referred to things there was no way of knowing from what had
appeared in Britain up to then, for instance that Nicholas Bodington, Buckmaster's deputy, had been in Paris during the fateful
summer of 1943 and that he, Bleicher, had known of his presence
there but had not arrested him. According to Bleicher, the reason
had been that it was more useful to the Germans to observe his
movements rather than risk tipping off the British as to the
extent to which F Section circuits had been penetrated. But he
was playing his own game too, and to forestall criticism from
the SD, should the question arise as to why the Abwehr had
made no arrest as a consequence of the Bodington visit, he
decided he had to sacrifice Simone – Vera Leigh – an easy
enough prey.

But Elizabeth Nicholas had done more than reveal the circumstances that tied together the betrayals leading to the deaths of
the eight women who ended up at Natzweiler and Dachau,
showing how each of them had been connected in some
way with the PROSPER group – connected, interpenetrated, and

compromised from the beginning. She had also done more than suggest that their own side was somehow implicated in what happened to them, either by an ineptitude at Baker Street so extreme as to be almost unbelievable or by a Machiavellian ruthlessness somewhere else in London equally hard to accept. She had discovered and published the identity of the fourth woman killed at Natzweiler, the hitherto anonymous companion of Andrée Borrel, Vera Leigh and Diana Rowden.

The solution to the mystery was simple, but like all simple answers to seemingly inexplicable things, it turned out to be a matter of asking the question in a different way. Up to now everyone, including Vera Atkins, had sought to establish the identity of British agents who had been transferred from Fresnes to Karlsruhe. But in fact the fourth woman was not British, she was French. Although she had been closely connected with the others and worked for a sub-circuit of the PROSPER network, she had never been to England and there was no record of her existence in any F Section files. Her name could be found in the records at Karlsruhe, but only by someone who thought to look under the dates of entering and leaving rather than under prisoners' nationalities. That someone was a friend of Elizabeth Nicholas with no other connection to F Section agents, SOE, or the resistance. The very unfamiliarity of it all may in fact have been what enabled him to approach the question from the fresh angle that, twelve years later, finally yielded the name of the woman who had died with Andrée Borrel, Vera Leigh, and Diana Rowden at Natzweiler.

CHAPTER 14

Sonia: The Fourth Woman

Plagued by illness, hospitalized with a spinal injury for which she underwent painful surgery, and occasionally bedridden for long stretches of time, Elizabeth Nicholas drew a sympathetic colleague of hers into her project, helping her search out sources and track down witnesses. Antony Terry was a correspondent for the *Sunday Times*, the paper for which Elizabeth Nicholas wrote travel articles, and he was on the spot, living in Bonn. Travelling around the country in the course of reporting from postwar Germany, he had seen the evidence of the Germans' killing factories himself, and made no secret of his disgust with 'the strange vagueness which always drifts into the voices of Foreign Office boys when you ask them anything which might revive nasty thoughts about the dear dear Germans who are now so schoen in every way.' In May of 1956 he wrote in a letter to Nicholas:

> In Dachau, unless the Germans or the hygienic Americans have pulled it down or scrubbed it, you can still see the big 'shower rooms' near the crematorium where the walls were (and when I was there *still* were) brown with the ordure from the victims who in their terror at being packed in tightly like sardines (children naturally not excepted) forgot themselves in a typically un-German and sub-human manner and besmirched the good clean Deutsche walls up to waist height, until the hissing of the Cyklon gas pouring in through the 'shower bath' nozzles in the roof gradually

killed them or made them ripe for the crematorium next door. Such typically non-aryan behaviour, one feels.[1]

In March 1956 Terry had written a piece on Bleicher's revelations, which had been appearing in the German and British popular presses. It was not hard for Nicholas to enlist him in her project and he undertook to do some legwork for her. It was Terry who found out the whereabouts of the ex-Gestapo officials Wassmer and Ott, who had brought the women agents to Natzweiler and Dachau, and who were now living in comfortable retirement on their pensions, and it was Terry who persuaded the British Embassy's legal department to provide information on the ultimate fates of the Natzweiler defendants. Röhde, Straub, and Berg, he was able to inform her, had been executed in 1946; Hartjenstein had been sentenced to death but died of an illness before the sentence could be carried out; Wochner and Bruttel had been sentenced to prison terms, then transferred to the French authorities, who had released them; and Zeuss and two others had been found not guilty. And it was Terry who interviewed on Nicholas' behalf the two women in charge of the section at Karlsruhe from which the three agents had been taken to Dachau.

The 'two old biddies who were working on the prison records back in the days of July 1944' shared the passion for regularity in all official matters which led so many bureaucrats in the vast Nazi killing enterprise to be able to produce, when required, proper records of the tortured and meticulous receipts for the murdered. 'I often discovered during years of interrogation of Germans,' Terry wrote to Nicholas, 'that they have, in fact, amazing memories (particularly about horrors) and recap all sort of things that astonish one, years later.'[2]

It was in his letter from Karlsruhe in March that Terry 'launched', as Nicholas later put it, 'his bombshell'.

He wrote:

In addition to the [prisoners] of British nationality, the following woman of French nationality was brought to

Karlsruhe from Fresnes on the same day, 13.5.44, and removed also on the 6.7.44 by the Gestapo.

She was Sonia Olschanezky, born in Paris 25.12.23. Profession, dancer.

Address: Paris . . .

Could it be possible that the fourth girl killed at Natzweiler was Sonia Olschanezky?[3]

Elizabeth Nicholas was sure that she was. She had only to prove that Sonia Olschanezky* had also worked for SOE. And four months later she was able to do just that. A dozen years after the killings at Natzweiler she was able to establish in two hours of combing the records at the Paris office of Libre Résistance, the association of former F Section *réseaux*, the identity of the companion of Andrée Borrel, Vera Leigh and Diana Rowden. The French too were keeping records, and while some were beginning the painstaking scholarship of compiling official histories, others recorded the activities of various groups of resisters and deportees in files open to anyone interested in perusing them. At the headquarters of the F Section *amicale* in the rue Paul Cézanne was a file for each one of some eighty *réseaux* that had operated under SOE direction. There was also a separate list of agents. On it under 'O' were the names Olschanezky, Enoch, and Olschanezky, Sonia.

Elizabeth Nicholas' notes of what she found under those two entries included the information that Sonia Olschanezky had joined the *réseau* in March 1942 as an *agent de liaison*, was promoted in November of that year to the rank of *sous-lieutenant*, was unmarried, had lived at 72 Faubourg Poissonière, and had been arrested on 22 January 1944. Her brother had joined in June 1942 and operated as a letter box, receiving messages from agents to be picked up by others, to avoid their coming in direct

---

* English sources and many books following them have spelled the name 'Olschanesky'. The family spelling, the one preferred by the surviving kin, and in the French records and on the plaque at Natzweiler is 'Olschanezky'.

contact. He had been arrested on the same day as his sister. The last entry read *déporté sans nouvelles*.

Among the files of the individual *réseaux* was one marked ROBIN (referred to on the British code list as JUGGLER) and in it the name of Sonia Olschanezky appeared again, this time with an address on the rue Bleue, only a short distance from the Faubourg Poisonnière in the neighbourhood of the Gare de l'Est.

Elizabeth Nicholas had not only identified the unknown fourth woman killed at Natzweiler, she had established that, like the three others, she too had been connected to the doomed PROSPER organization.

All of them had been linked to circuits which had been penetrated and whose radio sets were being worked back to London by the Germans. All of them were linked to Suttill, to Carte and Frager, Bleicher and Bardet. All of them knew too much about things the Germans – and perhaps others – would not want revealed.

The head of the ROBIN circuit for which Sonia worked, Jean Worms, had been in contact with Peter Churchill on the Riviera before being sent to England for training towards the end of 1942. Jacques Weil, who had been a member of INTERALLIÉ, the early resistance group penetrated by Bleicher, was an old friend of Worms. Weil became the second in command of ROBIN, which organized sabotage actions in the area of its base in Châlons-sur-Marne, about a hundred miles east of Paris.

Sonia regularly carried messages from there to Guy Bieler and Yolande Beekman in St Quentin to the north. She had been in contact with Prosper and his assistant Andrée Borrel; with Garry, whose radio operator was Noor, on whose captured set the arrangements were made for Madeleine Damerment to be dropped along with France Antelme; and with Sidney Jones, whose courier was Vera Leigh and who had worked in Marseille, where Eliane Plewman also operated. Even Diana Rowden, far away in the Jura, belonged to a group which had connections with the same circuits, used many of the same contacts, and received instructions via some of the same wireless sets – including those that were being operated by enemies playing the radio game.

And like the others, Sonia Olschanezky too had left behind a family uninformed of her fate. The families of the other three had all by now learned, from War Office communications, the Wuppertal trial record and other published sources, as well as what Elizabeth Nicholas had been able to tell them as a result of her investigations, what there was to know. But no one had ever connected Sonia Olschanezky with the Natzweiler affair. In the beginning Vera Atkins had thought that Noor Inayat Khan had been the fourth Natzweiler victim. The description seemed to fit. Brian Stonehouse's memory of a 'girl [with] very black oily hair . . . aged about twenty to twenty-five years' who was 'short and was wearing a tweed coat and skirt' could have been Noor, and Odette had thought a photograph of Noor she had been shown after the war looked like the seventh woman on the train to Germany. But when the facts of the deaths at Dachau became known, and revealed that Noor had been brought from Pforzheim to join the three other women from Karlsruhe, it was clear that it was some other short black-haired woman in her early twenties who had ended up in the furnace at Natzweiler.

Sonia's mother and a second brother were still living in Paris. They had no information from anyone about what had happened to her after her arrest. The only word had been a postcard she had written and perhaps dropped somewhere, and which some-one had mailed from Germany. It said not to worry about her, she was all right. It was postmarked from Karlsruhe.

All that was known was that when things got too hot for him after the arrest of Worms at the beginning of July 1943, Weil had escaped to Switzerland, leaving Sonia in charge of what remained of the circuit. She had eluded the Gestapo and managed to survive through the autumn until she was taken in January 1944, a few days after Guy Bieler and Yolande Beekman were arrested in St Quentin.

Her mother still hoped Sonia might have been alive in some

camp in the east liberated by the Soviets and, because of her Slavic name and Russian roots, been forcibly repatriated to the USSR. Madame Olschanezky had been living on hope, and little else, since the end of the war. Although, with Sonia, she had worked for the 'Buckmaster *réseaux*', as the F Section circuits had come to be called in France, the British government could do little after the war for those locally recruited subagents like her who were left behind by its London-trained agents, and the French government, while it provided pensions for those who had joined Gaullist groups, retained a certain ambivalence towards those who had worked for the British-led resistance organizations. In any case, Madame Olschanezky was not one to put herself forward. Her life had not conditioned her to do so and she was further weakened by grief for her husband and anxiety about her missing children. So she stayed on in the small apartment where she had lived during the war, waiting and hoping for some word from Sonia. It was there that she was visited in the spring of 1958 by a reporter and a photographer from the London *Sunday Pictorial*.

Elizabeth Nicholas' book was about to appear, and serial rights had been sold by her publisher for a five-part feature to run that summer. The paper wanted photographs of the women it was going to describe in headline-size type as the '7 ANGELS OUT OF HELL', and, with Elizabeth Nicholas once again bedridden, the feature writer preparing the series was delegated to approach Madame Olschanezky. It was agreed that at first she would say only that the *Pictorial* was planning a series on women who had fought in the resistance, but the first thing Madame Olschanezky did when they met was to ask whether the writer knew anything about what had happened to Sonia and beg her, if she could, to end the uncertainty in which she had been suspended since the end of the war. Like all of the next of kin of the missing agents, she wanted to be told whatever there was to know. And now she, who until now had been told less than any of them, finally learned what had happened to her daughter.

She learned it from her surviving son. It was he who made the decision that she should be told what the writer knew, and he told her himself. The photographer did not miss the opportunity a short time afterwards for a shot of two faces. An older woman is looking down at a picture of a younger one. The face in the picture is that of a young woman whom a British SOE agent who had only seen her once remembered almost half a century later as 'one of the most beautiful women I've ever seen.'[4]

Serge Olschanezky doesn't have a print of that photograph, which remained the property of the *Sunday Pictorial*. But he has others, a large box full of them – blurred snapshots and artfully lit formal studio portraits, images of the history of a family that no longer exists.[5] At seventy, his face is deeply lined and his full head of wavy hair is white, but when he speaks, remembers, smiles, and frowns, he looks much like the boy in the family group portrait taken in the 1920s – a delicate-featured dreamer in a sailor suit that matches the one worn by his sturdier dark-eyed brother. The two of them flank their mother, an ample and satisfied presence who is holding their strikingly beautiful baby sister, her hair curled, her dress beribboned and pleated, her expression clear-eyed and perfectly serious as she meets the camera's eye.

Their father was born in Odessa. He came to Germany to study chemical engineering and at a dance for young people given by the Jewish community in Liepzig he met their mother. She was passing around a tray and when she held it out to him, he took it from her, handed it to the friend he had come with, and led her out onto the dance floor. They were engaged to be married on 1 August 1914, the day Germany declared war on Russia and began what would later be called the First World War.

Mobilization meant internment in a prison camp for a Russian citizen, but his fiancée's father, a portrait painter from Minsk who had married into an old German-Jewish family of professionals, doctors and scholars in Mainz, appealed to some of the society figures and aristocrats whose portraits he had painted and they succeeded in arranging for the young man's release after six months on condition that he report every week to the police station in Chemnitz. Cut off from the support of his family in Russia and, as an enemy alien, with no possibility of employment as a chemical engineer, Eli Olschanezky took a job as sales representative for a manufacturer of ladies' stockings.

In September of 1916 Sonia's parents were married and set up housekeeping in Chemnitz, where their three children were born, Enoch in September 1917, Tobias (who took the name of Serge later, during the Second World War) in March of 1919, and Sonia on 25 December 1923. Their father did so well in the stocking business that he became general manager of the company, which exported its hosiery to a number of other countries, including France, Hungary, and Romania.

The family lived well in those between-the-wars years, with a chauffeur, a cook, and a governess for the children in their large apartment in a handsome brick building on a tree-lined street, the Hellenenstrasse, where abundant hospitality was part of the comfortable bourgeois life. In his seventies, Serge still remembered the party that was given in celebration when Sonia was born, with individual tables for four, each with a little lamp on it, and professional entertainment after the supper.

Every Saturday evening there were guests, with champagne cooling on blocks of ice in the bathtubs. Eli Olschanezky kept track of his friends' preferences in cigars, cigarettes, and pipe tobacco, and at every party each guest would find his own brand at his place. Costume balls were the rage for birthday celebrations, and invitations would be sent out two months ahead of time announcing the theme in order to allow time for costumes to be thought up, designed, and sewn. Helene Olschanezky made her children's costumes herself. In a faded sepia photograph taken before the party, the theme of which was fairy tales, Sonia is the princess, her brothers her knight and a chamberlain. They look at ease, and just slightly amused, in their royal raiment and uniforms.

In those days there were frequent trips to fashionable watering places, Eli preferring Carlsbad, which was supposed to provide a cure for the liver ailments to which he was susceptible, and Helene preferring Marienbad, the spa known for its weight-loss regimen. Pictures of the family in those days show Eli looking portly, leaning on his cane, his hat worn at a jaunty angle, Helene in a fashionable wrapped coat and with a flower in her cloche-style hat. Between them Sonia is dressed in a coat with fur trim at the collar and cuffs. The boys, as usual, are in matching sailor suits.

Serge remembers that when they were children, he was given an elaborate toy castle with a regiment of little soldiers. He never played with the soldiers, preferring to play at being a doctor, practising on Sonia's dolls. It was Sonia who played with the soldiers. And when he had trouble fixing his bicycle wheel, it was Sonia who did it for him, and repaired the family sewing machine as well. He remembers that she read a lot, and that he took her to school and to her dancing lessons.

Secular Jews, the Olschanezkys did not keep a kosher kitchen or observe the sabbath, but they celebrated major Jewish holidays and Eli contributed regularly to such Jewish charities as the Jewish National Fund. Helene told her sons the only reason for which they had permission to fight was if someone called them a 'dirty Jew'. There was a family tradition that in the holiday season Helene expected the children to give some of their toys to the poor. She told them they weren't supposed to pick the ones they were tired of but ones they still liked. She delivered them herself in neighbourhoods not usually visited by the well-to-do. Eli told his children that the more intelligence and education an individual had, the more he owed to others.

In the summer of 1926 the family left the idyllic life of Chemnitz and moved to Romania, where Eli had been invited to set up and take charge of a factory to make silk stockings in Bucharest. He oversaw the construction of the factory and brought workers from Germany. The label of the stockings pictured two charming little dark-haired boys in an oval frame and the trade name EnTo, for Enoch and Tobias.

The company remained in the name of Eli's Romanian

partners, since foreigners were not allowed to own businesses. The company operated round the clock, with the three hundred German workers putting in long hours and earning comparatively high wages, a revolutionary situation from the point of view of local businessmen who paid their workers a pittance. After three years, his partners stopped Eli's credit with the banks, without which the business could not function in the time lag between delivery of orders and collection of bills due. Eli Olschanezky turned to his lawyer, who advised him to leave the country and forget the matter. He refused, and insisted on paying all the debts outstanding out of his own pocket, in order not, he said, to allow his name to be dirtied. The family's villa was sold, along with such treasures as their piano. Serge still remembers his film projector. He was ten years old then, over sixty years ago. He made sure not to cry, he remembers. He says he could tell that his parents were already unhappy enough.

Once again the Olschanezkys left a pleasant life for one in a new country. They arrived in France in January 1930 and settled into a *pension de famille* in the rue de la Santé in Paris's Thirteenth Arrondissement. The two boys started school at the École Alsacienne near the Luxembourg Gardens. Enoch, the oldest, was always at or near the head of his class; Tobias, or Toby as the family called him, somewhere in the middle of his. The senior Olschanezkys spoke little French. They had brought little with them from Romania and with almost no money of his own Eli Olschanezky went into partnership in a lingerie shop. Once again he took to the road, travelling to Germany to buy merchandise, for which he paid on his own and which he sent to his partner. Once again he found himself cheated and dispossessed. And once again he found himself without legal recourse, whether by an unlikely seeming coincidence or some character trait of naïveté or idealism, of too much trust in others or too little sense of how the brutal realities of human nature are played out in everyday life. In any case, the aggravation of this latest crisis left him sick, demoralized, and unable to reestablish himself.

Serge doesn't remember his mother ever complaining. 'When life was good', he says, 'she enjoyed it. When things went sour, she sold her jewellery,' but never reproached her husband. The family moved once again, to cheaper and more modest quarters, and it occurred to Serge that, with no money coming in, it was his responsibility to help his parents. His childhood ambition of becoming a paediatrician no longer seemed possible. With no experience, and no working papers or any possibility of getting any, being both underage and unconnected as well as not a French citizen, it seemed to Serge that his best chances were in the hotel business. There was always food around, and a chance for extra cash tips. So, at fifteen, he got up one morning and, instead of going to school, went to the top of the Champs Élysée and worked his way down from the Place de l'Étoile, from hotel to hotel, asking if they could use a boy. After numerous rejections, one hotelier offered him a chance to work for three days and, if at the end of that time he seemed to be working out, the prospect of a permanent job. He took it. When he told his parents about it, his mother cried. He comforted her with the observation that he probably wasn't a good enough student to have become a doctor and eventually he would probably become the owner of a big hotel or restaurant. And the next day he took his brother to work with him and got him a job too.

It was Sonia who was the best student in the family. An early report card from the École de jeune fille in the rue de la Ville l'Évèque commends her progress in reading and recitation, translation, maths and geography. When she accompanied a friend to a classical dance class after school one day, she was invited to join in and eventually what at first seemed like good exercise became a passion. She had grace; she was gifted. She became a dance student, and when the manager of a children's theatre saw her in class one day she was asked to join the theatre company. Her parents said no at first, but she eventually won them over, and at the age of ten she began performing with Le Théâtre du Petit Monde on Thursday afternoons, the school holiday. Through the influence of a distant relative of her mother's, she appeared on television in a demonstration of the new medium at the 1937 International Exposition in Paris. While still a schoolgirl she was working now as a performer, appearing at school dances and private affairs. Her professional name was Sonia Olys. Her mother was still making her costumes, filmy tutus which she wears in publicity photos, looking elegant and ethereal en pointe, ballgowns in which she looks dignified and glamorous, tap pants in which she looks slightly naughty, sporting a jaunty hat and cane.

It's easy to see how Brian Stonehouse and Odette could have mistakenly identified a photograph of Noor as the woman the one had seen for only a few minutes and the other had travelled with under conditions of great stress years earlier. Noor and Sonia were both slight and graceful; they both had large dark eyes and full lips. Either could have fitted the description of Sonia by Jacques Weil's biographer as small dark girl with black eyes, intensely beautiful.' Noor had even been described as looking Jewish.[6]

As the 1930s, Auden's 'low dishonest decade', drew to a close, it was clear to everyone in Europe, and most of all to Jews, that bad times lay ahead. With war imminent, none of the Olschanez-kys was a citizen of France, the country they now lived in. Eli Olschanezky had lost his Russian citizenship when he failed to return by 1927, the date the Soviets had made the cut-off for post-Revolution returnees. Their status was that of refugees protected by France, but they were not, strictly speaking, nation-als of any country. The solution seemed to be military service, which automatically conferred citizenship, and Enoch joined the army in 1938, followed by Serge in 1939.

With streams of refugees arriving in France as one country after another was overrun by the Nazis, the competition for jobs became intense, and Sonia was among those who were not working because they were not French. At sixteen, living in German-occupied Paris, she took a domestic position as an au pair with a family. She was glad to have a job.

In May 1940, fighting with the troops that were overrun

defending Belgium against the tidal wave of Panzers, Enoch had been among those captured and shipped off to Germany. Serge was taken prisoner a month later. By destroying his papers, and with them the proof of his Jewish identity, he managed to wind up in a prisoner of war camp instead of being loaded on one of the boxcars bound for the east. In April of 1942 he managed to escape from Stalag 51 just outside Stuttgart with the help of an anti-Nazi Communist who was employed delivering wine to the camp. Hidden in one of a truckload of empty barrels, Tobias, who by now had become Serge, was driven to Strasbourg, where he got on a train to Paris.

In Paris, he had some difficulty locating his mother, who had moved again. When he found her, he learned that his father had died just a month before, in March. His liver ailment had got worse and there were few doctors still around who would treat a Jew.

In the early days of the occupation, enthusiasm in France for Pétain, the revered fatherly hero of the First World War, was second only to the Germans' enthusiasm for Hitler until he began to lose the Second World War. Pétain, whose attitude toward the Jews could at best be described as somewhere between distaste and indifference, had agreed to the Nazi policies and signed the racial laws soon after coming to power. By the end of May 1942 all Jewish men, women, and children were ordered to wear a six-pointed yellow star sewn on their clothing over the region of the heart. The *rafles,* or roundups for deportation, began that summer and the first transports left for Auschwitz, the Jews walking along the streets to the nearby railway station as Parisians stood and watched in silence. It can be said for them that, unlike Germans, Poles, and various Slavs witnessing such scenes elsewhere, they are not reported to have smiled or cheered.

In June 1942, when Eli Olschanezky had been dead for three months, the French police came to arrest him and Sonia. Her legal status had been defined as *'protégée française'*, but that protection was now withdrawn. Her mother's status was still listed on her papers as *'protégée roumaine'*, which meant she was not to be included in this roundup. Only Sonia was taken, to be interned at the camp at Drancy.

CHAPTER 15

The Tightening Net

Sonia Olschanezky had seen the progress of the Germans' efforts to achieve racial purity as their laws were enforced without objection by the French. First the yellow star to be worn by every Jew over six months old, then the prohibitions against going to school, practising a profession, doing business, using the libraries, eating in restaurants or sitting in cafés. By now Jews were not allowed to own telephones, to buy stamps, or to enter a shop until the hours when the stores would be sold out or already closed. They were prohibited from riding on any but the last car of the Métro. But if life seemed impossible, for those who remained it was still life, and preferable to what lay waiting for them in the east, where few of their countrymen seemed unwilling to let them go. The more anti-Semitic laws were passed, the fewer Jews there were left to be affected by them.

Only in France of all the occupied countries was there no need for the appointment of a Gauleiter to carry out the racial policies. France was the only country besides Germany to draft its own anti-Semitic legislation. Anti-Jewish laws were passed by French officials and enforced by French police, who rounded up and arrested the Jews themselves in broad daylight in the streets of Paris and processed them for internment in camps administered by French police at Pithiviers, Beaune-la-Rolande, and Compiègne in the countryside and at Drancy, on the outskirts of Paris, where French police handled the details of record-keeping and arranged for transport for deportation to the death camps to the east. There is no evidence that they found it difficult to round up their Jewish neighbours; their greatest difficulty seems to have been in securing enough trains at first. Most of the camps were located in the unoccupied zone, where hesitation replaced enthusiasm for the *rafles* only when it began to look as though it might not be the Germans who would be in charge of Europe when the war was over.

Not to be outdone by his chief, Pétain's premier Pierre Laval demonstrated his enthusiasm for the occupying powers by handing over Jewish children even before the Germans had asked for them. In the end, France sent seventy-five thousand Jews to the death camps, including ten thousand children, while the rest of the world, like the Christian French, stood by.

The camp at Drancy had been set up in a location convenient to Le Bourget railway station, next to the airport where Charles Lindbergh had landed. Its watchtowers and barbed wire were in full view of the apartment buildings in the surrounding neighbourhood, and men and women passed the place on their way to and from work every day. Everyone could see what was going on. Simone de Beauvoir wrote of having gone out to wave greetings to a young Jew she knew inside.

Inside the camp food was meagre and what there was was bad; sanitary arrangements were inadequate; together with the crowding, conditions made disease inevitable. The old and the young suffered the most. Many children, some as young as a few months of age, were left behind when their parents were deported. Confused and frightened, unable to understand what was happening to them, holding onto whatever bits of belongings had not been taken away from them, they remained in the camp, some of the older ones trying to take care of the smaller ones, until they too were loaded onto the trains to the east by the gendarmes, with Red Cross workers looking on.

When Sonia arrived at Drancy, the average stay was three to four weeks before deportation. Sonia managed to extend her stay by volunteering to take care of some of the children who had been separated from their parents. In the meantime, her mother was making frantic efforts to find a way to rescue her. Mme Olschanezky got in touch with some relatives in the fur business who had been left alone so far because their factory, manufacturing coats for the Wehrmacht's use on the Russian front, was classified as economically useful. Through their efforts an Alsatian German official was persuaded, for a not unreasonable sum, to produce the necessary papers attesting to the fact that Sonia was a *Wirtschaftswertvolle Jüdin*, a Jew with economically valuable skills, employed by the Germans in the fur industry. The certificate was produced and Sonia was freed, one of the few to walk out of Drancy not towards death but back to her life. She was eighteen and she would have two more years left to her.

She told her mother, who later told Serge, that she felt she had to 'do something to defend us. Others won't do it for us. We must do it for ourselves.' Her mother asked if she didn't think she had already lost enough. Sonia answered that if everyone said that, no one would do anything. But she didn't know where to go, how to find a way to 'do something.'[1] Then, through one of the families she had worked for, she met Jacques Weil.

Weil was a Swiss citizen who was doing business in Paris when France fell. He joined an underground group which was providing the British Secret Intelligence Service with information about activity at railway stations and ports, making use of his cover as a commercial travelling citizen of a neutral country and some contacts with former members of the Deuxième Bureau, the French secret intelligence service.

In October of 1942, shortly after her arrival, Weil was contacted by Andrée Borrel; in the following weeks she introduced him to Prosper and Archambaud. in January of 1943, when Jean Worms returned from training in England to head ROBIN, the sub-circuit of PROSPER referred to by the British as JUGGLER, Weil became his second in command. The new circuit would operate out of Châlons-sur-Marne, a pivotal point for the movement of troop trains to and from Germany. From its Paris headquarters behind a carpet warehouse in the rue Cambon, near the Place de la Concorde, its agents would fan out through northern France, maintaining links to those in the south as well.

Until they were sent a wireless operator of their own, Gustave Cohen, they used Archambaud's radio as their link with London. Meanwhile, Jacques Weil continued his association with SIS/MI6.

Sonia was attracted to the older, experienced man of affairs, and was eager to take part in the resistance underground. She was willingly recruited to the Worms/Weil *réseau*, at first as a courier, travelling regularly along the triangle formed by Paris, St Quentin to the north, and Châlons to the east. She was intelligent, capable, and resourceful, and she had steady nerves. Gradually, she began to take on organizational work and administrative responsibilities. Responsibility was one of the things she had been brought up to assume. After Worms' arrest Sonia gave half of whatever money came her way to the young teacher he had been living with who was pregnant with his child. Serge Olschanezky still has a snapshot of the baby boy, Worms' son, sent to Madame Olschanezky after the war.

In the early months of 1943 the ROBIN *réseau* began to be transformed into an agency of more active resistance, taking on sabotage operations in conjunction with PROSPER, in the widely held belief that summer would see the cross-Channel invasion. The long-awaited opening of a second front was expected by that autumn at the latest, an expectation that seemed to be supported by increases in arms deliveries and hints from London. Sabotage was stepped up all through that spring and ROBIN agents frequently met with PROSPER people to plan actions. One that Sonia took part in succeeded in blowing up a munitions train at Melun, on the Seine south of Paris.

All this time Sonia worked closely with Weil, and by now she had brought the other members of her family into the organization. To her mother and brothers she never denied the danger she was in, the risk of what she was doing. Her brother says, 'She was not one of those who revelled in it, she just accepted it.' In the autumn of 1942, after Sonia had been released from Drancy, she and her mother made their way to Annecy, in the Alps not far from Switzerland, to visit Enoch, who, like his brother, had escaped from a POW camp in Germany. Sonia convinced him that he could be more useful in Paris, and he returned to the capital and took a job as a barman at a nightclub in the Opéra district, at the same time working for the ROBIN *réseau*. The members of the family all maintained separate addresses now, so as not to compromise each other. As Suzanne Ouvrard, Sonia lived in one arrondissement, and Enoch, a sub-agent with the cover-name Robert Ouvrard, had a room in another. Serge never knew their exact addresses. Their mother operated as a letter box while caring for the children of a French family a few miles outside Paris.

Early in 1943, with the threat of invasion in the air, the Germans embarked on an all-out drive to eliminate resistance groups – with PROSPER, about which they seemed to know a great deal, a major target. The mobile direction-finding units were on Archambaud's trail and Weil himself, now, like all ROBIN members, a subagent of PROSPER, narrowly escaped a trap at a meeting that had been arranged at Gisors in Normandy and again while visiting an arms dump in Châlons.

In fact, on 21 June 1943,* while Prosper and his friends waited at a café outside the Gare d'Austerlitz in Paris for the arrival of the two agents from the Sologne, Culioli and Rudellat, and the two recent arrivals they were supposed to be bringing with them, the Canadians Macalister and Pickersgill, all four were already in the hands of the Germans. Within three days Prosper himself, Archambaud and Denise would follow them into captivity.

It has been a matter of frequent comment that both Pickersgill,

---

* This was the day on which resistance in occupied France suffered what was arguably its greatest disaster, the arrest of Jean Moulin, who as de Gaulle's emissary had succeeded in uniting the scattered and squabbling resistance factions and putting together the Conseil national de la résistance. Moulin was betrayed and taken at a meeting in Caluire, a suburb of Lyon, where he was given into the hands of the Gestapo's Klaus Barbie, who found satisfaction in seeing to it that Moulin was tortured beyond recognition before he was allowed to die, having said nothing.

who was sent to organize a new PROSPER subcircuit, and Macalister, his wireless operator, spoke atrociously accented French. There was not the slightest chance of either of them being mistaken for French or, in fact, for anything other than native English speakers. It was a fact duly noted by another newly arrived agent, a young Frenchman named Pierre Raynaud, who was to join Cammaerts' JOCKEY circuit as a sabotage instructor in the Drôme.

At seven o'clock on the morning of the 21st, Pierre Culioli, Yvonne Rudellat, and the two Canadians had set off by car for the railway station at the town of Beaugency in the heart of the château country of the Loire, intending to catch the train for Paris. In the trunk of their Citroën was Macalister's wireless set, several of the quartz crystals used to establish radio frequencies, and some messages written in clear English and addressed to 'Prosper' and 'Archambaud' among others. Seeing a roadblock ahead of them, they went on unconcernedly; such checks were routine. What they did not see until it was too late was the detachment of armed soldiers lining the road ahead.

They were stopped and directed at machine-gun point to the town hall, where their papers were examined. Culioli and Rudellat were dismissed, went outside, and were waiting in the car with the motor running, agonizing over whether to drive off while they still could or hope for the miracle it would take for the two Canadians not to be recognized for what they were, when they heard shouts that were unmistakably orders to bring them back. Culioli stepped on the throttle and made a dash through a barricade ahead, crashing into a cottage wall and bouncing onto a field. Yvonne Rudellat had been shot in the head and appeared to be dying; Culioli was uninjured. The Germans corrected that by shooting him in the leg and beating him up.

Rudellat was sent, unconscious but alive, to the hospital at Blois. Culioli was taken to Paris, interrogated at the Avenue Foch, and then placed in a cell at Fresnes, where so many of the F Section agents and their French colleagues were detained on their way to still worse places to the east. Before he was sent away, Culioli agreed to the terms of the pact explained to him by Gilbert Norman and, following Suttill's instructions as they had been explained to him by Norman, he wrote letters to several of the *résistants* who were hiding the arms that had been received by parachute from London. In them he asked, in order that no one should be condemned to death, that the arms be turned over to the bearers of the letters. What none of them knew yet was that there were worse fates than being shot.

In early August 1944, a little more than two weeks before Paris was liberated, Culioli, along with Gilbert Norman, Macalister and Pickersgill, Henri Frager and about twenty-five other British agents, left Fresnes for Buchenwald. Yvonne Rudellat joined Odette and a handful of other women of SOE at Ravensbrück, where she was marked as an NN prisoner, intended to disappear without trace. Her next stop was Belsen, where she arrived six weeks before its liberation, but not in time for her. Amid the walking skeletons and the emaciated corpses, the filth, the starvation, and the disease took their toll. She was buried in a mass grave before any of the liberators had found out who she was. Culioli survived to be tried as a traitor after the war by a French military tribunal because of the letters he had written to the members of the *réseau* asking them to turn over the hidden arms to the Germans. He was ultimately acquitted of the charges.

During the crucial summer of 1943, Weil learned from one of his many contacts outside F Section that Obersturmbannführer Kieffer at the Avenue Foch was extremely well informed about his activities. He concluded, he later told his biographer, that he 'was certain there was a traitor somewhere in their midst' and that 'Prosper too shared this feeling. He definitely suspected treachery and after a brief trip to London about this time he returned to Paris weary and despondent' and with a 'couldn't-care-less attitude.'[2] He says he told Sonia, 'He [Prosper] almost seems to have become a fatalist.'

Weil also said he was becoming 'more and more nonplussed [by] the happy-go-lucky attitude of some of the new recruits being sent from London,' who 'came with what seemed to him almost no preparation for life in a German-occupied country, and with cover-stories often so childish that he felt they could be penetrated by any really intelligent German within a few hours,' adding that 'he was becoming only too aware of the internecine warfare raging between various organizations in London,'[3] whose competitive, mutually antagonistic relationship seemed to him the counterpart of the battle between the Abwehr and the SD.

At the beginning of July Weil saw his old friend Worms arrested just as he himself was approaching a black-market restaurant in the rue Troyon very near the Étoile, where they had made an appointment to meet for lunch. They had been there often before, with Suttill and his lieutenants, Gilbert Norman and Andrée Borrel, who had all been arrested just a week before. The restaurant had been recommended to Worms by Henri Déricourt, the air movements officer, who had para-chuted with him at the beginning of 1942, and who had advised him against bringing other members of the network there since it was unwise to frequent the same place too often or to meet anywhere in public as a group. Worms never came back from Flossenburg.

Knowing what lay in store for him, a *résistant* and a Jew, if he were captured, Weil fled to Switzerland. Whether or not he and Sonia were lovers, whether or not she refused to go with him to Switzerland, despite his urging, because she would not leave her mother and brother, and whether or not she took on the direction of what was left of the organization when he escaped, no one will ever know. What is certain is only that although she was not directly employed by Baker Street, she was too closely connected with F Section circuits in Paris and St Quentin to escape detection.

By the time of the PROSPER disaster, with the Gestapo breath-ing down his neck, Weil was convinced 'his troubles had dated from the time of his association with the French Section of the British Special Operations Executive . . . at the end of 1942' and blamed treachery within the SOE, although not on the part of Buckmaster and his immediate staff who, like the agents who were arrested in the spring of 1943, were 'victims of events'. He referred to 'a young Frenchman' as 'the mysterious British courier-German spy' who was 'permitted to continue to function for a considerable time'[4] after warnings about him had reached London from a number of sources as early as mid-1943 – enabling the SD to photostat letters and orders passing between London and the field in France and to penetrate the PROSPER organization.[5]

Weil knew that there had been repeated warnings about the arrests and the captured radio sets, including those from ROBIN'S own wireless operator Cohen, and maintained that if 'some persons in Whitehall continued to receive and transmit messages to Paris as though nothing had happened . . . at least until early 1944,' knowing that the sets were being operated by the Germans, it could only have been on superior orders from the highest level.[6] And he suggested that these orders were part of a wide scheme of deception which also included Operation STARKEY, a mock invasion mounted in early September 1943 for the benefit of German radar screens on the northern coast of France.*

During that summer and autumn, left alone among the ruins of the Paris organization, Sonia had turned to Guy Bieler in St Quentin as her contact with London. Guy Bieler and Yolande

---

* STARKEY had been described by General Sir Frederick Morgan, Chief of Staff to the Supreme Allied Commander (COSSAC), in his 1950 book *Overture to Overlord*, as a feint intended to maintain German troop concentrations on the Channel coast throughout the summer and autumn of 1943, diverting them from the defence of Sicily and Salerno and weakening their forces on the Soviet front. About 'the great Underground Army deployed behind and among the Germans that was awaiting our actual arrival with growing impatience,' General Morgan wrote, 'it was quite impossible to tell them beforehand what we were doing,' adding, 'Equally we could not lie to them.'

Beekman were arrested in mid-January 1944 just as they were about to carry out a sabotage action on the St Quentin Canal, at the heart of the transportation system in the industrial north supplying German-run factories with engineering equipment for tanks, guns, and planes. The SD seems to have been well informed of their plans ahead of time. It is easy to see why. When their highly efficient direction-finding equipment led the Germans to Guy and his wireless operator, who kept a regular transmission schedule, sending from the same place at the same time for months in defiance of both training and common sense, their MUSICIAN circuit was shattered. When attempts to rebuild it were undertaken in the spring of 1944, the agents involved, as they travelled around the countryside of Flanders and Picardy, kept hearing about a Canadian officer who had already been there, gathering followers with promises of arms and supplies from the British. It was Joseph Placke, Goetz's assistant in the wireless section at the Avenue Foch, impersonating the captured Pickersgill, who had been sent to establish a circuit with the name of ARCHDEACON.

It was not hard for Placke to do. Macalister's set had been found in the trunk of Culioli's car complete with its codes and security checks, all nicely written down, and there was no backlog of previous transmissions to define his 'fist', or sending style. For the better part of a year large parachute drops were made to ARCHDEACON reception committes of local *résistants* in northern Lorraine organized by Placke, whose French was good and whose English was good enough for the French. He also provided the trucks which took the supplies off the locals' hands and which were of course driven by Germans in plain clothes and taken to German storehouses. London also sent a sabotage instructor and six agents into Placke's hands before suspicions were finally aroused at Baker Street by the failure of the new agents to send messages that had been verbally agreed on before they left as a means of indicating that they were safe. By that time it was May 1944.

When Weil had left for Switzerland the previous autumn he

had given Sonia all the information about the circuit's contacts and told her that London would be sending an agent, code-named Tiburce, to replace Guy. He would arrive by parachute in February and, once he had contacted her and she had had a chance to turn everything over to him, she could leave.

Baker Street did send a replacement for Guy, but he was met by a reception committee organized by Placke. Sonia was contacted in mid-January, and made an appointment to meet with the new agent on 21 January. She told her mother they would soon be able to start arrangements to get out on an escape line, but Madame Olschanezky thought it odd that London would send someone before the expected date. She urged Sonia not to go to the second meeting without contacting London for instructions. But who was there still at large whom Sonia could ask to send a message? She said no, she knew enough to be able to tell if he wasn't all right. They agreed that Madame Olschanezky would go with her as far as the neighbourhood of the restaurant where the meeting was to take place and wait for her at a café nearby.

On 21 January Sonia arrived as arranged at the Soleil d'Or in the Place de la Trinité, hard by the Galeries Lafayette. It was an early spring day, and she waited for the man she was to meet on the outdoor terrace of the café. When he arrived he was accompanied by three other men in a black Citroën.

When an hour had gone by and Sonia hadn't returned, Madame Olschanezky went to the restaurant and asked a waiter if he had seen the young woman she described. Yes, he remembered her. She had left with several gentlemen. Madame Olschanezky knew that could mean only one thing. She rushed off to find Enoch and told him what had happened and that he mustn't go to work that night. He told her he had left some important papers in his locker at the club and promised he would go just to retrieve them and leave immediately. But he didn't. The *patron* told him someone had been looking for him, left no messages but would call again later. Enoch thought there was a chance it might be someone with news of Sonia, and, after some hesitation, he decided to stay a while longer. At one o'clock in the morning the Germans came in with guns drawn and took him away. He never returned from Auschwitz. Conditions on the transport which took him there were such that of fifteen hundred men, women, and children, seventy-five arrived there alive, making the job of those who awaited their arrival that much simpler.[7]

While Enoch waited for news of her, Sonia had already been taken to Fresnes, where she joined Andrée Borrel, whom she had known, and the other six women with whom she would make the journey to Karlsruhe. Kieffer, to whom instructions had come from Berlin to transfer the SOE agents to Germany, seems to have decided on Karlsruhe because it was his home town, where he had been a member of the regular police force and where he still had family. He may have thought to save them, or to make use of them as hostages when the end came. If so, he did not reckon on the efficiency which led the prison officials to call them to the attention of the Reich Chief Security Office, the RSHA in Berlin. Their request to clear up the irregular situation of these women in 'protective custody' in what was an ordinary civil prison was answered with the instruction to have them delivered to Natzweiler for 'special treatment'.

CHAPTER 16

Trust and Treachery

While Elizabeth Nicholas might have been guilty of occasional lapses into sentimentality, she could not be accused of sensationalism. Not so the *Sunday Pictorial*, which published a highly condensed version of her book in five consecutive instalments in the summer of 1958. Sandwiched between advertisements for beer ('Happy Thought on Mr. Young-Husband's part to meet Mrs. Young-Husband after her morning's shopping and take her to the Local for a drink') and pills for pets ('vitamins, minerals and proteins so often lacking in a cat's domestic diet') was a typical Fleet Street tabloid feature. Under pictures of the agents Elizabeth Nicholas had written about was the exhortation to 'Look well at the faces of these seven girls. They are the seven vanished heroines whose fame and fate has been cruelly hidden – even from their families – by a smokescreen called "security".

'Security, rubbish!' it went on, and promised that 'The Sunday Pictorial will break through that smokescreen to disclose the appalling secret of their death, and the shame of how their heroism has remained unsung. We intend to raise these seven angels out of hell. We are proud to do so, and defiant of those who would prefer this heart-stirring and heart-breaking story to remain hidden for ever.' Readers were then told how Elizabeth Nicholas' investigation into Diana Rowden's past had led her to the others and promised the lurid details of 'their story of bravery and torture' in the coming instalments.[1]

And the details provided were lurid enough for even the hardiest reader, complete with 'the heavy breathing of armed guards', 'a bath of near boiling water', and verbatim quotations complete with 'dark eyes flashing' from unwitnessed conversations between people long since dead.[2] The instalment describing the journey from Karlsruhe to Natzweiler shares a page with an ad for a Glamorous Hair Competition in which a maker of shampoos offers the prize of 'a continental holiday of fairytale delight.'[3]

The series presented the bare bones of Elizabeth Nicholas' three-year battle against the 'official hostility and indifference' of the British authorities. It presented her argument that all of the 'girl secret agents' had been betrayed through the captured wireless sets being played back to England by the Germans pretending to be British agents, and that all could be traced back to some connection with Hugo Bleicher and the German penetration of F Section. And it accused the authorities of keeping the names of the dead women secret at the time of the Wuppertal trial not, as was claimed at the time, in deference to the feelings of their families, all of whom later told Elizabeth Nicholas they would not have objected to publication of their names, but as a War Office cover-up of official blunders. These were charges that struck a nerve in the postwar British public, which had already turned out its wartime leadership and was undergoing a reaction against the unquestioned faith in the government that had characterized the years at war.

The publication of the book itself later in the year brought more publicity, and demands for an official inquiry began to be heard. They were the product of another book as well, published at almost the same moment as *Death Be Not Proud* and dealing with the same general subject – SOE's French disaster. But while Elizabeth Nicholas had focused on the victims, Jean Overton Fuller's new book, *Double Webs*, was about the villain, whom she identified by his job, but not by name. However, his name had appeared prominently in Paris newspapers shortly after the end of the war, in 1946, and again in 1948.

Just as the exact fate of the women agents who did not return from occupied France would never have been known without Vera Atkins' efforts to trace them immediately after the end of the war, the details of the web of treachery and deceit that had brought them, and so many others, to that ending would never have come to light without the detective work of Jean Overton Fuller. Those details would have remained buried in the memories of a few individuals with good reason never to disclose them and, after their deaths, in whatever papers remained in the inaccessible storehouses carefully guarded by officials with no intention of ever letting them see the light of day. There is even reason to suppose that any clues that might have existed on paper were destroyed, whether by accident or design, shortly after the war had brought the existence of the special operations outfits to an end. Their implications were so momentous and so far-reaching that when Jean Overton Fuller began her research, innocently unaware of their possible consequences, she was warned by one of the first people she came to question that she should be careful from then on not to walk on the outside of the pavement. He told her she had become a threat – she did not know to whom – and he advised her to keep that in mind wherever she went from then on.[4]

And she was to go a long way from her original researches into the story of Noor/Madeleine. Their friendship had begun in a common ground of shared interests in mysticism, poetry, astrology. Like Madeleine, Jean Overton Fuller was idealistic, romantic, a little impractical. It made her at first glance an unlikely kind of detective – and may have partly explained her success at it. Whatever her beliefs, she did not share the cynicism that bred acceptance of so many evils once the war was over and so many people simply wanted to put it all behind them, to forget what had been done by whom to whom, and with what degree of connivance.

Somewhat naïvely, she went around asking questions. Each of her books in turn caused something of a furore in the press. But her discoveries kept leading her into new ones, as she befriended the men and women she had searched out and exchanged confidences with them in visits and in long letters. It was her capacity for intimacy, her tendency to become emotionally involved with the subjects of her researches, as much as her dogged pursuit of the facts, that explain how a free-lance writer with no previous experience of the military, of intelligence, or of what has come to be known as investigative journalism, could have uncovered a story of such staggering significance, of such complexity, so determinedly obscured by so many concerned.

Rebuffed by the English authorities at home, Jean Overton Fuller turned to some of the Germans who had been involved with the captured agents at the Avenue Foch, and had known about the pact and about the radio games, and to some of the surviving French members of the PROSPER network. Kieffer's interpreter, who had interrogated the British agents, was one of her main sources. Madame Balachowsky and others left behind by the subagents caught up in the events of June 1943 were others. Eventually, the trail led her to the person she was sure was at the hub of it all.

Henri Déricourt was a French pilot who arrived in London in the autumn of 1942 and, after passing through MI5's London reception centre, joined SOE at the end of the year. In January 1943 he was parachuted back to France to take up his duties as air movements officer for the French Section, responsible for arranging the Lysander and Hudson flights bringing agents in and out of the Paris region. Despite numerous reports from agents in the field received both before and after the PROSPER arrests suggesting that Déricourt was a traitor, and despite the reports filtering back of captured agents who had been shown copies of the courier, the secret mail sent to London via Lysander, Déricourt remained in place until he was finally recalled to London in February 1944. An official tribunal found insufficient evidence for a verdict of treachery, although it was established that Déricourt had been in touch with the Germans while working for SOE, and it was decided only that he should not return to the field. He remained in England until, shortly after D Day, he joined the Free French Air Force, was shot down over France, survived severe burns, and was awarded the Croix de Guerre.

In 1945 he began flying between Paris and London for Air France. In April 1946 he was arrested at Croydon Airport, where he had been found in possession of contraband in the form of English currency, platinum and gold. He was released on bail, allowed to go back to France on condition that he return to face trial, and appeared in the Croydon magistrates' court later that month. He was represented by a prestigious KC and got off with a relatively light fine, which someone paid anonymously on his behalf.

He returned to France and later that year was arrested by the French military authorities, who held him in custody until he faced a military tribunal in June 1948, five years after the betrayals of which he stood accused. At the proceeding, Nicholas Bodington of F Section appeared as a witness on Déricourt's behalf and told the court that he had authorized Déricourt to maintain his contacts with Avenue Foch, which he had known about and had referred to in a pencilled note (undated) found by M.R.D. Foot in Déricourt's file. It read, 'We know he is in contact with the Germans and also how & why.'[5] Questioned by the judge, Bodington stated unequivocally that he would still trust his life to Déricourt 'without hesitation'.[6]

In his memoir, the Abwehr's Hugo Bleicher had referred to a double agent named Gilbert who worked for the rival SD and revealed that in the summer of 1943 Bodington, then Buckmaster's deputy, had come to France and had escaped arrest, although surely 'Gilbert' must have arranged for his visit.[7] Bleicher surmised that Bodington's safe return to London would have served to demonstrate Déricourt's loyalty and put to rest the suspicions aroused by the accusations of Frager and others in the field against '*Gilbert – l'homme qui fait le pick-up.*'

Bodington had been sent in July of 1943 to investigate the extent of the PROSPER disaster, accompanied by another F Section agent, Jack Agazarian, who had been a wireless operator for PROSPER and on occasion worked for Déricourt. Agazarian had more than once transmitted to London the suspicions of agents in the field questioning Déricourt's loyalty. Agazarian, described by Foot as a 'handsome and dashing young airman',[8] was a member of Prosper's inner circle. He and his wife, an F Section courier, met with Suttill, Norman and Borrel regularly over meals, drinks, and cards, and he had at one time transmitted for more agents of different circuits than it was prudent for him to know. Suttill himself thought him something of a security risk and arranged for Agazarian and his wife to return to London. They left on the 16/17 June flight that brought in Diana Rowden and Noor Inayat Khan.

He was recalled from leave to accompany Bodington back to France on the July reconnaissance mission. All leads for making contact with any of the PROSPER agents were proving dead ends but the Archambaud radio was still working to London and came up with an address for a meeting. It is not clear, with all of the reasons for suspecting the source of the message, why either man had to investigate in person, but Bodington sent Agazarian, who went to the address given, in the rue de Rome near the Gare St-Lazare, to meet Archambaud on the 30 July. The Gestapo was waiting there for him.

Agazarian was a prize. He knew practically everyone and everything there was to know about F Section's activities in the north, and the Germans knew perfectly well that he did. He was killed at Flossenburg, a few weeks before the war ended, one of the unacknowledged heroes of F Section. It was his betrayal of which Déricourt stood accused in the dock in Paris in 1948.

The SD men brought to the French court martial seemed in their turn as reluctant as the British to see him convicted and gave evidence that his contacts with them had been of no real value to them. Both sides seemed to have their reasons for drawing a curtain over the whole matter of Déricourt's activities, although it was unclear exactly what those reasons were. No evidence was presented to the court concerning Déricourt's interception of the London-bound courier mail, which only came out later. He admitted to having accepted a proposition from the Germans that he work for them, but said he did it so he could carry on his work for 'the intelligence service' and save the

22. Brian Stonehouse

23. Henri Déricourt in 1962, shortly before he was reported killed in a plane crash

24. Major General
Sir Colin McV. Gubbins

25. USAAF B-17 'Flying Fortresses' making a daylight drop of supplies to the French Resistance in the summer of 1944

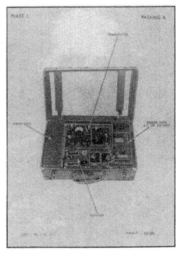

26. A Type 3 Mark II ('B2') transceiver set, carried by SOE wireless operators in the field

27. 'The House in the Woods', at Beaulieu, the estate of the Lords Montagu in the New Forest in Hampshire, where SOE agents were trained in security

28. Jean Overton Fuller in front of a display at Waterloo Station of the paperback edition of her book about Madeleine, 1953

29. Sonya Olschanezky in repose

30. Sonya Olschanezky in a publicity photo

31. The rustic Alsatian cottage in Struthof, before the war a skiers' restaurant, which became the gas chamber for Natzweiler. At the top of the exhaust chimney is the panel that was used to close it

32. The entrance to the camp, *Konzentrationslager Natzweiler*

33. The electrified barbed-wire fence surrounding the barracks. Beyond, the bordering forest and Donon Peak

34. The Cimitière national de la déportation, overlooking the site of the camp

35. The gallows used for slow public hanging of prisoners suspected of attempting to escape

36. The figure of a martyred prisoner at the base of the memorial overlooking the cemetery

37. The crematorium building

38. The crematorium oven. It could incinerate four bodies every thirty-five minutes

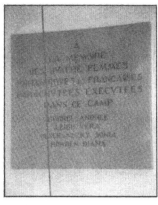

39. Stone dissection table used for experiments on prisoners on the effects of new gases being tested, on the results of typhus injections, and on sterilization

40. The plaque in the crematorium honouring the four women SOE agents killed there

41. The memorial tablet honouring the fallen members of the WTS/FANY, St Paul's Church, Knightsbridge

agents who depended on him. Yes, he had given SS Obersturm-bannführer Karl Boemelburg, Kieffer's immediate superior and head of the Gestapo's counter-espionage section in Paris, the location of several airfields, but only after making sure they would not be used.

To the president of the court, who commented that it was a dangerous game he had been playing, Déricourt replied, 'The more my merit!' The defence, conducted by a distinguished *maître*, a leading light of the legal profession, asserted that more than two hundred people had come and gone safely on Déricourt's flights (a grossly inflated figure but one there was no way of challenging at the time, no actual records being available). Among those he had seen off were a number of distinguished generals, eminent politicians, and leading resistance figures, some of whom were happy to offer testimonials in his behalf.*

Déricourt was acquitted, with Bodington's testimony the most telling evidence in his favour, and his decoration, which had been removed when he entered the courtroom, was restored to him, presumably along with his honour.

None of the facts about Déricourt's life after he was recalled to London were generally known at the time that Jean Overton Fuller began her research. Convinced by what she was told by former subagents of PROSPER circuits that he had betrayed the F Section agents through his contacts with the Germans and been responsible for the fates of Noor and many others, she tracked down former members of the Paris SD staff as well as former F Section agents and painstakingly combed through old newspaper files in Paris and in Croydon. Despite the omission of significant details, what she learned about both legal proceedings raised certain obvious questions. Who had come to Déricourt's rescue, and why? What was being hidden, and by whom?

---

* On the November 1943 night on which he received a party that included André Maugenet, code-named Benoit, on his way to join Diana Rowden in the Jura, among those Déricourt saw off from the same field was François Mitterrand.

Intrepid Jean got herself an interview with Déricourt himself, and put her questions to him. It had long been her belief, which she shared with Elizabeth Nicholas, that the Germans had decided to remove the F Section prisoners to Germany and then to kill them at the time of the invasion rather than risk having them liberated by the Allies because they knew too much about the radio game, and about certain double agents as well. Even in retreat the Germans intended to continue playing back captured radio sets, which they did well into 1945, and perhaps also to continue to make use of the services of undetected traitors. By now she had learned from former members of the SD staff at the Avenue Foch that Déricourt had been playing a double game. As Agent BOE 48, he handed over to Boemelburg the mail he was given to put on the planes returning to London, putting it aboard only after it had been copied at the Avenue Foch. It remained for the charming Déricourt to win her over, suggesting that it had really been a triple game he'd been involved in, although he was not at liberty to explain from what high places in London his orders had emanated and what ends they were intended to serve.

Their first meeting was a cat-and-mouse affair. Déricourt, personable and considerate, warned her against 'putting your nose into this stinking business.' He told her it was 'too recent' to tell the truth about it. 'Come back in fifty years and I'll tell you the truth.'9 He told her not to believe what he told her further than she wished. This she found 'touching'. And he denied that he had been responsible for the arrests of Prosper, Denise, Archambaud and the rest. That had been the result of the radio game. Furthermore, he insisted that he had informed London of the arrests as soon as they occurred and that the radio game had been intentionally kept up by London, deliberately sacrificing men and women in order to do so, 'to keep the Germans occupied. To distract their attention.'10

He had, he told her, informed London that F Section was penetrated from very early on, even before Prosper was parachuted into the field. His chiefs had known and had their own reasons for handling things the way they did. He did not think Buckmaster knew what was going on. He, Déricourt, reported to 'an officer of much higher rank.' In fact, he told her that he didn't think it was from within SOE that the crucial decision came. But seeing the extent of the penetration, he had decided to make his arrangement with the Germans in order to protect himself and those who depended on him, friends he had recruited into the section and the agents be received and sent off. He had not been responsible for what happened. Nothing he did could have made any difference. 'It was only a question of time. The network had been penetrated already from so many sides, it was bound to happen. The Germans did not need my services.'[11]

Thinking over what had gone on at their first meeting, Jean Overton Fuller said, 'The dreadful thing is – I like him!' But she also liked the Germans who had told her Déricourt had really done all those things she accused him of having done and which he did not admit to. Who to believe? Wondering why she didn't find him repellent, 'because I am very quick to react from anything foul,'[12] she thought perhaps the friend she was talking with was right. Déricourt was amoral. One did not sense a bad conscience in the man because he had no conscience at all. He was, in a phrase M.R.D. Foot was to use years later, not of this party or that but simply a '*Déricourtiste*'.[13]

Besides, they had found, when they met again and talked in a more relaxed atmosphere, that they had many 'kindred ideas', as she put it. He was a Christian Scientist, she a Theosophist – his near mysticism made for 'a deepening meeting point'. She could not believe he could have sent men and women to their deaths in cold blood. She felt in him a certain 'tranquillity'.[14] She asked for his astrological data and drew up his horoscope.

Nothing like the sympathy she felt for Déricourt, and for some of the former SD officers she interviewed, seems to have come over her with regard to any of the officials among her own countrymen. She did not find it hard to believe that some of them might have sent men and women to their deaths in cold blood. Even her friend Dame Irene Ward, a member of the government, thought it a distinct possibility that Déricourt was put into SOE by 'Intelligence proper' as part of some 'larger situation'.[15] They both agreed that British reluctance to reveal anything about what had happened could be explained by a hope, a vain one, that the French could be kept from ever finding out the mistakes that had been made in London which had cost so many French lives. In short, a cover up. That would explain a great deal, including the mysterious intervention at Déricourt's trials.

It was Déricourt's justification for his course of action (even hypothetically for passing the courier to the SD, which he still did not admit, even though his trial and its irreversible verdict were behind him, leaving him invulnerable to further legal actions) that it was worth it; it bought immunity for his air operations, all of which were successfully carried out unhindered. He considered it a small price to pay. Agents who died in Natzweiler, in Buchenwald, in Sachsenhausen, Flossenburg, Gross-Rosen, Ravensbrück and Mauthausen might not have agreed. Jean Overton Fuller wasn't sure. She had come to accuse, but stayed to admire, affected by what she felt to be the same sincerity, honesty, integrity – she describes it differently in different places – that impressed her in the Avenue Foch intepreter-cum-interrogator on whom she relied for much of her information.

Jean Overton Fuller was not the only one who liked Déricourt. Special Duties Squadron pilot Hugh Verity wrote that when he was told of the accusations against Déricourt he was 'shocked and incredulous. Henri was a good friend of mine.'[16] F Section's operations officer and Buckmaster's number two man, Gerry Morel, had also considered him a friend and had great respect for the efficiency and remarkable success with which Déricourt's operations were carried out. When told that Déricourt was reported to be in touch with the SD people in Paris, Morel volunteered to go over and bring him back for interrogation, at gunpoint if necessary. The operation was put off for more than a month until the bad weather broke and, early in February,

Morel flew over as the lone passenger on a flight that was to land on one of Déricourt's fields and collect several passengers to be brought back to England.

Morel was wearing his RAF uniform for the occasion and as he alighted from the Hudson his hat blew off in the slipstream. Of course it had to be retrieved and that bit of comic business may have made it difficult for him to maintain the stern and dignified demeanour necessary for giving orders. In any case, Déricourt refused Morel's. On the excuse that he could not leave immediately because he had to dispose of several bicycles he had brought along for the arriving agents he had expected to receive on the field, Déricourt promised that he would board a Lysander for the flight to England a few days later. He had business to wind up before he could leave. He explained later that he felt he had to make arrangements for the safety of the members of his FARRIER circuit, who included his friends Rémy Clément and Julienne Aisner Besnard, his assistant and his courier, both of whom he had recruited for SOE. Dr Goetz of the Avenue Foch was to depose after the war that Déricourt had spent his last evening in Paris dining with him and Boemelburg and that the table talk had been about what Déricourt would say when he got to England.

Déricourt kept his promise and then some. He was on the field when the plane that had been sent to fetch him set down but he was not alone. He had brought his wife along. She had come, wearing what Hugh Verity later described as 'an expensive looking fur coat', for what her husband described at the time as 'a shopping trip to London.'[17]

Verity and Buckmaster received Déricourt at the flat in Orchard Court, where, all of them comfortably seated in spacious armchairs, they acquainted him with the accusations that had been made against him of being in contact with the Germans in Paris. With no show of emotion of any kind he told them, after a slight pause, that he kept up with his German acquaintances from his prewar flying days, supplying them with black market oranges, in order to protect his operations.

What his friends thought of his explanation at the time is not recorded. They had plenty of opportunity to reflect on it in the years to come. But it was decided 'at a very high level', according to Verity, that Déricourt should not return to France while the war was still on. Despite the doubts about Déricourt, Verity 'still felt that he was a friend and a great partner in our operations.' So naturally enough, 'as a gesture to cheer him up a little, my wife and I arranged a small party for them [and] went off to the Savoy Hotel for dinner and dancing.'[18] It was only many years later that it occurred to Verity that the expensive looking fur coat Mme Déricourt wore for the occasion might have been paid for with money paid to Déricourt for information which led directly to the arrest and death of four French agents of the resistance.

By that time Verity had learned that at Déricourt's court martial in France one of those who offered evidence in his behalf was an agent named Robert Lyon, who had travelled with a Colonel Bonoteaux in Verity's Lysander and been received on the field by a Déricourt-arranged reception committee. In 1953, in his capacity as a member of a commission investigating the fate of deportees, Lyon came across Bonoteaux's file, from which he learned that his travelling companion had been arrested shortly after they had parted on the day of their arrival. Bonoteaux had died in a concentration camp. Lyon was convinced that Déricourt had fingered Bonoteaux, a fact which Déricourt admitted to Jean Overton Fuller after his acquittal, adding that he had given away three others as well – one of them the Maugenet who was to have joined Diana Rowden and John Young at Clairvaux and whose capture led to their arrest and death.

In repeating that confession to Hugh Verity, Jean Overton Fuller added that Déricourt's eyes had filled with tears as he told her. He said, 'You must not think I am a monster.'[19] He had had to do monstrous things, he admitted, in order to keep up his end of the dangerous game he played, but he was no monster. Although she believed him, others came to wonder whether the chicken farm he bought after the war was paid for, like Mme

Déricourt's fur coat, with the money – reportedly some four million francs – given him by the Germans in exchange for the information about the flight carrying Maugenet and the others. For her part, Jean Overton Fuller maintained that the Germans didn't need Déricourt to tell them about the Maugenet flight. Arrangements for it had been made, on Pickersgill's set, by Placke.

Verity remained puzzled by the problem of 'what made him tick' and years later he asked M.R.D. Foot, who by then was familiar with all of the material on Déricourt in surviving SOE records as well as in captured German files, where he thought Déricourt's loyalties had really been. It was then that Foot coined the phrase that, 'at heart, he was a *Déricourtiste*.'[20] Déricourt's second in command, Rémy Clément, who had been closer to Déricourt than anyone except possibly his wife, thought that described his old friend perfectly: ambitious, unscrupulous, and arrogant enough to think he could deal with anyone and outsmart them, but trustworthy as far as his own friends were concerned. And that remained the consensus on *le Déricourtisme* for some time to come. By that time Henri Déricourt had been reported to have died in an air crash while flying over Laos in what was then French Indo-China. It was not possible to make a positive identification of any of the bodies found amid the burned wreckage of the plane, which inevitably led some to speculate that Déricourt had faked his death in order to begin a new life somewhere else.

From the Germans she interviewed while researching her book on Déricourt, Jean Overton Fuller learned that their possession of the messages that had been intended for London had had a devastating effect on the captured agents, who inferred that they had been betrayed and, according to their interrogators, concluded that the treachery originated in London. It led some of them to provide information they might otherwise have withheld. It almost certainly is what led Prosper and/or Archambaud – the other Gilbert – to make the pact with Kieffer that resulted in the wave of arrests, and ultimately in deportation and death for so many. She also learned that, while none of Déricourt's flights were intercepted, many of them were observed. Agents of the Gestapo, most often members of the notorious Bony-Lafont gang of gangster collaborators, followed many of the newly arrived agents from the landing fields to the train stations from which they set off for their destinations. On arrival, they would occasionally be arrested, more often followed. From then on they could be kept under surveillance until the Gestapo was ready to spring.

As Overton Fuller travelled around Germany seeking out former members of the SD it occurred to her that the penetration of the French Section was in part a result of the German control of the Netherlands Section. When London began to call for the return of one of the N Section agents, the Germans decided on a scheme whereby they would send to France two of their own men posing as SOE agents. Since the F Section agents would not have met any of the N Section agents, the Germans had only to set up plans and passwords on the radio they were playing back, and send their men off to a rendezvous. The plan was for one of the two to be captured in a mock arrest. This would explain his failure to return to London and, since it would take place in full view of some of the F Section agents who would be allowed to escape, word of what had happened would get back to London.

One thing went wrong with the otherwise perfect plan. When the Germans arrived at the address they had been given in the Square Clignancourt, and asked for Gilbert, meaning the Air Movements Officer, they were referred to the wrong Gilbert.

Every agent was given a code name, for use in messages exchanged with London; a field name, for use in the field among fellow agents and their French colleagues; and a cover name, by which to move around in occupied country, which appeared on all identification and other official papers. In practice, although their true surnames might not be known to others in the field, the PROSPER group were in the habit of calling each other by their real first names, such as Francis – or François – and Gilbert.

This was destined to prove a source of great confusion in the crucial events involving Gilbert Norman, code-named Archambaud, and Henri Déricourt, code-named Gilbert.

When Archambaud – Gilbert Norman – was presented with the supposed SOE agents, he explained that, while he was also called Gilbert, he was not the Gilbert they were looking for, and offered to put them in touch with the right one, the Air Movements Officer. Their cover was so successful, as was the entire Nordpol operation, that one of the two, posing as a Belgian patriot while shepherding Allied personnel via an escape line that was allowed to function in order to further the deception, was awarded a Military Cross. After the war, an embarrassed British officer informed him that the award would have to be annulled.

The controversy generated by the publicity for her book brought Jean Overton Fuller letters from a number of men and women who had been involved in the events it dealt with. By the time she added their testimony to what she herself had gathered, she was certain that London had been receiving information about the radio game from various sources very early on. And she had a visit from a former agent now living in French Equatorial Africa who came to tell her about his own experiences.

Pierre Raynaud, code name Alain, had been parachuted onto the field where he was received by Pierre Culioli on the night of 18/19 June, just after the Canadians Pickersgill and Macalister. With orders to proceed south via Paris, Raynaud decided that, rather than accompany the party travelling by car the next day, he would make his own way to join Francis Cammaerts in the south-east.

Raynaud told Overton Fuller he was convinced that the British could not have been taken in by the radio game and that they continued it as part of a strategy decided in London, knowingly sacrificing the agents who dropped to German receptions, a belief Overton Fuller found widely held among the French. The English, on the other hand, maintained that such a possibility was inconceivable and that the only explanation was 'muddle', deplorable but honest mistakes made in the confusions of the time and the difficulties inherent in the transmission and analysis of coded messages.

Without Jean Overton Fuller, it is possible that none of what gradually came to be revealed about what had happened in France would have come to light. The chance coincidence of her friendship with Noor Inayat Khan, based on a common interest in various forms of spiritual beliefs, started her looking into the matter of what had happened to her friend. Noor's story led her to Starr's, and his to Déricourt. Their confrontation had unexpected results. Her villain became her hero. He would remain the central figure of books she continued to write about the German penetration of F Section over the years. And the questions she had raised, along with the two other women who became preoccupied with the history of F Section, finally forced the British government to break its silence and come up with some answers.

CHAPTER 17

Questions

One of the rejection letters Elizabeth Nicholas received while she was looking for a publisher for *Death Be Not Proud* said, 'I found much of it fascinating, but frankly I am fed up with books about the war.'[1] Not so, evidently, the British public, especially when it was a matter of spying, secrecy, or deception, and most of all when it concerned official dereliction. Elizabeth Nicholas' and Jean Overton Fuller's books were widely reviewed and discussed. 'MISS FULLER RAISES CLOAK AND DAGGER STORM', read a headline in London's *Sunday Despatch*[2] and even in the United States *Time* magazine devoted most of a page, with a picture of Diana Rowden captioned 'Burned alive as a decoy?', to the public furore aroused by the two authors' charges, that 'London's S.O.E. security seemed incredibly lax' and that 'S.O.E. was totally fooled by a French-born double agent code-named "Gilbert" [who] passed pertinent documents to the Gestapo.' Noting 'Gilbert's' defence that he was actually working for the British in a capacity he could not reveal in order to 'keep the Germans occupied, to distract their attention,' the *Time* writer said, 'The thought that the seven girl agents, and a hundred others, might simply have been decoys handed over to certain death in order to mask other intelligence activities was an unpalatable one for many Britons.'[3]

One of those who found it most unpalatable was the Conservative Member of Parliament for Tynemouth, Dame Irene Ward, who had herself written a history of the FANYs[4] in which she had included the stories of a number of the F Section agents. She and the other two women authors had shared certain information as it came their way and followed up various leads supplied by the others as their respective researches progressed and, although her own book, a kind of authorized biography of the service, contained nothing but praise for anyone involved in its exploits, Dame Irene as a politician was not the babe in the woods she may have seemed as an author. She was happy to challenge the government officials who seemed to her to be determinedly keeping the truth hidden, limiting access to the facts about things that had happened during a war that had been over for ten years now on the grounds of the continued need for official secrecy.

Early in 1956 she had raised the matter in the House of Commons of why SOE files could not be made available to other writers as they had been to the authors of the various 'success stories' that had been published with official help which 'led people to believe that an amateur organization, bravely manned and devotedly served by British and French agents was a match for the German Intelligence Service.'⁵ Elizabeth Nicholas described the women F Section sent into occupied France as 'for the most part girls in their early twenties, telephonist, shop assistant, clerk; speaking, some of them, imperfect French; whose lives had been led in the simplest, most ordinary surroundings' and who, after a mere few weeks of training, were sent 'to pit themselves against German counter-espionage services manned by men of the utmost shrewdness, highly trained, with many years of experience in that field' and controlled from London, she added, by mere 'amateurs'.⁶

In reply to Dame Irene, Lord John Hope, the under secretary at the Foreign Office at the time, said that the SOE files could not be made available to the public because it was a secret organization. A member of the House added that far too much harm had already been done 'by amateur authors rushing into print and cashing in on wartime experience in our secret services' and suggested that 'rather than encourage such publications', Lord John should invoke the Official Secrets Act. Lord John concurred, 'We are bound to bear security in mind first and foremost.'⁷

The honourable lady had another go at him in June, when she asked Lord John in the House of Commons why the SOE files had been closed only after publication of *The Starr Affair* and he again referred to 'reasons of security'. It was hard at the time to see what security matters could be breached by allowing access to the personal files of those agents who had not returned from the field or what secrets could remain after the revelations of Giskes and Bleicher about the radio games, the numerous memoirs and histories that had already appeared in France, and the almost unlimited information available in official sources there.

And that is where matters stood until the publication of the two books almost simultaneously in the autumn of 1958 gave Dame Irene the occasion to bring SOE up again in the House of Commons and once again F Section and its agents were in the headlines. 'MP ASKS ABOUT SPIES', 'DAME IRENE WARD DEMANDS INQUIRY', 'MP DEMANDS ANSWER ON SPY CHARGE', 'TELL US IF NAZI SPIES WERE IN OUR SECRET SERVICE'.[8] The tabloids did not seem to have grasped the nature of the organization they were referring to in their headlines, and it seemed doubtful that reporters had read the books, but no matter. The issue was joined. As Dame Irene wrote later,

> I communicated my views in 1958, with certain disturbing books by two of my friends, Mrs Elizabeth Nicholas and Miss Jean Overton Fuller, to the then Prime Minister (Mr Macmillan) and begged him to initiate an informed history covering our part in the resistance movements in Europe. To my satisfaction, he agreed that the time for action had arrived and he personally negotiated with the Treasury for £5,000 to obtain a historian to write the first of the series on France.[9]

As a matter of fact, Dame Irene had communicated her views in a way that was bound to illicit some concession. She put the matter to the Foreign Secretary in a letter asking point blank whether 'Gilbert' had been in the employ of the

Foreign Office, in response to which she was assured that he had not been. The Foreign Office categorically denied that he had been 'one of theirs' or that they had had anything to do with the defence at either of his trials. Which brings to mind the retort of Mandy Rice-Davies, a principal in the 1963 government scandal that came to be known as the Profumo affair, when told that Lord Astor had categorically denied her account of their sexual shenanigans. 'Well,' Miss Rice-Davies had famously remarked, 'he would, wouldn't he?'*

The consent to an official history might well have been intended in part to deflect attention from the issue of Gilbert and to buy time for everyone to calm down, as well as to put the case as it would emerge from what documents were available.

The decision may also have been dictated in part by the desire of Mr Macmillan's government to placate the French, many of whose postwar leaders had been active in resistance movements during the occupation. They were aware, even if they did not subscribe to it themselves, of the belief held by those of their compatriots who had suffered as a result of the PROSPER arrests that the British had knowingly betrayed SOE agents and their French subagents to the Germans as part of an intricate deception scheme. In the late 1950s those leaders would be influential in deciding the form that the European Common Market would take and thus Britain's place in it. The British faced de Gaulle's hostility on two counts: his desire for France to dominate the EC countries and his resentment of the ongoing 'special relationship' between Britain and his particular *bête noire*, the US. Anything that could be done to salve the general's pride was worth considering.

'For two years,' as Dame Irene wrote later, 'the search for a

---

* It is one of history's little ironies that the reply delivered to Dame Irene in the House of Commons in December of 1958, stating categorically that 'for security reasons it is not possible to allow members of the public to have direct access to the archives of the Special Operations Executive' was delivered by none other than John Profumo.

suitable historian continued. This was then in the hands of Mr Edward Heath, then Minister of State at the Foreign Office, who swore myself and my friends to silence.'[10]

That silence was to last for four years, during which time the three women kept their word and their silence about the project underway. Meanwhile in 1961 the Foreign Office chose an Oxford don, M.R.D. Foot, to draft an account of SOE's French Section, and invited him to spin the straw of what remained of the F Section archives into the gold of an official history.

An army officer throughout the war, Foot had been a member of the Chief of Combined Operations' intelligence staff from 1942 to 1944. He had also been attached to SAS headquarters. On a special mission behind enemy lines in post-invasion France, he had been captured, wounded in an escape attempt, and awarded the Croix de Guerre. He had relevant experience, appropriate academic credentials as a professor of history and politics, and a particular interest in Second World War European resistance movements. The assignment seemed made for him, although there was no way of foreseeing how controversial it would turn out to be.

What had got the official history project started was Dame Irene's 1958 motion in the House of Commons calling for an investigation into the effectiveness of the Special Operations Executive 'in the light of the doubts raised.' The spokesman appointed to answer those doubts in the press was Colonel Buckmaster, whose own account of things often seemed addled to a point suggesting that he was either unusually dim or unusually ill-informed about what went on in his own outfit. His own books were so full of factual errors, on the level of who did what and when and where, that Elizabeth Nicholas was able to compile a fifteen-page list of them. One example among many was his identification of the Canadian Pickersgill as the principal agent operating a network covering a vast region of north-east France. Pickersgill, of course, never operated anywhere, having been arrested three days after his arrival, imprisoned, and eventually killed at Buchenwald.

Elizabeth Nicholas was particularly bitter about Buckmaster's inaccuracies, as she was about the official help given the authors of such upbeat accounts as the book about Odette. She wrote to a friend,

> I feel, as you do, extremely strongly about these matters. Men and women died monstrous deaths serving with SOE, and it is no subject for semi-fictional cheap journalism. It is deeply distressing that the services of the dead should be so lightly valued that no effort is made to write of them accurately. The fact is that when Audrey Whiting interviewed B[uckmaster] about this, he said that the book [*They Fought Alone*] had been ghosted, and he was so bored with the subject, he could not be bothered to vet the MS properly. If the subject bores him, he should leave it alone.[11]

Of course, Audrey Whiting's brand of journalism was hardly less sensational than Buckmaster's, but with her it was a matter of style and with him of fact. In his position, his critics felt, more could justifiably have been expected of him.

What Dame Irene had referred to as 'the doubts raised' by the two latest books on F Section and the replies by its defenders were by the late 1950s sharing space in magazine articles and newspaper columns with another affair involving agents of SOE's French Section. At issue was what France's *L'Express* dubbed *l'affaire Odette*.[12]

The book about Odette published in 1949 had been a tremendous success, a best seller at the time and the foundation of a film starring Anna Neagle as the wartime heroine. The film premiered both in London and in Paris. At the London opening great crowds turned out to see the King and Queen and other members of the royal family, ambassadors and ministers of various countries, representatives of resistance movements side by side with what the press described as 'luminaries of the film world'. The Paris opening, attended by the President of the Republic, was no less spectacular, and press accounts of it could not be missed by anyone living in France at the time, including some former associates of Odette during the five-and-a-half months she had spent working as a courier in the south of France from the beginning of November 1942 until her arrest with Peter Churchill in the middle of April 1943. Their former colleagues were affronted by what they claimed to be an exaggeration and glamorization by the book and the film of the role she had played in resistance activities and the consequent adulation she had been receiving, which included England's highest civilian honour for courageous conduct.

After the war, Odette and Peter Churchill had married and were later divorced. Resentful of her growing celebrity, the group of French subagents of the *réseau* to which Odette and Peter Churchill had belonged wrote a letter to a French air ace who had provided a preface to the French edition of the book, saying that his 'good faith had been imposed on'. Neither that letter nor one to the president of the Association nationale des cadres de la résistance received a reply. According to *L'Express*, 'Odette, the sacred national heroine, received at Court and covered with decorations, had become untouchable.'

When it was announced early in 1956 that a sequel to the film about Odette's exploits was being planned, Francis Basin, who as Olive had been involved in early F Section activity on the Riviera, called for a 'jury *d'honneur franco-britannique*' to sort out what was truth and what fantasy in the growing literature devoted to the exploits of Odette. Nothing happened until, in the wake of the new wave of publicity on the books that were appearing about SOE, in November of 1958 the *Sunday Despatch* of London ran a six-column headline reading: 'SIX FRENCHMEN QUESTION THE EXPLOITS OF ODETTE AND PETER CHURCHILL'. The six former resistance workers challenged Churchill and Odette to name any of their acts of sabotage. Two other newspapers, the *Daily Mail* and the *Daily Telegraph*, rushed to the defence, and Odette herself issued a statement accusing her accusers in turn of bad faith.

Peter Churchill told newspaper reporters he would demand an

inquiry himself unless the French retracted their allegations against himself and his former wife, Odette, GC – now Mrs Hallowes. He pointed out that Odette had been sent as a courier, not a saboteur. And there the matter rested, as far as the British public was concerned.

But the article in *L'Express* in February 1959 re-opened the issue. The French former *résistants* who were attacking Odette and Peter Churchill included, in addition to Basin, the Baron Henri de Malval, president of the Association des anciens internés de la Gestapo à Fresnes, whose luxurious villa had for a while served as headquarters for Churchill's group; the former head of CARTE, André Girard; and the widow of Henri Frager.

In fact, de Malval had reason to be bitter towards Peter Churchill, who had a way of hanging on to old messages he had exchanged with London and, against all security rules, was carrying de Malval's phone number when captured, along with a message directing agents arriving on the French coast to go straight to the baron's Villa Isabelle, with the address, all in clear. The Gestapo had shown it to de Malval when they came to arrest him.[13]

In a letter to Elizabeth Nicholas the following summer, a foreign correspondent for an English newspaper wrote to her about the 'Odette hunt', which he called 'a very strange affair.' His letter went on:

I gather that there is a tacit agreement that the French resistance men won't move if they are satisfied that there will be no further sanctification of Odette in plays, films, etc. . . .

The pity is that on a vastly diminished scale Odette comes out of it rather well . . . She has once tried to end the nonsense by sending her GC back to Buckingham Palace, but the odious Churchill got them out of that one and it was put down to her sufferings, her wonderful modesty. By divorcing Churchill she feels she has gone some way towards making amends, and no doubt she has been persuaded by the SOE boys that to do more would open Britain to Communism and atheism and cause spinsters to curse God on vicarage lawns.[14]

In the spring of 1964 it was finally announced, in answer to a question by Dame Irene in the House of Commons, that a draft of the official history of French Section had been completed and that His Majesty's Government had decided in principle that it was 'suitable subject to further detailed scrutiny, for publication by His Majesty's Stationery Office.' The announcement, even before the publication, led to explosions in the press and Dame Irene was on the mark in prophesying further 'furious repercussions' once the book itself appeared.[15]

But the real fury came from another quarter. In his account of the role played by Peter Churchill on the Riviera, Foot explained that Churchill's assignment was to act as liaison between CARTE and Baker Street, which explained why, to the annoyance of his French colleagues, he did little if any sabotage work. It was not part of his job. But while giving Churchill his due for the kind of nerve and skill he had demonstrated in various dangerous manoeuvres, Foot criticized, with some degree of acerbity, both Churchill and Odette for their role in the turmoil that brought down the Riviera circuits.

This was too much for the gallant captain and the national heroine. Odette complained bitterly that Foot had never spoken with her (he had interviewed a few former agents and staff members in addition to relying on the files made available to him) and that she had not been shown the manuscript before publication (some former French Section members had been given a chance to comment on a draft). Odette's lawyers insisted on changes in the text and Peter Churchill brought a libel suit. There was an out-of-court settlement in which Churchill was awarded what the press referred to as 'substantial damages' and in 1968 the history had to be reprinted in an amended edition. It was an episode that served to discourage the commissioning of any further volumes of SOE history for public consumption for years to come.

But these were tangential matters, intriguing bits of marginalia in a work whose main thrust was to record the creation and accomplishments of the French Section of SOE during its four years of activity. The basic narrative does just that, and, while it is difficult if not dizzying to read any account of what went on in the field that attempts to deal with persons and events in anything like their real complexity, Foot's official history stands as a model of its kind, partly because of his elegant style and dry wit. No irony escapes him and his praise of individuals he deems worthy is impressive because his tone is neither sentimental nor angry. But it does have a subtext.

The history was commissioned, after all, in response to the charges that had been brought against F Section by authors maintaining that unsuitable and insufficiently trained women had been sent into the field, that they were sacrificed as a result of either gross incompetence or betrayal or a combination of both, and that the results, even if it were possible to explain London's actions in terms of good intentions, were not worth it. The game had not been worth the candle. The actual achievements of SOE in France had not justified the means.

Foot's narrative began with the creation of the unprecedented special organization and the rivalry and hostilities against which it fought its first battles on its home ground. Intramural squabbling and back-stabbing were the precursors of the struggle against the real enemy across the Channel. There was the rivalry between the British-controlled F Section and the RF Section, run by de Gaulle's Free French. There were the interdepartmental struggles for power born of the dislike and distrust both the Foreign Office and the War Office felt at finding themselves bypassed when the new secret organization was placed under the aegis of the Minister of Economic Warfare instead of either of their jurisdictions. The Secret Intelligence Service, MI6, was threatened by the agenda for subversion and sabotage which was designed to attract the attention of the populace, gain its confidence, win adherents, and prepare for an eventual uprising. What MI6 needed was quiet and obscurity in which to gather intelligence and pass it on in stealth. The military felt distaste and contempt for a body of amateurs undertaking what it saw as paramilitary adventures without the necessary background or training. Professional officers in general agreed with the Chief of the Air Staff, who thought that dropping 'assassins' in civilian clothes was not only a gamble, it was unethical.[16]

He may have changed his thinking during the course of the war, as the nature of the enemy and what would be required to defeat them became clearer, but up until the very end the Air Staff remained reluctant to divert aircraft from bombing raids to SOE operations. They argued that it made no sense to divert aircraft to the special-duties squadrons from the strategic bombing offensives then successfully attacking Germany just in order to supply unproven resistance organizations which might or might not eventually prove effective at the time of invasion.

Foot showed that F Section's record in industrial sabotage compared favourably with that of the much less economical RAF bomber command. It took the massive resources of a full-scale RAF raid to knock out a factory at Montluçon in 1943. Back in production in 1944 the same factory was put out of commission by a two-pound plastic bomb planted by an F Section agent. All told, SOE was a bargain, in terms of both lives and money lost, according to Foot, who pointed out that both General Eisenhower and the defeated German military commanders agreed that the resistance organized and armed and trained by SOE in France had shortened the war by six months. Rail sabotage and attacks at the Germans' rear areas kept vital Panzer divisions away from the Normandy battlefields long enough after the landings to enable the Allies to consolidate their positions. Without the activity of resistance groups that owed their beginnings to the British, the beachheads might never have held.

Foot also pointed out how resistance groups following the retreating Germans made way for de Gaulle's triumphant entry into one liberated town after another, assuring him the role of national saviour as his people took over communications and picked up the reins of government. The irony was that de Gaulle, determined to consolidate his still precarious political power, rejected the very agents who had paved the way for him and made it possible for him to assume power. There is a legend attested to by Francis Cammaerts that when de Gaulle denounced George Starr as a British mercenary and ordered his immediate departure from the country, the leader of the WHEELWRIGHT circuit, which had defended the south-west so effectively as to make the general's return possible, demanded a private interview with de Gaulle. Starr assured an intermediary that what he had to say would take only a moment. It was, the story goes, '*Mon géneral, je vous en merdre.*'[17]

If de Gaulle's peremptory and unceremonious dismissal of the most gallant and effective of the French Section officers was motivated by his need to gather all existing strands of power, whether held by Communists or British officers, in his own hands, it was also his revenge for the slights he felt he had endured on the part of the Anglo-American leaders. He had been kept outside the corridors of power, where decisions were made and policies determined, by Roosevelt's dislike and the early pro-Pétain policies of the American State Department. And the British, although they had done so much for his cause, he saw only as serving their own. SOE took no political sides in France and organizers like Starr were as willing to work with Communists as Gaullists as long as they would help fight the Nazis. The reluctance of the Allied powers to recognize him unequivocally from the very beginning of the war as the legitimate head of a post-war government was neither forgiven nor forgotten. More than twenty years after the Normandy landings, pulling France out of the NATO military alliance, de Gaulle told the American Secretary of State he wanted every American soldier out of France. To his everlasting credit, Dean Rusk asked him whether that included the dead Americans in the military cemeteries.

De Gaulle had had his own agenda, which was to return to France as a victor leading a victorious people who had risen up spontaneously to overthrow a hated conqueror, thus reestablishing the myth of 'heroic France the invincible', France the glory of civilization, and restoring French honour. In this telling there was not only no place for any heroes but the French, there was no place for a history of widespread collaboration, for the existence of an enthusiastic Milice or an industry of informers, and above all no acknowledgement that only France, of all the occupied countries, had itself, at the hands of its own government and its own citizens, organized and administered the shipping of hundreds of thousands of innocent Jewish men, women, and children to the agony of the death camps in the east. Many individuals, for the most part in the villages and countryside of rural France, had helped and hidden Jewish friends, neighbours, and even strangers, but official France had rounded up its Jewish citizens for the transports to Auschwitz. Civilized France had done that on its own, making it unnecessary for the Germans to occupy themselves with the matter.

While British and American soldiers were still fighting their way inch by inch across the country, de Gaulle flew back to France and walked through the streets of its towns. His people were installed in key positions in the town hall, the postal and telegraph office, the railroad station, preventing the Communists – who in the event had been the most effective *résistants* – from seizing the reins of power for themselves. Although Communists and fellow travellers were accepted into the provisional government if they agreed to support the Gaullists, the Party was prevented from seizing power. And all along the way of his triumphal progress, the general proclaimed a myth. It was that 'the whole of France, of France alone', had fought to win this victory and that it was the French themselves who had liberated themselves. It was a myth that served, as de Gaulle had known it would, to bind his bleeding nation together and substitute pride for shame. The only thing it cost was truth, a commodity which must have seemed, in the midst of all the other shortages and shambles of those days, not worth as much as certain other things.

Foot's history touched on all the larger issues of Britain's participation in French resistance as the background to an account – incomplete but the best that could be expected from the surviving records made available to him – of day-to-day operations. In the end, it was by detailing the activities of many of the individual agents in the field as they built up circuits, of their successes and failures at a kind of clandestine warfare that would become common in the decades to come but was unprecedented then, and interweaving those accounts with that larger background of political purpose, that he arrived at his answers to F Section's critics.

CHAPTER 18

Answers

Whether they got the story quite right or not, Jean Overton Fuller and Elizabeth Nicholas – two women with no official authority of any kind – aided by a like-minded MP convinced by their arguments, were responsible for bringing the matter before the public and forcing the government to tell its own side of the story.

The heart of the indictment of SOE drawn up by the 'three-headed dragon, all feminine', as Jean Overton Fuller herself styled them,[1] was that an organization of amateurs who had no real understanding of the field they were entering and no experience to be guided by, misread the situation and underestimated its opponents, shrewd professionals, and sent into the field young people whose few short weeks of training in no way prepared them to elude the older experienced Germans. The kind of knowledge they needed for their survival was not anything that could be taught during a few weeks at a special school. How to recognize double dealing, how to cope with it, are things that only years of life experience can teach.

'What qualifications other than idealism and bravery had young girls like Denise and Madeleine to pick their way in that complex underworld into which they were dropped?'[2] asked Jean Overton Fuller. She recalled the unworldly young Noor and asked what hope a dreamy girl like that could possibly have against an agent like Placke. To have sent these young people into urban areas crowded with Germans and their agents and informers, to meet in crowded cafés, make contact with strangers by means of a password in some busy place, was to sign their death warrants. They never realized that the Germans' aim might not be to capture them immediately but to observe them, to keep a watch on their activities. Many of them in the towns and cities were under constant surveillance, thinking they were safe only because they hadn't been arrested.

Most of the agents who survived operated in remote and mountainous regions, like those belonging to WHEELWRIGHT in Gascony, led by George Starr, and Francis Cammaerts' JOCKEY in the south-east, although even in an out-of-the-way hamlet in the Jura Diana Rowden could not be protected against betrayal. And members of those same networks based in urban areas – in Lyon, Marseille, Toulon – were subject to the same dangers as those in Paris.

M.R.D. Foot's mandate was to put the case for F Section in the context of wartime strategy and politics, to defend its actions and their results against the charges that had been brought against it by outsiders. His history was meant 'to show that the dead deserve honour, and that SOE's effort was not made in vain.'[3]

To the charge that the women who did not come back and too many others like them were amateurs, Foot responded that so were many of the SD and Gestapo staff they were up against. Kieffer had been a police inspector before the war, but Goetz had been a teacher and most of the other SS staff were more likely to have had careers as some kind of criminals before the war than as professionals in counter-espionage. He also pointed out that many of F Section's most successful agents were also amateurs drawn from civilian life rather than from the ranks of the military.

Cammaerts too was an amateur, but in the event proved uniquely suited by temperament to the clandestine life, a thoughtful and cautious man with an instinct for people and one whose security measures were impeccable. On arriving in France he had sized up the situation on the Riviera and elsewhere and cut himself out, lying low until he could make his own way to the Drôme-Vaucluse-Var area of Provence, where, as Roger, he would take his time gathering a trustworthy group of competent men and women. The well-trained and well-disciplined members of his JOCKEY circuit, like those of George Starr's WHEEL-WRIGHT, were still in place on D Day to rise up as planned and significantly delay the arrival of German reinforcements.*

But what of the decision to send Noor? Beaulieu had advised against sending her in much stronger terms. To Colonel Frank Spooner, the army regular who headed the security school, she was too sensitive, too inexperienced, too vulnerable to be sent into enemy territory. He had considered both Noor and Odette, he later told Jean Overton Fuller, too emotional and impulsive for the work at hand and had gone out on a limb to say so, but Vera Atkins had disagreed with him and Buckmaster had backed her up. She never forgot it ('One knew them . . .').

These two were not the only agents whose qualifications were questioned. Sometimes the doubters proved right and sometimes they proved wrong. And, as Foot pointed out, no one was sent

---

* But even Cammaerts' luck ran out eventually, proving that even the most cautious of men would be up against shrinking odds over time. Arrested by the SD at a roadblock near Digne, about ninety miles from both Marseille and Nice, he was imprisoned in the cellar of the SS headquarters there with a pair of fellow agents. When his courier, the beautiful, brave, and resourceful Polish countess Krystyna Skarbek, known in SOE by her *nom de guerre* Christine Granville, heard of his capture, she undertook one of the most dramatic exploits recorded in SOE lore.

When the Nazis invaded Poland Krystyna Skarbek had organized escape routes through the Balkans to the Middle East to rescue both Polish airmen and British prisoners of war. Eventually, she became a British agent operating out of Budapest and was the first woman dropped into occupied France from Algiers, landing on the Vercors plateau to join Cammaerts. When she heard of his arrest she immediately arranged by wireless for a drop of two million francs to be sent from Algiers, and managed to ransom the three agents by persuading a Gestapo agent that if he helped them escape he would be taken along with them to the rapidly advancing Allied lines and freed, whereas if he refused he would be dealt with by the local maquis. He chose wisely. The war in Europe would not be over for another nine months, but there was no longer any doubt about who would win it.

over who didn't know what to expect from the Gestapo if caught. The routine sadism of the Nazis, who had built their political system on the habitual use of torture to reduce men and women to beasts and slaves, was the commonest of knowledge. It was, after all, one of the reasons F Section's recruits had for enlisting in the struggle to defeat them.

Andrée Borrel was an amateur who seemed uniquely suited for the job at hand. She did not have to worry about passing as a Frenchwoman, she was one. She could move around the country with the assurance that comes only with familiarity and her manner was that of millions of other young Frenchwomen entering a shop, stopping for a traffic light, ordering a drink in a café. As for Noor, she had a skill that was so valuable it could easily seem to outweigh all other considerations. She was French-speaking and knew the customs of the country, even though she lacked most of the necessary traits for an agent in the field – aggression, patience, and emotional self-control. More important than these shortcomings, though, she was a trained W/T operator at a moment when there was an acute shortage of them.

Communications was the vital prerequisite for everything SOE had to do – for organization as well as for operations – and the disruption of communications was the highest priority of the enemy. Francis Cammaerts, speaking of his remarkable wireless operator Gustave Floiras, who sent a record 416 messages for him over the unprecedented period of fifteen months, said, 'Without your radio operator you were a pigeon without wings.'[4]

SOE was dependent on a number of things over which it had little or no control: the moon, the weather, the willingness of the RAF to provide transport, and the ability to keep lines of communication operating between its offices in London and various rooms in farmhouses and city apartments in an enemy-occupied country sealed off from the outside world. There men and women might be taking it on themselves for reasons that could only be guessed at to act in ways that defied the rules of security they had been taught. The recruitment of subagents in the field was a particularly risky manoeuvre. The more people involved in a circuit, the less secure it was. The more people in his or her own circuit or others an agent knew about, the more dangerous he or she would be if captured.

Writing some twenty years after the events in question, Foot pointed out how misleading it could be to look back and focus on some particular activity, some isolated series of events during that far-away time. Things seem deceptively simple in retrospect. They were not so at the time. SOE's activities in France were a tiny part of the vast matrix of the war raging on several fronts and involving millions of people in myriad ways. There was, one might say, a lot going on. Furthermore, it was a new kind of organization, engaged in unprecedented work. The people in charge had to do a lot of guessing, to find their way through trial and error, see what worked and what didn't, and often by the time they found out it was too late to make effective use of the knowledge.

One of the easiest misunderstandings people fell into as they looked back on what had gone wrong had to do with the imprecision of the wireless communications of the time. Despite training, despite the system of checks and double checks intended to guarantee the integrity of an agent's messages from the field, sending conditions in the field often made it difficult if not impossible to decipher parts of the messages received. There was natural atmospheric interference, jamming by the German wireless interception service, and haste under difficult conditions contributing to human error, all of which could make for difficulties. Agents transmitting under pressure could make mistakes that were unintended as well as the intentional ones designed as security checks. And at each of a number of stages there was fresh opportunity for error to creep in. In the operator's coding of the message, in transmitting it, in receiving it clearly, in the decoding, in the teleprinting process − only after all of these would some form of the original message given to the operator reach the desk of Vera Atkins, Morel or Buckmaster.

Sometimes there would be a string of characters the decoder had not been able to make sense of. A jumble of letters and figures would have to be puzzled out by a member of the staff making guesses on the basis of what was known about the sender's circumstances and associates – often very little. Checks were often omitted in a crisis, and when they were included the final message as received and decoded often contained enough other errors and inadvertent mutilations to make it unintelligible to the FANY signaller decoding it at the reception station before passing it on to a senior member of the staff at Baker Street.

One example among many is a message delivered to Vera Atkins' desk reading: 'IMI THRMY SAYG ABLE TAKE TWHGVE CONTTT?S G??U?D AFFLY BBBR MASSAGE MIEUW TORT KUE ???IIS.' Applying her considerable knowledge and intuition, she was able to translate that apparent gobbledygook into: 'IMI TOMMY SAYS ABLE TAKE TWELVE CONTAINERS GROUND APPLE BBC MESSAGE MIEUX TARD QUE JAMAIS.'[5]

It seems rather remarkable not that the staff were sometimes wrong but that they were so often right.

The autumn of 1942 had seen changes that affected both Allied strategy and tactics. Forced labour conscription, the hated STO, had begun in the late summer and started the movement into the hills by the young men who would form the guerrilla army known as the maquis. It was in them, and not the phantom 'secret army' originally envisioned, that the best hope for resistance lay. The effects of Operations TORCH and ATTILA, the Allied landings in North Africa and the immediate German takeover of the previously unoccupied zone of Vichy France, were also rearranging the pieces of the puzzle. And it was clear that something would have to be done for the Russians. Stalin had begun to demand a cross-Channel invasion to force the Germans to relieve the pressure on the Soviet front. And if a full-scale invasion was not yet feasible, at the very least the Germans would have to be distracted.

In the face of these larger developments in early 1943 the 'madly insecure'[6] early CARTE organization was to be superseded as SOE's leading circuit in France by Frager's takeover of what was left of it (DONKEYMAN), together with a new circuit built by PROSPER on the ground of Vomécourt's ruined AUTOGIRO. They started off compromised by the penetration of the earlier organizations and soon compounded their troubles by ranging too far and failing to maintain the kind of watertight security arrangements among themselves that saved other threatened circuits from complete destruction when an individual agent's luck ran out. PROSPER's overlapping circuits and snowballing sub-circuits were dangerously widespread, ranging as they did from the Ardennes to the Atlantic, and the kindest thing that can be said about the apparent carelessness of the thirty agents under Prosper's command and their numerous recruits in the field is that they were more trusting of Providence and each other than they had any reason to be.

The PROSPER inner circle made things easier than necessary for the Germans by acting with a kind of stylish bravado that made them more conspicuous than any agent had a right to be. Suttill, Norman, Borrel and Guerne regularly lunched together in a black-market restaurant near the Étoile and met in the evenings at a café in Montmartre; they spoke English in these public places and seem to have made little effort to be discreet. 'They forgot how many Paris waiters were in the Gestapo's pay,'[7] Foot observed. There was the story about them demonstrating a Sten gun in a café they habitually met in near Sacré Coeur. Some of this behaviour can be attributed to character, some to earlier experience. Even his enemies seemed somewhat awed by Francis Suttill's 'magnificent' persona; Déricourt compared him to Ivanhoe.[8] And Andrée Borrel was used to taking chances; her months on an escape line had imbued her with a sense of cameraderie in danger.

Allowing for all of which it is still difficult to account for such behaviour, considering what they had been taught at Beaulieu, except by saying that personality is a more potent force in determining behaviour than precept. But it would be wrong to put their actions down to mere carelessness. It is difficult for those who have never been placed in extreme situations to judge the feelings of those who have. Perhaps the panache under pressure was intended to dilute the awful boredom, to neutralize the constant anxiety. They were aware of the brutality and terror they ran the risk of confronting if caught and they were practising gestures of denial in the face of fear. Andrée Borrel behaved no differently under arrest than she had in a Paris café. Perhaps she had been practising courage.

Once they fell into German hands, every one of the F Section agents captured as a result of the wireless game disappeared. All of them, with the exception of John Starr and one other who escaped, were killed by the Germans. The Allies were not meant to discover what had happened to any of their agents captured by the secret services. If Vera Atkins had not taken it on herself to interrogate the surviving German staff officers immediately after the war, the fate of the British agents who had not come back would never have been known. And if Elizabeth Nicholas and Jean Overton Fuller had not undertaken their searches and published their books about them, the stories would never have been made public.

Foot's judgement was that a combination of bad security in the field, penetration by double agents, and 'undue gullibility' back in London had brought about the disasters of summer 1943. These things had made possible the reading of the London-bound reports sent via Lysander from agents in the field and the playing back of captured sets in the radio game. Ultimately they had made possible the avalanche of arrests of hundreds of French subagents.

But while acknowledging the existence of the rumours he had been brought in to lay to rest, Foot dismissed out of hand the belief on the part of many of the French who had been involved that the PROSPER circuit was deliberately sacrificed by the British as part of an elaborate deception scheme to distract the Germans from the invasion of Sicily that summer.

Despite official denials and Foot's protestations, it was not an entirely unreasonable hypothesis. The Sicilian assault, planned by Roosevelt and Churchill at Casablanca early in the year, was aimed at knocking Italy out of the war, eventually gaining a toehold in southern Italy, and at the same time mollifying Stalin temporarily by engaging German forces that might otherwise have reinforced the eastern front. But at the time Foot wrote, little or nothing was known about the role of deception schemes in Allied strategy and the accusation was easy to dismiss, particularly in the presence of so many instances of lax security and betrayal in the field. It didn't seem necessary to go much further to look for causes of the disaster that befell F Section's agents in the Paris area than their own conduct and a measure of bad luck. 'The real wonder,' Foot said, 'is not that Suttill and his friends were caught, but that it took so long for so many Germans to catch them.'[9]

As for London, it was ineptitude, not treachery, that Foot laid at the staff's door. They were lacking in 'imaginative perception of what things were really like'[10] in occupied France. Questions none the less remained. How could Baker Street have 'overlooked' the many reports of the arrest of agents with whose sets they went on exchanging signals for weeks, sometimes months afterwards? How could they have ignored the absence of an agent's security check, provided for the very purpose of alerting them to his distress or to his absence? (Maurice Southgate, the resourceful and highly successful organizer of the STATIONER circuit, one of the only three of more than forty British agents sent there who were still alive in Buchenwald when the camp was liberated, reported having met a number of agents in captivity who had vainly tried to alert London to their predicament by leaving out their security checks. He said he 'would very much like to know what the hell the check was meant for if not for that very special occasion.' Buckmaster, with his usual degree of astuteness, remarked that Southgate's was 'clearly the report of an extremely tired man.'[11]) Foot can offer no satisfactory answer. Some staff officers were brighter than others, it was a matter of bad coordination – the issue is left at that.

About what was actually accomplished by SOE in France, Foot has quite a lot to say. In the days and weeks after D Day, guerrilla ambushes and sabotage actions behind the lines delayed and distracted German troops and kept reinforcements from reaching Normandy until it was too late to repulse the Allies. The slowdown of troops was partly due to air attacks and to railway workers' sabotage and the Communists were particularly effective in the cities, especially in Paris, but SOE agents and SOE weapons had prepared the thousands of maquisards and other resisters who came out all over the country, particularly in the rural south-east and south-west.

A crack SS armoured division ordered up to the Normandy beaches from the region of Toulouse took two weeks longer than the three days it should have taken to get there. Another Panzer division raced from the Russian front to the Rhine and then took three more weeks to cross France. The delays bought the time necessary to secure the Normandy bridgehead, where things were touch and go for the first few days. The Panzers of the Das Reich division were harassed all the way along the route by agents of F Section circuits blowing up its fuel dumps. Railroads made unworkable by recalcitrant railway workers and by sabotage with SOE plastic explosives had to be abandoned; unusable railroads meant the troops had to move on the roads, where SOE-armed and trained snipers were lying in wait for them. Telephone lines were cut, making enemy communications difficult and forcing them to use wireless telegraphy, which could be read by SOE operators. All this had the additional benefit of weakening the Germans' fighting effectiveness, sapping their morale along with their energy.

When the Allies came ashore on the Riviera a little more than two months after D Day, Heslop's MARKSMAN circuit in the Haute Savoie, Starr's WHEELWRIGHT in the south-west, and Cammaerts' JOCKEY in the south-east held open the route along the lower Rhône valley all the way up to Grenoble, enabling the Allied forces to advance in pursuit of the retreating Germans.

Was the effort expended by SOE in France worth its cost, including that of the lives lost there, the men and women, young and old, who did not come back? That question was the subtext of Foot's history.

In France, SOE had, with all its blunders and its occasional failures, sought out the first stirring of resistance, organized the resisters, armed and trained them, and made it possible for them to rise up in support of the Allied invasion of the Continent. In turn, the army of resistance created primarily by the British made it possible for the French to lift their heads up again and to believe de Gaulle when he told them their honour was restored to them.

Foot's ultimate answer to SOE's critics had to do with the men and women who undertook to prepare the way for an armed resistance movement in conditions fraught with risk for them and for those who joined with them. It is an answer that has often been quoted since, and bears quoting again at some length:

> To the question why people with so little training were sent to do such important work, the only reply is: the work had to be done, and there was no one else to send. On 6 June 1944 a sacrifice was made on the Normandy beaches which represented a comparable spending of some lives to make straight the pathway for many more; though the later sacrifice has received none of the notice devoted to PROS-PER – partly because no women were on the spot, and because the whole forlorn business was over in an hour and a half; mainly because it was a recognizable part of an ordinary operation of war. Before the main invading forces could actually set foot, a little after sunrise, on the NEPTUNE coast, three battalions of British sappers had to go ashore at low tide with the first light of early dawn, and make safe the mine-laden obstacles strewn on the beaches. Three-quarters of them were shot down at their work; but they did it. Suttill and his colleagues were doing a similar indispensable

pioneers' task; their fate was no more agreeable for being so much more protracted, yet their relatives also can feel they died to some good purpose.[12]

It was an answer meant to comfort and to reassure, and to lay to rest the suspicions and rumours that had hovered over SOE's French Section since the end of the war. It should come as no surprise that it neither lulled the suspicions nor put an end to the rumours, both of which were about to be given new life from unexpected quarters.

PART THREE

Sifting the Ashes

After such knowledge, what forgiveness? Think now
History has many cunning passages, contrived corridors
And issues, deceives with whispering ambitions, guides us by
    vanities. . .

Neither fear nor courage saves us. Unnatural vices
Are fathered by our heroism. Virtues
Are forced upon us by our impudent crimes.
These tears are shaken from the wrath-bearing tree.

From T.S. Eliot, 'Gerontion' in *Collected Poems, 1909–1935*

CHAPTER 19

The Deceivers . . .

'It is a double pleasure to deceive the deceiver.'
Jean de la Fontaine, *Fables*, Book II, fable 15

Following the publication of Foot's book, the curtain of secrecy gradually began to be lifted from some of the wartime records in Great Britain and in particular in the United States. Formal liaison between the United States' Office of Strategic Services and SOE had begun shortly after America's entry into the war at the end of 1941. OSS files in the National Archives in Washington contain records pertaining to SOE dating from the time that cooperation between the two services had begun and include such documents as the 1948 *Secret War Report of the OSS* to the US Joint Chiefs of Staff, declassified and made public in 1976.

In 1975 and 1976 the National Archives opened the records of the OSS's London Research and Analysis branch it had received from the State Department and, beginning in 1980, it began to release files made available by the Central Intelligence Agency. These included the London War Diaries of the OSS, the CIA's precursor. These histories of OSS's various branches included that of special operations, in which there remains a considerable amount of material relating to SOE. And in the Public Record Office in London thirty years after the end of the war researchers were finally able to consult minutes and memoranda of the War Cabinet as well as some official files containing papers of such bodies as the Chiefs of Staff, the Joint Planning Staff and the Foreign Office, and the correspondence and working papers of various ministers and other officials who had been involved in high-level decision making.

What began to emerge from all this was the extent to which deception had formed a major part of Allied strategy and the tactics by which it had been implemented. And the nature and extent of that strategy and the way in which those tactics were conceived and how they were implemented raised new questions and shed new light on the fate of Prosper, his closest associates, and those hundreds of others who shared their fate.

One of the first important facts that came to light was the degree of acrimony which characterized the relations between SOE and MI6, the Foreign Office, and the regular services, as well as, in the case of F Section, de Gaulle. In the case of de Gaulle, it was not clear at the beginning how much support the general actually enjoyed among the French still in France while it was an indisputable fact that there were French men and women who were willing to work with the British but not willing to swear allegiance to the general. The best that SOE could do under the circumstances was to create the parallel RF section alongside F. As Bickham Sweet-Escott, a versatile senior SOE staff officer who at one time headed the Gaullist RF Section, put it, 'The scope for muddle was immense.'[1]

That there would be some factionalism and competitiveness between departments was to be expected but the intensity of the jealousies, ambitions and misunderstandings that abounded in the early days eventually became minefields of conflicting interests ready to explode in recriminations and self-justification. The Foreign Office was concerned with questions of who would be in charge of Europe after the war, MI6 worried about subversive operations interfering with intelligence gathering, Bomber Command objected to diverting aircraft for special operations, and no one trusted the amateurs at Baker Street.* At least not until

---

* Disdain for SOE had persisted, in some quarters, well beyond the war years. The reviewer of a book dealing with British policy in Greece during the Second World War wrote in the influential and widely read *Times Literary*

they had something to show for themselves besides plans. As one historian put it, 'SOE appeared to the Foreign Office and Chiefs of Staff as an unruly sixth-form schoolboy unable to keep his grubby fingers off the tablecloth while constantly demanding second helpings when there were none.'[2]

And for quite some time SOE had little enough to show for its efforts on the Continent. Among the headaches in the first tentative months of SOE's existence was MI6's grip on SOE's wireless communications. Until the early summer of 1942 MI6 sent and received SOE's messages to and from the field at its station in Bedfordshire, from which they were sent to London by teleprinter for decoding by MI6's staff before being passed on to the SOE country-section. MI6 also provided the documents such as identity papers and ration cards on which an agent's life could depend. It was no wonder that SOE was anxious to set up its own wireless organization and produce its own forgeries. But MI6's head, Stewart Menzies, and his deputy, Claude Dansey, jealous of their position in Whitehall, were also concerned about their intelligence organization on the Continent, constantly threatened by SOE agents' conspicuous sabotage activities. Malcolm Muggeridge, who belonged to MI6, known before the war as the Secret Intelligence Service, would recollect, 'Though SOE and SIS were nominally on the same side in the war, they were, generally speaking, more abhorrent to one another than the Abwehr was to either of them.'[3]

As late as eight months into the war, in the early summer of 1940, there was not a single British agent anywhere in western Europe. Little organized resistance existed in France, and the weather of the terrible winter of 1941/1942 severely limited the possibilities for actions in Europe. Yet by spring of 1942 SOE had scores of agents inside Europe and throughout the Middle

Supplement (18 March 1965) that among SOE's 'higher executives many displayed an enthusiasm quite unrestrained by experience, some had political backgrounds which deserved a rather closer scrutiny than they ever got, and a few could only charitably be described as nutcases'.

East and North Africa. It was only in late 1942, as the Allies began to take the offensive, that SOE really got off the ground, and by the spring of 1943 it was functioning in every theatre of the war, with its emphasis on building up secret armies which would rise up to support an eventual liberating Allied invasion. The long hot summer of 1943 provided 'wonderful moons for the Lysanders' and special duties pilot Hugh Verity recorded an increasing number of flights into France from April through to the September harvest moon.[4]

The second important fact that emerged from the growing number of documents that followed Foot's official history of F Section was how vastly more complicated than anyone had dreamed at the time was the invisible strategy of the Allied high command. It began to appear that it had not been the powerful armies levied against the enemy or even those in the shadows that had been the decisive factor but a long-secret component of top-level policy involving some armies that existed only in imagination – strategic deception.

No one was better placed to describe that component than J.C. Masterman, whose report on *The Double-Cross System in the War of 1939 to 1945*, written shortly after VE Day, had to wait over a quarter of a century before Her Majesty's Government approved its publication in 1972. In it, Sir John, as he was by then, described the wartime counter-espionage operations of MI5, the internal security agency, which had captured and turned German agents sent to Britain and used them throughout the war as double agents to mislead the Germans about Allied intentions in a number of crucial campaigns. The Germans never knew that it was MI5 that ran their entire espionage network in Britain.

Masterman's report on the counter-espionage work of the Twenty Committee (also referred to as the Double Cross Committee from the Roman numerals XX and the obvious pun), which coordinated the manipulation of double agents by MI5 with the military services, showed how those agents' wireless communications were used to deduce the enemy's intentions and then to influence their plans by deceiving them about Allied intentions. Since a good deal of truthful information had to be passed on in order to establish the credibility of the eventual lie, 'a nice assessment of profit and loss', as Masterman put it,[5] had to be made constantly. It was the function of the Twenty Committee to analyse and coordinate knowledge of what was going on in the various branches of the services and intelligence departments so that the Controlling Officer of Deception and ultimately the Chiefs of Staff could make the decision as to what information and misinformation could be given to the Germans.

'It was always in the back of our minds', wrote Masterman, 'that at some time in the distant future a great day would come when our agents would be used for a grand and final deception of the enemy.'[6] That grand and final deception would, of course, involve the time and place of the invasion of western Europe.

Deception policy for the rest of 1943, however, was aimed at holding German forces in western Europe and the Mediterranean rather than having them moved east to reinforce the Russian front. Towards this end, Operation STARKEY was set afoot over the summer with the intention of convincing the Germans that a large-scale landing was coming in the Pas de Calais. It was part of the overall camouflage and deception plan called COCKADE, the aim of which was to relieve the pressure on the Russian front by focusing the Germans' attention on supposed threats in western Europe.[7] By this stage of the war, in the summer of 1943, strategic deception plans for all theatres of the war were coordinated by the London Controlling Section (LCS), a small and highly secret group that met in Churchill's War Cabinet headquarters and was led by the Controlling Officer of Deception, and were then submitted for approval by the Chief of Staff to the Supreme Allied Commander (COSSAC) and later by Supreme Headquarters, Allied Expeditionary Force (SHAEF).

The LCS would soon be designing another grand scheme intended to mislead the Germans into thinking not only that the invasion would come later than actually planned but, even after the invasion had begun, that the Normandy landings were only a diversionary operation to be followed by a major assault in the Pas de Calais. It was an elaborate plan involving information supplied through the MI5 turned-round wireless agents; the creation of a fictional army complete with dummy tanks and assault craft stationed on the English coast where enemy aerial reconnaissance would locate it seemingly poised to attack far to the north of the actual landing beaches; and stepped-up resistance activity in the north of France, where increasing arms drops would accompany increasing sabotage and guerrilla operations. As far as the agents in France were concerned, it was literally a game that involved playing with dynamite.

This plan, however, would hardly have been possible if not for the fact that by 1943 the British were reading a good part of the wireless traffic of the German high command, having broken their supposedly unbreakable codes. They had, in effect, been eavesdropping on the enemy's top-level secret communications.[8]

That extraordinary achievement – with the development of the atomic bomb, one of the two best-kept secrets of the Second World War – had been made possible by Polish Secret Intelligence Service deciphering experts who obtained one of the commercial enciphering machines known as the Enigma, which had been adapted by the Germans for military use during the 1930s. The Poles managed to make two copies of an early form of the machine and its coding wheels and turned them over to their French and British opposite numbers in Warsaw on the eve of the outbreak of the war.

Machine ciphers were thought to be indecipherable; they could be read only if another machine had been set to the same keys on a wheel that rotated to provide an unending number of possibilities. But using information supplied by a German officer of the Reich's cryptographic bureau and a Polish Jew who had worked at the Enigma factory in Berlin before being forced to leave Germany, a group of brilliant Polish and French decrypters working in France penetrated the ciphers and the wizards at the Government Code and Cipher School, the cryptanalytic headquarters at Bletchley Park, succeeded in duplicating the increasingly sophisticated machine, something like a primitive computer, and cracking its keying procedures despite their nearly infinite complexity.*

The top-secret and uniquely valuable intelligence produced by Enigma was code-named Ultra. It was to become an inestimable strategic advantage. Ultra intercepts eventually provided the Allies with details ranging from the German order of battle to news of experimental weapons and even included Hitler's own instructions to his generals in the field. Ultra made it possible for the Allies to see not only what the Germans were planning to do but what was going on in the Germans' minds and how much of the material being fed to them by the double agents controlled by MI5 and coordinated with the military by the Twenty Committee they were buying. It was undoubtedly used in the planning for the events of the summer of 1943 in France, the grand deception scheme of which STARKEY was a part.

In the summer of 1942 things had still looked bleak for the Allies. But by the autumn of that year, with the victories at El Alamein and at Stalingrad, things were beginning to look brighter. Hitler had reached the limits of his greater Reich. From then on, he would gradually be losing ground. Although it remained an official secret for thirty years afterwards, Ultra had been a major factor in the success of the Allied victory in North Africa that had turned the tables and for the first time made an Allied return to the shores of Europe seem a realistic possibility. It would eventually be revealed that Ultra had provided intelligence crucial in the Battle of Britain at the beginning of the war, and later to the crushing of the submarine fleet that had menaced Allied shipping supply lines, two of the most critical moments in the war.

But valuable as it was, the Ultra material posed its own

* David Kahn's definitive work on cryptanalysis, *The Code Breakers*, had introduced Enigma to its readers in 1967, but the full significance of the use to which it was put would not be fully revealed for another half dozen years.

problem. It had to be used sparingly. Action taken on the basis of information it provided ran the risk of tipping off the Germans to the fact that their signals were being read. They never did realize the fact. And, until the early seventies, the existence of Ultra and the use made of it was known to only a handful of those at the very top of the chain of command. The distribution of the Ultra material had been in the hands of Menzies' MI6 and those involved were bound by the Official Secrets Act. (It has been said, perhaps apocryphally, that Churchill threatened that any of those entrusted with knowledge of the Ultra material who divulged the secret would face a firing squad.)

As the existence of Ultra became known, there began to be questions raised and reproaches levelled about various disasters – operations launched too soon with too little, bombing raids on undefended English cities, agents walking into traps – that it was suggested could have been prevented by acting on the information provided by the Germans' decrypted secret wireless traffic. Because the details of messages received remain secret and may never be declassified, it remains a moot point what was known, how it could have been used, and most of all whether and when it should have been. It would require an exquisite calibration of risks and benefits in the context of long-range strategy to answer such questions of tactics. No answers were forthcoming, but the questions would be raised in countless pages over the years since the signals were received, decoded, and passed on from Bletchley to the decision-makers of the Allied high command.

At the Teheran conference towards the end of 1943, Churchill told Roosevelt and Stalin, 'In war-time, truth is so precious that she should always be attended by a bodyguard of lies.'[9] He was putting before them OVERLORD, the overall strategy for the coming invasion of Europe, and explaining the necessity of deceiving the Germans, by means of a vast and far-reaching plan that would be code-named BODYGUARD. Its object was surprise, and surprise was a necessity if the landings on the Normandy coast were to succeed. It would be a contest between ingenuity and might, between pretence and Panzers.

Hitler's armies were still huge, their armour was still powerful, and the Atlantic coast was heavily fortified. The Wehrmacht, if no longer invincible, was still highly efficient, still capable of doing deadly battle. If Hitler's generals knew what to expect – not just that invasion of Fortress Europe was imminent, but where and when it would begin – there was a good chance that they could beat it back. Even if NEPTUNE, the initial landing operation, succeeded in establishing a beachhead, breaking out and moving on would have to depend on catching the Germans off guard and gaining time before they could reinforce their troops in Normandy.

BODYGUARD had a number of tactical components. The one designed to protect NEPTUNE, the initial assault phase of OVER-LORD, was code-named FORTITUDE. By means of orchestrated rumours, misleading newspaper accounts, planted radio signals, dummy planes, tanks and ships – some of them constructed in the prop workshops of the Shepperton film studios – arranged to be seen by enemy aerial reconnaissance, false reports of move-ments of fictional troops and high-level staff, it was intended to create the impression that invasion was coming north of the actual site and later than the actual date of the planned assault. It was also meant to create the impression that they, the Germans, had put all this together and figured it out on their own.

The members of the LCS, the super-secret agency coordinating strategic deception schemes as part of the British military's Joint Planning Staff, knew that in order for such schemes to succeed, they had to be known to as few people as possible and they had to seem entirely plausible. What that meant, for one thing, was that even some of the men and women involved might not know that what they were involved in was a cover operation. The hundreds of little details and larger events designed and staged to fool the enemy might end up fooling those on one's own side as well. Nowhere would this prove more significant than in the case of the special operations agents and those men and women they had recruited, trained, worked with and depended on in occupied France. There was a special relationship of trust between the SOE organizers and the *résistants* in the networks made up of what the one called their circuits and the others their *réseaux*. In neither language had they been prepared for some of the tactics of the war of special means being waged in a cover even denser than their own war in the shadows.

It was inevitable that as more and more operations involved more and more people, some of them would talk. Rumour and gossip could be counted on to spread the word of what was expected. Among the British, the French had a reputation for having loose tongues. Ben Cowburn, an outstanding F Section organizer whose prudence enabled him to survive longer than most agents in the field, was later quoted by Foot as saying, 'Ninety-five percent of the people arrested were caught simply because their friends had been incapable of keeping their mouths shut.'[10]

Among the elements that converged to create the impression that a cross-Channel attack at the Pas de Calais was imminent – rumours, press reports, supposed troop movements of imaginary divisions in phantom armies described by turned agents, aerial photographs of dummy camps, ships, tanks and planes, fake radio signals – was the fomenting of unrest on the northern coast of France, where stepped-up resistance activity would suggest that the expected amphibious attack was about to be launched. To provide the right touch of authenticity necessary to spring the trap being laid for the Germans, SOE parachute drops of arms, ammunition and explosives would increase and so would sabotage operations. The danger in this labyrinthine strategy was that resistance forces might themselves be lured into the trap, rising up too soon and falling into the ready hands of the Gestapo.

London was aware of the danger, but hoped to be able to keep the resistance groups it had built up from going too far too soon. The BBC would broadcast the various circuits' alert messages – telling them to stand by ready to act within a fortnight – but not the subsequent action messages instructing them to take action within the next forty-eight hours. The planners were well aware that they would be bringing the resistance groups 'to flash point expectations of relief before the winter' of 1943 only to disappoint them.[11] They judged, and the Chiefs of Staff agreed, that in the end the deception would be found acceptable by the western Europeans in the light of the success in the Sicilian and Italian campaigns that the deception was intended to assure.

In the end, although BODYGUARD as a whole accomplished its ends, the STARKEY component was a failure. The Germans did not fall for the elaborate ruse and did not rush to defend the Pas de Calais area. It was not, however, as great a disaster as it might have been. The resistance, despite increased acts of defiance and sabotage undertaken all over north-western Europe that late summer and autumn in the belief that invasion was at hand, was not destroyed and would live to fight another day – on D Day and after. But one dark cloud hangs over the whole affair. If Prosper and other agents in the field were not let in on the fact that STARKEY was an elaborate game, in which they in effect became pawns, and if they acted on the belief that invasion was really set for the autumn of 1943, did that lead them to relax their security precautions while at the same time increasing their activities? Was that the cause of the mass arrests in the Paris area early that summer? Was the PROSPER tragedy set in motion by the way in which the STARKEY deception was carried out? Had F Section agents in the field been deliberately misled in the interests of 'authenticity' for the sake of STARKEY?

It was a view held by many of the French, who bitterly maintained that the British had been responsible for the disaster that had overtaken so many of their people that fateful summer of 1943, sacrificing them in order to save the lives of the servicemen who would mount the invasion.

. . . and the Deceived

One of the embittered Frenchmen who believes that F Section agents were deliberately misled for the sake of larger strategic goals is Pierre Raynaud.[1]

He met me one hot sunny afternoon at the bustling railway station in Avignon, a compact man with a square jaw and a bald head, moving purposefully, the perfect image of a tough irregular soldier. Within minutes, as we drove through the dry summer Provençal countryside, he was talking as though we'd been discussing F Section for years, in a degree of detail I found it difficult to follow, referring to names and places I didn't always recognize, scowling with annoyance if I interrupted to ask a question.

We had never met before. I was prepared by his early letters – pages of closely written and sometimes illegible information, interpretation, charges, evidence – for an enthusiast. Listening to him as we drove furiously toward his house near Mt Ventoux, I realized I was in the company of a man in whom enthusiasm had turned to obsession. Which, of course, did not necessarily mean he was wrong. I was intrigued.

I had been following a trail of people that had begun with Vera Atkins and through her I had met former British agents like Brian Stonehouse, Odette Hallowes, Lise Villameur, and others. I had been kindly received and given helpful information by the official in charge of transmitting whatever information could be gleaned from existing files held by the Foreign Office. I had been in touch with historians and journalists, museum curators, and relatives of former agents long dead. But none of these would have thought of referring me to Raynaud, and perhaps for good reason.

As a young French subaltern, Pierre Raynaud had managed to escape to London, where he had been picked up and trained by F Section. Dropped into the Sologne, he was met by a reception committee led by Pierre Culioli and Yvonne Rudellat, who were doomed to be captured in that fateful last week of June 1943. He decided to make his own way to join Francis Cammaerts at Montélimar rather than travel together with Culioli, Rudellat, and the two Canadians who had been parachuted the night before. Before parting with them, he had handed over to them material that had been given to him to bring to agents already in the field. It turned out to be obviously incriminating evidence that sealed the fate of those on whom it was found. What was also found on the Canadians, according to Raynaud, was the address of the Laurents, where Gilbert Norman and Andrée Borrel were arrested three days later.

Having avoided the disaster that overtook the others, he reached the south and – as Alain – became an instructor of sabotage groups for Cammaerts' vast JOCKEY network. A year after his arrival, shortly after D Day, he took charge of the Third Battalion of the French Forces of the Interior (FFI), the maquis of the Drôme-Sud. After the war Raynaud went on adventuring in one trouble spot after another – first in what was then French Indo-China and then in Algeria, finally settling down as a finance official in French Equatorial Africa. Over the years he continued to mull over his experiences in SOE and in particular the events of those days in June 1943 when the net had drawn in so many of the French Section agents and subagents and he himself had so narrowly escaped sharing their fate. His suspicions only grew with time. He remained convinced that a purposeful curtain of lies had been drawn over the reality of what had been done and by whom and with what motives.

In 1983 he retired to a house in the area of the Drôme where he had once operated for SOE and began to devote himself full-time to research on F Section's activities in the field and their communications with London, unearthing scores of documents in the French National Archives and writing hundreds of letters to former agents and SOE officials. He challenged official accounts of some dates of arrivals and departures of agents from the field, sought to determine the number and texts of W/T messages sent and received more than fifty years earlier, and took issue with many of the accepted versions of events and of the roles played by various agents, both British and French. In the process, he amassed a mountain of information and antagonized a goodly number of people, mostly among the British.

Reconstructing contacts, meetings, conversations attested to in depositions, in documents in official files, in postwar trials, and in personal correspondence, he began to assemble, piece by piece and section by section, the parts of an enormous puzzle, convinced that when he put them all together they would demonstrate the truth of his belief that he and the Canadians had been dropped into a trap. He began building a vast collection of documents, writing endless letters to former agents and officials, sifting clues to explain discrepancies in what records remained, determined to establish an archive secured for future historians.

During the two days I spent with Raynaud and his wife he talked almost non-stop, sometimes in English, sometimes in French, smoking as he paced, while I took notes furiously in an effort to keep up with him. What emerged from his explanations, accusations, descriptions, diatribes, was a theory, a mass of evidence to back it up, and a passion so intense that it could only work against him. Tact was not part of his nature, and he had managed to alienate many of those he had tried to enlist in his cause, particularly among the English, although some of his old companions among the French who were recruited in the field share his perspective on the events of June 1943.

He is convinced that the PROSPER agents were meant to be caught, in order to give information to the Germans about the time and place of the invasion which the agents actually believed to be true although it was not; in order to placate the Russians by demonstrating how weak the internal resistance was and therefore how unfeasible the possibility of invasion any time soon; and in order to protect Déricourt's position by eliminating those agents who had come to suspect him. Déricourt, he believes, was originally a German agent who had been turned by the British.

He maintains that the SD knew from the courier passed on to them by Déricourt that the two Canadians, Pickersgill and Macalister, were bringing new radio crystals and 'skeds' for Archambaud, and that Raynaud was bringing instructions. An exploding canister on one of Culioli's drop fields focused the attention of local authorities on the Sologne at just that time, and thus Raynaud believes the trap was set. The captured agents had on them the instructions for Archambaud, in clear, as well as his codes and security checks. It is Raynaud's contention that these were intended all along for use by Placke in the radio game. The Germans would think they were fooling the British, who would be well aware that it was not their agents who were transmitting and could plant disinformation about the coming invasion plans. Of course, for the STARKEY deception plan to work, they would have to let some of their agents be sacrificed to maintain credibility.

Raynaud set out to put together everything that could be gleaned from the records of the Germans as well as of the French and British. It is an enormous undertaking, and it became clear after a few hours of listening to him and looking over copies of some of the documents he has amassed (originals are secured elsewhere) why he said that a full understanding of the whole complicated situation would require weeks, not a mere two days.

What interested me most was that he knew so many of the agents involved in the part of the story I had set out to tell.

He had met Noor at Tempsford while both were waiting to be flown over. He remembers coming across her sitting and poring over a railroad timetable. It seemed clear to him that she had no idea what it was all about, what she was going into. It did not even seem to occur to her, he thought, that the trains were not still running on the prewar schedules, or that she would not simply be able to go to a station and board a train. He is convinced that it was intended that she be caught. He also has evidence he thinks may indicate that she expected to leave on one of Déricourt's flights shortly before her capture but was left behind on the field at the last moment.

Sonia he describes as Weil's mistress, and says 'she was certainly betrayed [by another member of the ROBIN *réseau*]'. Diana he knew at Wanborough, where they trained together for three weeks. 'She was a good girl,' he says, 'she did good work – very, very decent.' He believes that Benoit (whose real name was Maugenet) was one of those who were sent to be caught, which was bound to lead to the capture of Diana and Young. Of Andrée he says that after her arrest she was not interrogated. 'They had nothing to learn from her,' nor from any of the F Section agents. Nothing, that is, that they didn't already know through the courier mail passed on by Déricourt or the radio games.

Raynaud had met Vera Leigh in London in the spring of 1943. Neither told the other of being in SOE, but when she gave him her post office box number so they could write to each other, he saw that it was the same as his. He describes her as '*pas très jolie, moins "parisienne" qu'elle ne le pensait certainement*' (not very pretty and less the Parisian type than she thought herself). Vera, whose French was that of a native, worked from the beginning of the occupation with the PAT escape line, taking downed Allied airmen to Spain. When she arrived in London around Christmas of 1942, joining SOE was like a continuation of her work in PAT, '*mais ses expériences ne lui avaient pas appris la prudence*' (her experiences had not taught her to be cautious), as Raynaud puts it.

Vera was very friendly with Julienne Aisner, Déricourt's former mistress who was by then his assistant, and saw her almost every day. Raynaud thinks Vera learned about Déricourt's contacts with the Germans, which Julienne certainly knew about, and says, 'Vera believed Déricourt was so powerful, there was no risk as long as she was in his track.' She worked for Frager, whom Bleicher had tipped off, through Bardet, about Déricourt's contacts with the rival SD. Bleicher had thus betrayed a German agent on orders, Raynaud suggests, from Canaris, the anti-Hitler Abwehr chief. Raynaud believes that Vera was about to be arrested by the SD and that Bleicher felt he had to arrest her himself because he feared that, in the hands of the SD, she might reveal knowledge of Déricourt's activities that would lead back to him as the source of that knowledge.

Both Frager and Bardet warned her that she was in danger, but she refused to believe them. In a letter of which Raynaud has a copy, Frager wrote to Buckmaster in October 1943, only a few days before she was taken, that he was tired of warning her uselessly ('*ses mises en garde inutiles*'): 'J'ai interrompu la séance *ne voulant pas perdre mon temps à cause d'une charmante petite dame qui n'a jamais autant réfléchi que de puis qu'elle est agent secret de Jeannette*' (I broke off the meeting, unwilling to waste my time on a charming little lady who never thinks beyond being a secret agent of Jeannette). After the war Bardet claimed to have warned her the very morning of her arrest that if she went to the rendezvous in the Café Mas she would be taken and that she should get out of Paris immediately, but '*Elle n'a pas voulu me croire*' (she didn't want to believe me).

Raynaud points not only to Vera's having stayed in an apartment in the shadow of both Bleicher and the SD and going to her prewar hairdresser, but having kept up her link with the PAT escape line, 'a foolish and dangerous thing to do.' According to Raynaud, at the beginning of September 1943, Vera told Frager she had hidden two US pilots in the Paris suburbs in order to pass them on down the line and that someone had slipped under her door a note purporting to be from the resistance saying that two officers would be coming by in German uniforms in a German car to collect the fliers and take them to a landing field for a pickup. But it was not a moon period, so it was impossible for there to be a flight scheduled. Frightened, she turned the job over to Bardet.

According to Raynaud's sources, the very day after Suttill's arrest – and not, as others have said, after holding out for forty-eight hours while undergoing torture – he wrote the 'deliver to bearer' letter saying that all arms and ammunition, everything must be delivered, without exception, and sent the SD off with it to his agent and friend Darling in Gisors. In German archives Raynaud found testimony from captured agents who said that Suttill seemed very much at ease at the Avenue Foch, and that he had been heard to ask the Germans, when they returned from Gisors, 'Did you look in the *faux grenier*?' As for Norman, in everything he did, Raynaud says – including a disastrous visit to Andrée Borrel's family while in custody of the SD – he was executing the orders given him by Prosper in the belief that their subagents would be spared according to the terms of the pact that had been ratified by Himmler's RSHA headquarters in Berlin.

Raynaud's revisionary history touches on countless details, including such matters as the fate of Agazarian, another agent he maintains was deliberately delivered to the Germans because of what he knew, and the notorious business of the lost CARTE list. Raynaud says the list of names did not end up in the hands of the Germans but was given to a French police commissioner in sympathy with the group, who returned it to CARTE. The arrest of the Tambour sisters is said to have been a warning from the Abwehr to the British, who ignored it, that the SD was on to PROSPER and that the circuit was in danger. And there are accounts of double and triple dealings such as the Bleicher-Bardet-Frager connection which leave one's mind reeling. All of these cross connections, ignored messages, corrected dates, operational details, form the base of Raynaud's revionist version of the history of SOE in France.

Raynaud believes that, by means of deception at a high level, 'the British were giving PROSPER to the SD'. He is convinced that what Churchill told Prosper in London in May was that there was no hope of invasion that summer; he would have to hold out until September of 1943, and that Prosper was also instructed, if captured, to talk, and to deliver the arms in exchange for a promise to spare the agents' lives. He imagines Churchill saying to Suttill, I ask a great sacrifice of you. Give them everything and all our people will be saved.

Jacques Bureau, Prosper's radio technician, has said that Prosper spent only a week in England in May 1943, and that he spent the remaining weeks before his arrest anxiously travelling among the circuits of his vast network, which were receiving enormously stepped-up deliveries of arms and ammunition and a flurry of messages indicating that the moment for the uprising was near. Bureau adds that on his return from England Prosper seemed depressed and said to him, 'It won't be long for us now.'[2]

What Raynaud maintains is that 'the British power structure', which he characterizes as 'the establishment, Oxbridge types, bankers and wealthy investors, Jews and Freemasons', sent men and women to be caught in order to effect the destruction of the circuits that posed a threat to Déricourt and might interfere with his mission in the interests of STARKEY and FORTITUDE. It was essential for the success of the deception plans that the Germans trust Déricourt as a source of information regarding the time and place of the Allied invasion. Raynaud thinks officials at a high level were protecting Déricourt in his dangerous position – and hiding the complicity of MI6 and the LCS in the affair – by seeing that all agents who had sent messages reporting suspicions about him and those whose own sets had been used in the radio games were killed, including the women who ended up at Natzweiler and Dachau. It is a chilling thought.

Raynaud describes SOE as 'a reservoir of possibilities' for the LCS, the XX Committee, and MI6. His painstaking reconstruction of dates and texts of messages – who was arrested when, who reported the arrests and when – seems to indicate that Déricourt was suspected by many agents and that the arrests of those whose radios continued to transmit in German hands were known to those in London even as they pretended to be exchanging messages with them in good faith. He insists they lied about the number of radio games, the number of agents, the number of flights, in order to further their deception plans and in order to keep the secret forever. He says bitterly, 'It was all for nothing, in Holland and Belgium as in France. The Germans were not fooled. The wrong people were praised and decorated after the war. The British should have paid tribute to their victims in the end and thanked them after telling the truth about what they did.' Instead, he says, 'The lies continue.'

Repeatedly, he returns to his conviction that he himself was one of those who were sent to be caught. He says he had to make repeated efforts to have his ID papers include a newly required stamp he had learned about from a French newspaper, and that when it was finally produced it was dated 27 February, when the regulation did not go into effect until the first of March. What saved him was deciding not to go with Rudellat and Culioli and the two Canadians, whose accents appalled him, but to go on by himself. Otherwise, he would have been in the car when it was stopped.

As he tells these stories, and particularly as he talks about what happened afterwards, he seems to have total recall of every one of the names, dates, and places involved in hundreds of operations. And he insists on reading every word of the endless pages he has amassed on every aspect – no summaries. There is a certain maliciousness in his mimicry of those whose words he supposedly recreates, pursing his lips and half-closing his eyes as he speaks in a high voice with a French-tinged English accent, but he does catch something of their manner. As I watched and listened to him, bullet-headed, stocky, cigar-smoking, I was reminded of Erich von Stroheim in *La Grande Illusion*.

Raynaud goes on working obsessively, possessed by a mania, a little paranoid perhaps. But of course he may be right . . .

He goes on working, although few others seem to care. His correspondents eventually find him irritating, grow impatient with his constant inquiries and comments on minute details. He speaks of 'poor Jean; she fell in love with Déricourt,' and in fact explains everyone's disagreements with him in terms of their character or interests, never considering that they might have reasons as persuasive to them as his own are to him. Jean

Overton Fuller was one of the numerous recipients of pages and pages of closely written comments and queries, badly typed on legal-sized pages with hardly any margins, such margins as exist heavily annotated in a minuscule almost illegible hand, and who no longer respond to his letters, another source of bitterness.

Raynaud says he has placed the material he has painstakingly assembled over the years in a French government archive, where it will eventually become available to historians. He jokes about being killed by 'them', but adds, 'It's too late. It's all there.'

CHAPTER 21

After Such Knowledge . . .

Although Raynaud seems to have mastered thousands of details and carefully archived them, historians have not yet had a chance to judge the credibility of his theories and the evidence for them.

This has not been the case with a group of Anglo-American investigative journalists who independently have come to share a similar conspiracy theory about the downfall of PROSPER. They may not have the detailed facts that Raynaud has amassed but they make up in creative imagination and boldness what they lack in hard evidence. Working together and separately, they have published their views in various volumes. The view of BBC writer/producer Robert Marshall, novelist Larry Collins and James Rusbridger, a former MI6 agent[1] is that Prosper was disinformed as part of the deception schemes COCKADE and STARKEY, designed to pin down German forces in north-western France by pretending imminent invasion in order to keep them from reinforcing the Russian front; this resulted in a relaxation of security by the PROSPER agents, who thought they were on the verge of coming out of hiding but were in reality being encouraged to plan for a non-event. By that time, of course, PROSPER had been thoroughly penetrated. And by the time STARKEY was mounted in the autumn as the climax of COCKADE, Prosper, Denise, Archambaud and all those hundreds of others were in German hands.

What the journalists added to the by-now familiar facts was the charge that the network, already known to be doomed, was betrayed to the Germans by British intelligence – MI6 – as part of the deception scheme.

Maurice Buckmaster confirmed some of these claims when he told an interviewer in the 1980s that in the summer of 1943 he had been instructed to bring Prosper back for an interview with Churchill, who 'sent for Francis Suttill because he wanted to increase the amount of sabotage operations and general unrest in the west of France so that he could have some defence against Stalin's claim that we weren't doing enough to help bring German divisions out of the Eastern front and back to France.' He added that Suttill 'was encouraged by Churchill to run enormous risks, to overlook the security training he'd had in SOE training and produce violent explosions in the Paris area so Churchill could say to Stalin, "Now look what we're doing, we're doing all this." '[2]

Marshall's book, *All the King's Men*, set forth the conspiracy theory as strongly as possible. Déricourt, runs Marshall's argument, was recruited by Claude Dansey of MI6 and planted in French Section in order to ruin the rival service. He was used to mislead the Germans, who thought he worked for them, by passing on misinformation in the courier he handed over to them, but he also made it possible for them to trail incoming agents, decode radio messages, and in effect caused the arrest and deaths of hundreds of British agents and their French resistance associates and, not incidentally, the discrediting of SOE. There is a repelling description by one of his colleagues of 'Uncle Claude', as he was known in MI6, clapping his hands with glee when he heard the news of the PROSPER disaster.

What had not come out earlier, and had not even been dreamed of when Foot was writing his history of the section, were Marshall's assertions that Déricourt's German contacts had been known to MI6 from the beginning, that he had been passed on to F Section with Dansey carefully concealing his own role in the matter lest his motive be suspected, and that Buckmaster's deputy Bodington ('a secret agent *manqué*'), hoping for a position in MI6, had really been working all along in Dansey's interests. According to Marshall it was Bodington who had introduced

Déricourt, his old friend of prewar Paris days, to both the SD's Boemelburg and his opposite number Dansey. All of this is supposed to have been concealed from Buckmaster and the rest of F Section staff.

Buckmaster had also either lately remembered, or was reluctant to seem to be about the only one who didn't know, or now at last felt free to tell Larry Collins that MI6 had often intruded on his turf and that MI6 had sent messages to various resistance groups without F Section's knowledge.[3]

But the most striking testimony came from Harry Sporborg, who had been a principal figure in SOE. Sporborg had been private secretary for SOE affairs to Lord Selborne, Hugh Dalton's successor as Minister of Economic Warfare, had previously supervised SOE activities in northern and north-western Europe, and had been vice-chief to Gubbins, all positions which put him in touch with activities on a level above the country-section staffs. As Gubbins' deputy, it was Sporborg who oversaw the investigation of the charges against Déricourt in February 1944. In an interview shortly before his death, Sporborg stated that at the time of the investigation MI6's people had gone out of their way to play down the charges and that he was convinced that Déricourt had been acting as an agent of MI6. He admitted that he had no proof, but was unequivocal about his conviction. He said, 'SIS would never have hesitated to use us to advance their schemes, even if that meant the sacrifice of some of our people.'[4]

It was a shocking statement, and Sporborg added that those who were involved in 'these things' were bound never to admit anything afterwards, never to reveal what they had done. 'You must go to your grave still resolutely denying that it ever happened.'[5] Which, of course, is not quite what he himself had done. Why that is so remains another unsolved mystery.

The conspiracy theory of PROSPER's downfall was a view that Foot's quasi-official account had dismissed, but that was before the scale and extent of Allied strategic deception was known. Even the existence of the LCS remained hidden until three years after *SOE in France* was published and twenty-five years after D Day.[6] And not until 1972 did documents surface at the National Archives in Washington which established conclusively that planning for COCKADE and STARKEY had involved deliberate deception not only of the enemy but of F Section agents in the field in France, who were not informed until long after Prosper, Archambaud, Denise and all the others were on their way to the death camps that STARKEY was only a rehearsal for things to come.

One of the F Section agents recruited in the field, Jacques Bureau – Prosper's radio technician – also is convinced that the PROSPER agents were used to deceive the Germans about the time and place of the invasion, but he sees it as an indispensable, a justifiable strategy for defeating the Nazis and saving countless lives. His attitude is one more of sorrow than of anger, an acknowledgement of the tragic ironies of the situation rather than an indictment of the British. He believes that Suttill and Norman behaved honourably, following orders that were designed, although neither they nor the French Section staff were aware of the fact, to set up the radio games that, along with Déricourt's passing of the mail, would keep the German forces in the north-west of France in a constant state of expectation of invasion there between the spring and the autumn of 1943, when they might have been used against the Allies on other fronts. Although they were unaware of it, as he sees it the weapons he and the other PROSPER agents wielded were the lies that successfully protected the real invasion plans.[7]

What did these conspiracy theories, of those who witnessed the fire – Raynaud and Bureau – and of those who were sifters through the ashes – Marshall, Collins, Russbridger – add up to? Not much, according to M.R.D. Foot. It is hardly surprising that his judgement of the Marshall book was dismissive – 'a good story . . . a bad piece of history'[8] – but in giving it short shrift he brings to bear the authority of the historian's sober judgement against the journalist's sensational assertions and makes it hard to dismiss his own counter arguments. He does not doubt that

Dansey had the bad taste to revel in the PROSPER debacle, but points out that that is hardly proof that he brought it about. The proof in the end amounts to little more than Jean Overton Fuller's account of her conversations with Déricourt in which he implied he had been planted in SOE to follow orders from somewhere higher up in London.[9] What he had been, Foot insists, is a German plant, but loyal to neither their side nor that of SOE – loyal in the end only to himself. He was in it for what he could get out of it, and remained so to his end – if indeed it was his end – when he presumably went down flying for a heroin ring in south-east Asia.

That Déricourt approached Boemelburg and offered to work for the SD on instructions from Claude Dansey of MI6 can only be conjecture. There is no actual proof that Dansey exploited the F Section agents for the sake of penetrating the SD. Prosper's downfall can, on the principal of Occam's razor, be explained without invoking the agency of Dansey. There was the undeniable fact that the PROSPER network – some sixty interconnected circuits consisting of over a thousand French subagents – had been hopelessly compromised from the start by penetration of German double agents, by their own gallant carelessness and indiscretion, and later through the various radio games. PROSPER's lack of security seemed to be at the bottom of the network's downfall and the PROSPER agents were, according to Foot, 'riding for a fall'. Alas, sighs Foot, another bad book on the secret services.

The Marshall book is full of errors, both small (names of people and places misspelled) and large (errors of fact such as people's positions, their relationships, the places of their deaths). Hastily put together, it was not difficult to sniff at, citing its sloppiness and inferring that its conclusions were as questionable as its form – shaky at best. Still, as with any conspiracy theory, it is harder to disprove than to design. No diary entry or memo of Churchill's meeting with Francis Suttill survives to establish whether or not 'he was told',[10] as Marshall unequivocally puts it (how does he know?) by the Prime Minister himself that the invasion would take place at the Pas de Calais in early September of that year. But in the absence of proof one way or the other, there is always that grain of doubt, those unexplained connections . . . And there would always be someone to pick them up.

The death of the heroic Prosper, like that of the young President Kennedy twenty years later, aroused some instinct, some primal distrust of those in authority, a feeling that they must share complicity for allowing such wrongs to have been done. Above all, there is the sense that only a need to hide something can explain the long official silence, the locking away and partial destruction of the only records that might have established the truth of what happened. And so the belief in a cover-up persists. If there was no intrigue, no guilt, ask the conspiracy theorists, why the secrecy? Wartime confusion, bureaucratic muddle, remains the only answer they are likely to get.

Even if perfidy is ruled out as the cause of the PROSPER disaster and incompetence is the verdict, the question remains, Whose incompetence? Foot had thought it was that of Prosper and his agents, insufficiently attentive to security matters, a judgement that had to be tempered if not reversed with the eventual disclosures regarding strategic deception and the extent to which Prosper and his people were encouraged to increase their activities, and thus their risks, in the spring and summer of 1943 in connection with STARKEY.

In summing up everything she had learned about the German penetration of French Section, Jean Overton Fuller had agreed on incompetence as the cause of the disaster, but blamed SOE's staff rather than the agents themselves. She went over the behaviour in London: ignoring the reports of the arrests of Norman and the others, continuing to respond and to send to his radio signals, chiding him for omitting his security check, continuing to drop arms and ammunition to the German-controlled circuits and even arranging on Norman's radio the rendezvous at which Agazarian would be taken. And in the end she divided the responsibility between a grossly negligent French Section staff in

London, the presence of 'too many people in the organization' both there and in the field, and the disclosures made to the SD by Déricourt – without belabouring the whys and wherefores of his actions. Moving away from the view of 'a diabolic master-plan in London' she too had come to believe, by 1975, that the warnings about the arrests had been discounted in 'a kind of psychological inability to grasp that the worst had happened.'[11] She had joined the ranks of the muddle theorists.

Ever loyal to her own image of Déricourt, Overton Fuller reasserted her own faith in him again after summing up every-thing she had learned – which was very much – and everything she had come to believe – which was very forgiving.[12] She had maintained friendly contact with him from 1957 until he abruptly broke off their correspondence with no explanation in 1961. It was not until 1965 that she learned of the report of his death. True to a promise she had made him, she kept away from Déricourt's widow. He had not wanted his wife to read Overton Fuller's 1958 book about him. Despite the fact that she was already prepared to justify his behaviour, that book had been inconclusive. Now she felt she had found more of the answers to the mystery surrounding the man she had come to 'esteem as a friend'.

Her final views on Déricourt were intended to answer Mar-shall's accusations, as well as those of Rusbridger. Analysing them in detail, she was able to show the absence of real evidence for what was claimed, and the circumstantiality of the case, identifying misquotations and errors, and ultimately, although they disagreed on many other things, agreeing with Foot that the prosecution, 'irresponsible' and 'deplorable', had no real case, only a theory.

Her own theory was, not surprisingly, kinder to Déricourt. It also turned out to be kinder to those in London who were trying to win the war. She pointed out that, although tactics exploiting the agents in France might have been discussed in plans for COCKADE, there was no evidence they had been acted on. The PROSPER agents were compromised from the beginning – by the

CARTE connection, the Bleicher infiltration, the radio games, and their own carelessness. Déricourt had seen their vulnerability as soon as he arrived in the field and, dismayed, had taken his 'own measures', as he put it, to protect himself, the friends he had brought into the circuit, and his operation. He had bought the safety of the agents he flew in and out at the price of passing over to the enemy material in the courier that was inessential,* and with the promise of providing the date and place of the invasion, a promise, according to Fuller, that he never intended to keep.

By the time Overton Fuller felt free to go looking for them, after the death of Mme Déricourt in 1984, Déricourt's private papers and pilot's log book, as well as the manuscript of the memoir he had written in novel form, had been acquired by Robert Marshall. They had been found in the same two-room apartment in the rue Pergolèse in which Mme Déricourt had lived with her husband in 1943, next door to the Abwehr's Hugo Bleicher and a stone's throw from the SD premises on the Avenue Foch. It is possible that Déricourt himself may be heard from on the subject of his treachery if his own book is published some day. In the meantime, his admirer would end her account of him with the judgement: 'It was a loyal treason.'[13] Or as Déricourt himself had put it in one of his letters to her, in her book 'the villain turns out to be . . . a good villain.'[14]

Unlike the dramas of novelists, journalists and broadcasters, the view of the desperate events in England and France in 1943 which may yet stand the test of time is not a story of wicked cold-hearted men sending unwary innocents to their deaths. It is a view which sees instead a story of the brilliance and resourcefulness of an imaginative handful of men who managed to fool the enemy in ways that made it possible, against the odds, to defeat them. In fact, FORTITUDE, the cover for the Normandy invasion,

---

* She disregards the fact that the Germans made good use of this material to demoralize captured agents.

turned out to be the most successful wartime deception since the Trojan Horse. The lasting achievement of the deceivers was

> to build up in the minds of enemy intelligence a totally erroneous idea of available Allied operational strength . . . [T]hey believed their opponents capable of delivering multiple attacks, and had in consequence to spread their forces so thinly to meet them that the actual assault, when it came, achieved overwhelming local superiority.[15]

It is not easy to convey the sense of urgency hovering in the background of those crucial events in 1943/44; the desperation of the struggle, its complexity, the uncertainty of the outcome, and what it was all about. Not just some abstract 'power game' between roughly equivalent sides but the struggle to escape domination by an unequivocally evil force. What price was a reasonable one to pay for freedom from subjugation by the Nazis, with their society built on terror, their economy built on slave labour, and their ideology committed to murdering men, women, and children they defined as subhuman? It was a price paid in many lives. Was it worth it?

Half a century has passed. What, I wondered, having come this far in the story, do the men and women who still remember their part in those events believe? And so I set out to find some of them and ask.

CHAPTER 22

. . . *What Forgiveness?*

I had met Vera Atkins at the very beginning, when I set out to discover who they had been, those names on a wall in the crematorium at Natzweiler, and how they had come to end up there. I wrote to her, explaining my interest and asking for her help, and she replied, inviting me to visit her in the East Sussex village where she 'saw the war in', as she puts it, and still lives when not in London.[1]

The woman who opened the door was still every bit as imposing as she is reported to have been when she interrogated Nazi officials about the missing F Section agents. Her grey hair swept back from a strong-featured face, walking stiffly and slowly but purposefully, as she does everything, Vera Atkins settled me in her narrow parlour and, once we had both been provided with generous gins with bitters, made herself and her memories available, as she has to countless historians and print and broadcast journalists over the years. Her reserved manner takes on a tinge of irony when she speaks of most things. When she talks about 'the girls' she seems distanced, talks more slowly, looks beyond me . . .

She talked about her search for the truth about their fate and about the ceremonies, thirty years later, at which a plaque had been placed on the wall of the crematorium at Natzweiler reading '*À la mémoire des quatre femmes britanniques et françaises parachutées executées dans ce camp*' followed by the names Borrel Andrée, Leigh Vera, Olschanezky Sonia, Rowden Diana. The four women's remaining relatives had been invited to participate and there was a guard of honour from the WAAF and from the FANY. 'The evening before the ceremony we sang songs of the resistance in the moonlight. It was a tremendously moving occasion.'

Telling how she had managed to have an SAS driver take her into the French Zone, how she had insisted on being allowed to question Kieffer of the Paris SD as well as the Natzweiler camp officials, how she had prevailed on the British Embassy in Paris to provide her with a huge Union Jack for the 1975 Natzweiler ceremonies, she speaks with a kind of quiet firm authority that makes it clear why no one can refuse her anything she requires – a flag, a driver, the chance to interrogate a prisoner. (George Millar, whom she had interviewed for French Section, later wrote, 'The woman knew she could master anyone in trousers.') That irresistible determination had shown itself in the trial held in the Zoological Gardens at Wuppertal in 1946. Was it really a zoo, I asked. She thought a moment, then said she didn't remember the surroundings. 'It was just a building. It could have been a zoo or it could have been the Grand Hotel. I was too churned up with other things to notice.'

She had been talking with me for hours about her duties in SOE, about how things had been organized, how the first people were recruited and trained, when she stopped, sighed, then said, 'Yes, well, let's get on with it. I'm sorry. I don't think anyone realizes it is a considerable strain talking about all this. One has to think back nearly fifty years and when I talk about these people it brings back a whole lot of other things and it is not a subject I particularly enjoy. And, you know, since '45 in all those years I've never been without somebody who was writing. Never. I do it,' she said quietly, 'as a sort of moral duty.'

I had asked all the questions I had come with. Now I asked her what *she* thought should be emphasized in all this. What did she think it was most important to remember?

'Well,' she said, 'I have to take the war as a whole. I have the greatest admiration for these people and they were people I liked, but I can't say they are more deserving of being remembered than – I feel that one mustn't turn them into anyone more heroic than, say, the young pilots of the RAF, going out and knowing perfectly well that of the group that was setting off from a particular aerodrome, some of them, perhaps as many as half, would not return.

'I don't know what one should remember or what one should forget. I think one should remember forever that Germany – a civilized country – was capable of evolving this theory of the master race, and what they did on the basis of it to the Jews and the Poles and the gypsies and in all the occupied countries in which they creamed off the intelligentsia. The Germans were very easily led. I think that is something that needs to be remembered: how easy it can be to manipulate a whole nation. Intimidation is a terrible thing and its exercise is increasingly potent, but there will always be an uprising of natural decency. There was resistance by some in Germany, but they were few and far between. Most people just went along with it.'

On another occasion, talking of the agents she had known, she said, 'Ordinary people sometimes reveal quite unexpected strengths. These people had no doubts about the importance of defeating Nazism. They undertook risks feeling it was a duty; they made a voluntary sacrifice.' The explanation for the PROSPER disaster, she maintains, is that 'it was started in '42. That sort of thing can last just so long. There were so many local informers among the French. There was collaboration all around, and betrayal.' Suttill she describes as 'sober, sensible, secure.' The radio games? 'Mistakes and carelessness. George Noble [Bégué] was receiving the messages; he knew what it was like in the field. They often omitted checks, transmitting under difficult conditions, just left them off. It's impossible to judge fifty years later, when you were not there, what it was like.'

Like everyone else who was involved, I thought, she believes what she needs to believe. She does convey a sense of moral right in this sea of deceit, although of course she may be as self-serving in her own way as the rest of them. It is a matter of the need for belief in what one has done. Especially at the going down of the sun.

The last time I saw her we met in London. By now my interests had followed my knowledge into matters I hadn't dreamed of when I first went to see her three years before. She made it clear that she thought I ought to leave the murkier aspects of 'all that' alone, concentrate on the women's lives before they had been sent into the field. That was what would interest people the most – learning what the women who undertook such work had been like. To disagree seemed pointless, and I was aware of a frailty and a sadness in her that I had not seen before. She was going to the theatre that evening to see a production of Kafka's *The Trial*. It struck me as a particularly appropriate choice.

What of French Section's official historian, I wondered, now that so much has been revealed that was unknown to him when he wrote? He answered my request for a meeting with an invitation to the Special Forces Club,[2] where photographs of the F Section officers line the wall along the staircase. There they all are, smiling or sober, in uniform and at the moment when everything still lay before them, those who would return and those who would never come back. Among them is a watercolour by Brian Stonehouse of a scene remembered – the figures of four women walking single file, one carrying a coat, one with a ribbon in her hair . . .

In this place so evocative of the subject we had met to discuss, the afternoon's talk ranged over many things. Like Vera Atkins, although they might disagree on many other matters, M.R.D. Foot too still believes that insecurity and muddle can account for the PROSPER disaster. He does not believe that MI6 ran Déricourt, or that Churchill met with Prosper in order to mislead him about the invasion plans.

'The first rule of a historian', he says, 'is that if there are two explanations, one simple and one complicated: go with the simpler one. They were insecure. They got in the habit of all meeting together, chattering away in English. When you get into the field you find it's so different from anything you'd been prepared for or expected or imagined, you're tempted to disregard what you've been told. They simply forgot their training, or chose to ignore it.'

Foot thinks it was Gilbert Norman, and not Francis Suttill, who made the pact with the Germans, and that the relationship between Déricourt and Bodington was simply that of two greedy and self-centred men, not part of anyone else's plan. He maintains that the value of the resistance set in motion by SOE in France proved crucial at the moment of the invasion and afterwards and that 'what matters is that there were these people who were willing to chance their own lives to protect a way of life, what they saw as a world worth fighting for.

'After the war,' he says, 'we saw the plan Germany had for England. Think what life would have been like for us if they had won.'

Brian Stonehouse's memories emerge in unpredictable detail. He returned against all odds from nearly a year in solitary confinement at Fresnes followed by two years as an NN prisoner in Mauthausen, in a slave-labour detachment in an armaments factory, then in Natzweiler, ending up still alive at Dachau when it was liberated. 'Afterwards,' he says, 'I closed the door.'³ For a short time after the war he was stationed in the British Zone of Germany, where he recognized one of his former interrogators among the Germans employed by the military government, but he chose not to exact revenge. What he wanted was to put the past behind him. He went to the United States towards the end of 1946 'to get away from it all,' and lived there for the next thirty years as a fashion illustrator and portrait painter. He returned to England in the late 1970s and, as he puts it, 'hit the top in London,' where his commissions included a portrait of the Queen Mother that also hangs in the Special Forces Club.

By now he was ready to deal with his memories, taping his reminiscences for the Imperial War Museum and becoming the subject of a BBC documentary. In it he answers some of the questions he is always asked about his wartime experiences. He talks about how young he was, only twenty-three, and how full of idealism when he was recruited for French Section. He knew the risk of capture and interrogation, brought home most clearly when a departing agent was given the cyanide pill that was intended as a last resort. Still, he ignored what he had been taught at the special training schools, operating his radio from the same place and staying on the air much too long.

'There was no one else to do it,' he says over tea in his Queen's Gardens flat. 'I was a babe in the woods despite all the training we'd been given. There was so much to be sent and there was no other radio in the Lyon area. Someone had been caught and I was the only contact with London.'

A signal had been arranged whereby the owner of the château would cut off the electricity at the main switch if any strangers were seen approaching, then turn it on again. When the lights went out Stonehouse knew something was up. He made frantic efforts to hide his set and aerials, but it was too late. Caught, he decided to abandon his cover story and say that he was British so that his parents would be able to trace him.

Stonehouse and his courier were arrested by Vichy French police accompanied by Germans in plain clothes Later, he was told that they had been betrayed.

'There was so much denunciation in France,' he says. 'When I go to France now, there's always something shady about the people my age.' And he tells of a visit to the château where he'd been arrested so many years before, and hearing that the daughter of the family was having trouble finding domestic help. He suggested she do what he had done in the States, 'find someone on the dole and pay them in cash.' She had tried that, she told him, but someone had denounced the girl she'd hired to the authorities. 'My God,' he said, 'you haven't changed.' Later, at the cocktail party given in his honour for 'the local bigwigs', the other château owners, someone remarked that the Germans didn't like talking about the last war. There was a lull in the conversation and someone said, '*Et les Français non plus*' (Neither do the French). With a wry smile, Stonehouse adds, 'At least with the Germans you knew where you stood.'

Stonehouse's cluttered flat is recognizably that of an artist. An unfinished canvas rests on an easel and there are portraits and still-life studies on all the walls. On a table beside a lamp is a drawing he made in Dachau. It is of the crematorium. Seeing me looking at it, he says, 'That was done just the day before the liberation. I was making sketches all the time, but most of them disappeared. The few I have left survived because of a German prisoner who took them out and left them with someone in the village. Yes, of course the people around the camp knew what was going on. How could they not? Dachau was in the middle of the village.'

How did he survive the brutality, the slavery? 'I don't know,' he says at first, but then goes on to talk about the group of four British agents who managed to stay together in the camps. One of them was Guérisse, the Pat O'Leary of the escape line. Some instinct for self-preservation, Stonehouse thinks, and talks about those prisoners who didn't have it, the ones they called the 'blanket people', who just gave up. Of course, he adds, he and his friends were never tortured, never experimented on. 'Dachau was a great camp for experiments on human beings, Jews and gypsies.' He adds that it was important for him never to do anything in order to survive that would mean he couldn't sleep at night, would not be able to have 'a tranquil heart.

'You had to remain a human being. That was how you won. They wanted to make us into beasts. Behaving like men, not letting them destroy the human being in us, was how we won.' And he talks about a young French prisoner standing at the edge of a quarry where he was waiting to be shot starting to sing the Marseillaise. Stonehouse is visibly moved and cannot go on for a moment. Then he says, 'The thing I've been trying to do is make sure none of this is forgotten before we all disappear. We did it for the future. It would have been night and fog for everyone.'

CHAPTER 23

A *Few* Good People

A short distance from Pierre Raynaud's present home in the countryside of the south of France is the house of his former chief Francis Cammaerts.[1] They could not be farther apart in their views on the past they once shared.

The English agents come down squarely on the side of 'decency'. They simply can't believe in the deliberate sacrifice of agents. 'Not possible,' they say. They insist that it was a matter of 'muddle', of honest mistakes, mistakes that sometimes had horrible consequences, but that were committed in ignorance and confusion, in the heat of a moment that is hard to reconstruct today.

Francis Cammaerts dismisses as 'a fantasy' the theory put forward by those like his one-time deputy Pierre Raynaud and the BBC's Robert Marshall that Déricourt was run by MI6. He thinks men like Bodington and Déricourt became double agents because 'they had a freak sense of adventure and thought it was a clever way to play it.' As for the radio games, he sees no need to infer a conspiracy when 'the human factor' is enough to explain what went on. 'At the end of the war', he says, 'we all came back with bitter recriminations, boiling with fury about what had happened that shouldn't have and what hadn't happened that should have. But we came to realize that it was a consequence of London being out of touch with actual conditions in the field, while we were out of touch with what was going on there, with the degree of confusion at Bletchley, where conditions could only be described as chaotic.'

The French have a more Byzantine cast of mind when considering these things, and many are still defensive about their role in the Second World War. Until recently there was a kind of national denial by those who had participated in it of the total moral collapse when war began, of the lack of a will to fight, of the abandonment of their men by the officer class, fleeing with their women to save their own skins, of the weary cynicism that said, Someone will rule over us, it might as well be the Germans as the English, of the willing collaboration in the anti-Semitic measures that doomed so many innocent French men, women and children forced to wear the yellow star, and of the widespread belief in 1940 of the inevitability of a German victory.

It took a blind stubbornness to believe in the possibility of eventual German defeat in that first year of the war, and it is that quality that saved Europe, or at least held off disaster for a moment long enough for history to take a new direction. And, to their everlasting credit, it belonged to the British, and to them alone.

Some of them were undeniably heroic, and any account of those includes Cammaerts, the organizer whose saboteurs and snipers prevented German reinforcements from reaching Normandy until three weeks after the invasion; it was a distance they could, without interference, have made in three days. Had they done so, the Allies might very well not have been able to establish their positions and hold their ground in the face of German heavy armour. Later the men and women of the JOCKEY circuit and the maquis they had armed and trained managed to clear the way and hold open the Route Napoléon from Cannes to Grenoble for the American forces that landed on the Riviera in August 1944, one of the major contributions made by the resistance to the Allied cause.

Cammaerts brushes aside the word when it's applied to himself. 'The real heroes and heroines', he says, 'were the ordinary French people with whom we lived and worked, especially the housewives who made the process of living possible. In France from 1942 to 1944 the middle-aged and the old were as active as the young – often more so. It was sad that in those days they

289

cooked up the name *sédentaires*, which sounded like "armchair heroes". In fact it was those who stayed at home and continued to work and lead an apparently normal life, thus badly exposed, who provided the essential background against which the refugees in the hills and mountains, the Jews and Socialists, Free Masons and politically independent were able to carry out the more active role. The housewives, the elderly, the children were absolutely essential to us. I never used a paid lodging, a hotel or boarding house. Each and every night I slept in someone's home and so made them and all their families liable to torture and execution. No "hero" would have survived without the environmental support of *L'homme moyen ordinaire*.' It is those ordinary French men and women among whom Cammaerts lives today, in nominal retirement. Much of his time is spent travelling about the countryside in which his circuit operated, contacting old helpers, paying, one might say, old debts.

'Recognition of their services by governments after the war was clumsy and often led to misunderstandings,' he acknowledges in response to the charge that has often been made that the ordinary people who had given so much were abandoned once the war was over. 'The King's medal for courage was awarded to some eighty or ninety people in the south of France in 1947. Unfortunately, there was no provision for posthumous decorations, something that would have been appreciated by the kin of those who had been shot or died in the camps. And since the medals were distributed in alphabetical order, a M. Albert who had been in the resistance for six months at the end might receive his before a M. Rousset who had been a leader since the early days got his.'

The closest thing to anger or bitterness I heard Cammaerts express had to do with the double standard he felt was practised by French Section's staff. Vera Atkins, he says, concerned herself only with the men and women who were English officers, an attitude he found prevalent among the senior staff towards 'their people' as distinct from the subagents recruited in France. (I myself had heard references by those I had spoken with to 'our chaps', but had assumed it, perhaps naïvely, to be inclusive of nationality as well as of gender.) This relic of English snobbery Cammaerts finds especially galling in the case of his courier Christine Skarbek and his radio operator Auguste Floiras.

As we drove along a narrow road winding up towards Cammaerts' house he pointed out a bridge on which he had stood and talked with Floiras on another summer afternoon almost half a century earlier.

Floiras, who tirelessly and faithfully transmitted a record number of messages for JOCKEY, got no help from the British when the war ended and he returned to civilian life. As for the French, when Floiras returned to his civil service department where he had worked before the war the Marseille authorities refused him any compensation for the years he had spent in the resistance, a reflection of de Gaulle's attitude towards those who had worked with the British.

'It was not done as it should have been for everyone. But there are some explanations other than wilful neglect,' Cammaerts says. 'After 6 June 1944, men and women who joined the Forces françaises de l'intérieur, the Free French army, were military recruits. It was easy to keep track of them. The people who tended to get overlooked were among the tens of thousands of *sédentaires*, those men and women who stayed at their jobs and the many middle-aged and elderly living at home who risked reprisals on a daily basis by aiding SOE and helping escapees and evaders. Many of them were arrested and deported. In the confused conditions after the war there were attempts to identify them and distribute some compensation. But, unlike military recruits, some of whom would pretend afterwards that they had been *résistants* all along, they were not organized. They were not neglected so much as not recognized.' While they were rewarded and helped in many cases, not all were identified, a situation Cammaerts himself is involved in correcting to this day, tirelessly seeking out survivors and their widows and organizing memorial ceremonies at which those who participated in the resistance are remembered and honoured.

Andrée Borrel's sister lives in a suburb of Paris and tends a small shop that sells trimmings and supplies for jewellery-makers on a busy narrow street in a commercial section of Paris.[2] In her seventies, she is troubled with arthritis and walks slowly and with a cane, but still gives an impression of strength. She has long ago accepted what happened to her sister, but has not forgotten the other things that happened as a result. She does not read English and has little idea of the vast literature that has appeared since *Death Be Not Proud* was published in 1958, followed by the articles in the *Sunday Pictorial*. She has copies of those and keeps them, along with a few photographs of Andrée – in her nurses' uniform at the beginning of the war, in tennis garb and smiling over her racket somewhere in the south of France, in her FANY uniform, looking straight out of serious eyes – and only enough other keepsakes to fill a small box. Among them is Andrée's certificate as a Red Cross military nurse, dated January 1940; a receipt from the Marylebone Ladies Rifle Club in Devonshire Place, London, for annual dues for 1942 of forty-one shillings and sixpence; and the little tobacco pouch Andrée used as a change purse that she still had in her possession and threw out of the window of the Zellenbau that afternoon in Natzweiler. It was retrieved by the Belgian prisoner Dr Boogaerts. On a slip of paper inside it he found her name. After the war he gave the little pouch to Léone Arend.

Mme Arend attended the official ceremonies held at Natzweiler in 1975, when a plaque commemorating the four women who died there was unveiled in the crematorium, but daily life goes on in its inexorable way, with the cares of family, illness, making a living, births and deaths. The years have passed and she has not been aware of the continuing interest in the events of the summer of 1943, although to her they remain vivid.

When Andrée returned to Paris as Denise in the autumn of 1942 she got in touch with her family and continued to see them, sometimes arranging to meet Suttill and Norman in the Arend flat in the rue Caumartin. To her family they were François and Gilbert.

After her arrest, Andrée managed to smuggle messages out to her sister. Written on bits of cigarette paper and hidden in the hems of her clothing sent home to be laundered, a system the prison authorities allowed as an economy, the notes went unnoticed at first. Some of the linen was washed, notes and all, before Mme Arend was aware of their existence. Finally, alerted by a sympathetic prison matron, she began finding and reading the messages. For the most part they assured her that Andrée was well, asked her to reassure their mother, and requested little things from home – a sweater, a notebook, some hairpins – ending with kisses to all. They could almost have been letters written home from a business trip or a vacation. Those letters Mme Arend still has, crumpled, torn, yellowed, almost indecipherable.

But there were others. Mme Arend remembers them clearly. In one Andrée wrote '*C'est Gilbert qui nous a tous vendu*' (It is Gilbert who sold us all out) and in another, '*Gilbert nous protége*' (Gilbert is protecting us). She also wrote, according to Mme Arend, that Gilbert was present at the '*bidon*' (phony) trial at which she and the others were interrogated. She warned her sister not to trust him.

But by that time it was too late.

Andrée's sister and brother-in-law, like Sonia Olschanezky's family, had been drawn in to the operations of the *réseau*, providing a meeting place, allowing a transmitter to be stored with them, occasionally carrying messages to a letter box. Andrée tuned in to the BBC, listening for the coded *messages personnels*, on the radio in their apartment. Andrée's colleagues François and Gilbert had become friends of the family. Gilbert Norman had even spent some nights in the apartment. Thus when, on a July evening about a month after the PROSPER agents had been arrested, Gilbert Norman turned up at the home of M. Arend's parents in the company of three Germans in civilian clothes, the old people asked them in. M. Arend the elder willingly produced Gilbert's wireless set at his request and sent for his son so the younger Arend could come up with the parts he himself had not been able to find. All of them, taking their cue from Gilbert Norman's easy demeanour, assumed that he was in the company of friends, Germans who had been bribed or for some other reason were working for the Allies. Nothing was said to disabuse them and no one suspected that Norman was in fact in the custody of the Germans.

Cigarettes were passed around, *apéritifs* were offered, and in the conversation that followed, the elder M. Arend mentioned that his son was a *réfractaire*, avoiding conscription into the STO, the forced labour service compulsory for men his age. One of the Germans politely asked to see his papers, and pocketed them. A few minutes later Gilbert Norman and his German companions left, as casually as they had come.

Other Germans came a few days later and arrested Arend. At the Avenue Foch he was questioned, with Gilbert Norman present. He was asked about the arms and explosives the Germans had been searching out but was unharmed and was left with the impression that Gilbert Norman was cooperating only in order to save those whose role in the network was most vital. He would have time to reconsider as he was moved from prison in Paris to Compiègne and from there to Buchenwald.

Robert Arend was one of the lucky ones who survived to return home. After the liberation, his wife contacted the British authorities hoping to find out what had happened to her sister. She told them about the letters Andrée had written to her from Fresnes and was asked, she remembers, to give them to an SOE officer named Hazeldine to be copied, after which they would be returned to her. It seemed a reasonable request; some of them might contain information of significance to the authorities.

Time passed, and she did not hear from London again. So Mme Arend wrote asking for her letters to be returned. No one, she was told, could find any such letters and there was no record of there having been any received by the Foreign Office or by any of its departments. No one had any recollection of having been given the letters. Sincere regrets were expressed.

Eventually, copies of some letters were found and were returned to Mme Arend. The letters about mundane matters, little requests, reassurances, were there. The letters mentioning Gilbert were not. They have never been found and the official word is that no such letters ever existed, or at least never came within the purview of the Foreign Office. Only Mme Arend remembers them.

She did not know that there had been another Gilbert involved in the affairs of the PROSPER network. It would have been irrelevant, she says. They knew only one Gilbert and they knew him only by that name, not by his field name or the code name that would have been used only in communicating with London. The Gilbert she knew, and that she knows her sister was referring to, was Gilbert Norman.

Was he a traitor? There are those who say that it was Suttill who made the pact, which Norman only carried out according to his instructions. No one will ever know. Suttill was shipped off to Germany shortly after his arrest and the conclusion of the pact and killed at Sachsenhausen. Norman remained at the Avenue Foch, went along with the Germans to persuade the luckless *résistants* to give up the arms and ammunition they were hiding, and encouraged newly arrested agents to cooperate with the Germans interrogating them, saying it was pointless to hold out, since the Germans already knew almost everything anyway.

Among those who believed he had betrayed them were British officers and French subagents who saw him at the Avenue Foch when they were arrested. One who believed him innocent and fought for years to have his name cleared was his father. Until his own death, every year on the anniversary of his son's death the elder Norman placed a memorial notice in *The Times* reading, 'In loving memory of Major Gilbert Norman, DLI, executed at Mauthausen September 6 1944, victim of enemy barbarism and SOE ineptitude.'

In the spring of 1989 *Voix et Visages*, the bulletin of the Association nationale des anciennes déportées et internées de la résistance, carried a notice about an American writer asking to hear from anyone who had known Andrée Borrel, Vera Leigh, Diana Rowden or Sonia Olschanezky. Among the replies was a letter from Odette Fournier, née Mathy. She had known Diana Rowden as Paulette in the *réseau* to which she and her parents also belonged. She wrote that Paulette had been a frequent visitor to their home in Lons-le-Saunier. On 18 November 1943 Paulette had come to the Mathys' house with an Englishman 'who in reality was a spy.' That evening Paulette was arrested along with another English agent, Gabriel, at Clairvaux-les-Lacs. Later, the Gestapo had come for Odette and her parents. Her mother and father never returned from deportation. Some time in February 1944 Odette Mathy saw Diana at Fresnes, but wasn't able to speak with her. Two months later she left for Ravensbrück.

'I still remember her very well,' she wrote, 'in spite of the fact that I was only eighteen at the time. She was a great friend and we took part in several missions together.'

That summer I visited Odette Fournier and her husband, Georges, also a concentration camp survivor, in a modest little house outside Toulon.[3] Among the family photographs and religious pictures was a framed painting of the French and British flags flying beside each other, and superimposed on them two photographs, one of a handsome dark-haired man under which was printed 'Gabriel', the other of a half-smiling young woman with a slightly protuberant upper lip, under which was the name 'Marcelle'. Like 'Paulette', Marcelle was one of the names by which Diana Rowden was known in the field. Across the bottom, beneath the flags, was written 'Arretés par la Gestapo le 18 Novembre 1943.'

On 19 November Henri Clerc, a wine merchant of St Amour who was a key member of the local resistance, had received a message at the place where he had gone into hiding shortly after the arrest of John Starr in the late summer. Before going to ground he had had occasion to work with the two agents he knew as Gabriel and Paulette. Diana had spent several nights under the Clercs' roof in the summer weeks after her arrival and they had bicycled together on several moonlit nights to set flares and wait to receive arms drops on the fields outside the village. He admired her energy and her steady nerves as well as her poise and graciousness, although he and his wife had some reservations about her command of French. It was good enough, Mme Clerc agreed, for her to make a purchase at the local boulangerie, but would not have convinced anyone with reason to be suspicious of her claim to be a Frenchwoman.

While in hiding, Clerc had kept in touch with Diana. A few hours before she was arrested, Diana had met with him over a drink at the Café Strasbourg in Lons, a meeting place and mail drop for the members of STOCKBROKER. She had brought along the newly arrived member, never suspecting he was about to betray them all. The three of them had parted amicably and M. Clerc had not yet heard about the arrests when he received word the next day that Diana had called his sister's house to leave a message asking him to meet her at the café.

Some instinct made Clerc uneasy. He went to the rendezvous, but his feeling that something was wrong made him cautious. When he walked into the café the first thing he saw was his friend and fellow résistant, M. Mathy, flanked by two unmistakable Gestapo men. Neither Clerc nor Mathy showed any outward sign of recognition. Mathy remained impassive as Clerc sat down, gave his order, drank it slowly, paid and got up and left. An hour later he was in the hills with the maquis. Mathy was not so lucky.

His daughter and son-in-law are typical of those decent, matter-of-fact French men and women who formed the backbone of the first body of résistants. They were asked to help out and they did. When they returned from the horrors of the camps they had enough to do rebuilding their health and then their lives. There was a living to make, children to raise. They never expected any honours, nor even any recognition, and they got none. They joined an association of men and women like themselves who met occasionally to confirm the experience they had shared and only they seemed to remember, but as the years went on they met less and less frequently. Instead, they made use of a newsletter to keep up with each other's doings, the occasional political career, items documenting the occupation years, reminiscences of the camps, and a growing number of obituaries.

They are surprised that a writer from the United States is interested in these things, in them. When she leaves, they insist that she take along something that is obviously precious to them. It is a book about the camps called *La Déportation*. The text is as simple as the title. It is the pictures that are heartbreaking. They will never lose their power to shock, but how many people look at them any more? The Fourniers have no idea, but they will keep one copy for their children and grandchildren and send the other one out into the world.

CHAPTER 24

Epilogue: Out of the Darkness

Every great war changes the world. It is fought to preserve something which inevitably, by the time it ends, no longer exists. Thus its heroes come to acquire mythic stature. We don't see people like them any more. Better perhaps, worse certainly, but never again the same.

The First World War was entered into in a spirit of brio. Young men marched off to war in splendid uniforms to a nightmare of mud-filled trenches, poison gas and endless unimagined carnage. Afterwards, the countries of Europe mourned the loss of a generation of their best, the flower of their youth, their dreams, their hopes for the future. And vowed, understandably, not to permit that future to include such meaningless – as it had come to seem, for what had it really accomplished? – butchery.

The next generation inherited an outlook of cynicism as the legacy of its fathers' war, and a tone of irony in which to express it. In Britain, they resolved never again to fight for King or country. In America, they returned to business as usual. In France, a bitter and exhausted population could see, by the time it came to matter, no reason to prefer *les boches* to *les anglais*. If someone were to overtake them, it hardly seemed to matter who it was. The Germans could be friends as easily as the English could be enemies. There was plenty of precedent for both. What mattered most, to most people, was keeping warm, keeping fed, getting ahead, and, if possible, getting rich doing it.

The men and women who joined the resistance, as different as they were in their characters, their backgrounds, their motivations for accepting the risk that went with the adventure, had one thing in common. They were willing to fight against what was clearly an evil – a society that, although nominally modern, developed, cultured, and sophisticated, was driven by primitive tribal superstitions expressed in the racial myths that provided the justification for killing those outside the tribe. The cult of the charismatic leader preaching exclusion, hate, cruelty and murder found enthusiastic acceptance to an extent that surprised an innocent, or perhaps thoughtless, world.

There are always, everywhere, power-hungry leaders ready to create such systems and others ready to follow them. We need to think about what values construct and unite societies, ours and others, if we are to be saved from them. Without the will to fight, the belief that there are things worth dying for, we will die anyway, for nothing more glorious than our decadence or more honourable than our cowardice.

The men and women of the resistance saw this and, among the myriad other reasons they may have had as individuals, chose to engage in the fight. Like Sonia Olschanezky explaining herself to her mother, they all said at some point and in some way, If I don't, who will?

They saved us all. Until next time. The world goes round, and human nature reasserts itself in new generations of the alienated and enraged and new generations of those who reason that anything is better than fighting and risking death. Who can blame them? But who, when it comes down to it, will save us next time?

In the war against the Nazis, resistance meant doing something instead of doing nothing, and it took many forms, in France as elsewhere.

The Arends and the Fourniers are ordinary people, hardly cast in the heroic mould. How did they come to be *résistants*? It was simple. Someone asked them to do something. They did it, then something else the next time they were asked . . . Like those who went the other way, many of them just drifted into it. They drifted in the direction they did because of the nature of their impulses, their characters. It starts with a decisive moment of decency, of saying yes, I will help, of feeling – whether it is expressed verbally or not – I can't do otherwise. Or with turning the other way, shutting the door, pulling down the window blind. Most people went that way, and when the tide of events turned and they saw which was the winning side, they pulled up their blinds, came out of their doors (some of them in uniforms, wearing their old medals, and often they even collected some new ones for being on the right side). Of course, the worst actively collaborated, in some cases with an enthusiasm and enterprise in rounding up Jewish children, or torturing their fellow countrymen, that surprised even the Nazis. Everywhere, in every time, there are the heroic, the decent, the apathetic, and the evil. A matter of – what? The degree of acceptable sadism? Of empathy for other human beings? At what moment does the character crystallize and determine what one will do, how one will behave in extreme situations?

The men and women of PROSPER worked in the dark, when the Allies' return to the Continent seemed like a tiny point of light at the end of a long dangerous tunnel. What they did made it possible for others who came after them to succeed at what they had started. By that time they, and many of their helpers, were in the purgatory of prison or in the hell of the concentration camps or, what could only have been a mercy for some of them, already dead. And by that time it seemed that everyone had been on their side from the beginning – *Résistants de '44* appeared everywhere, to share in the excitement, the comradeship, the thrills of the moment, to put on an old uniform or a new armband and strike a blow for *la patrie*.

It should not be forgotten how much courage it took to go into that darkness at the very beginning, when there was so much to fear and there were so few friends, and to stay at one's post despite the danger and the fear. They were the point men who went before the rest, and if their service turned out to consist of a sacrifice, they should be honoured for it not by being pitied but by being accorded the dignity that goes with having volunteered to serve as soldiers do.

We are in a better position to make a judgement about their service – or their sacrifice, if that is what it was – than those who considered the question in the years immediately after the war. Since then we have learned that strategic deception had been a – if not the – decisive factor in the victory over Nazism, a system based on brutality and terror designed by men intent on degrading and dehumanizing other human beings and then destroying them. The Nazis had created a bureaucracy of human annihilation to carry out the largest atrocity in history: slavery, genocide and the creation of a new race of men without compassion. The men and women involved in saving the rest of us from a world run by believers in Hitler deserve to be remembered not just for what was done to them but for what they did. Whatever else could be said of them, they practised the virtues of courage and self-sacrifice, living a principled life in the face of the world's persistent perils.

Lise Villameur said they were 'ordinary women'. Serge Olschanezky said they were 'like soldiers'. What is left are their names on a wall. Their presence there suggests that the actions of individuals make a difference, that history is not just the working out of impersonal forces.

The tangle of evidence for the proliferating theories about the fate of British agents of resistance in wartime France should not obscure a few simple truths.

In 1940 the threat of Nazi world hegemony and the concentration camp society it would entail was a real possibility. The Axis powers loomed as a seemingly insuperable coalition. Facing an apparently invincible and pitiless enemy, Churchill understood that not all acts of war are carried out on the battlefield. At his instigation, a new kind of soldiering came into being, directed by a group of planners working in secret. Their object was to win the war and minimize human suffering in the long run. That some would have to suffer in the short run to achieve their aim was a necessary trade-off, part of the inevitable tragic aspect of human affairs.

With the German attack on Russia in 1941 re-entry into

Europe became a distinct possibility and the invasion of England less certain. From then on Allied strategy and tactics were aimed at the single overriding aim of landing on the Continent and liberating the occupied countries. The means included, in addition to military operations, subversion and sabotage from within and deception engineered from without.

The architects of the strategic deception plans have been described as cold men heartlessly inventing schemes with no thought of those who would become entangled in them. But the business at hand in those desperate hours was to win the war. When they decided to exploit every opportunity, who knows what they felt, how they slept at night. How is what they set in motion different from sending young men of the RAF up in planes knowing half of them wouldn't return, or sending sappers ashore on those deadly invasion beaches knowing they had even worse odds? A little more calculating, perhaps, but any less necessary? It was an unfortunate but inescapable paradox that in order to defeat the Nazis it was sometimes necessary to meet them on their own terms, adopting measures that were not always consistent with the principles of the Western democracies. It was that or accepting their destruction. Compromising on principle was certainly preferable to annihilation.

SOE itself was an organization driven by improvisation. It had no precedents; there was no relevant body of experience to guide its leaders, no manuals for them to draw on in designing or carrying out its functions. They had to figure out what to do as they went along. It required flexibility and adaptability and, inevitably, some of the decisions turned out to be wrong ones.

The recruitment of women for operational duties was one of their departures from previous norms. The women who volunteered to be put down behind enemy lines had various motivations. To some it was an interesting job, a way out of the routine office chores or driving that had been their only other options. For some there was the excitement of the unknown. Some loved France and some England. All hated Nazism. But whatever the motives of the women who joined, they, like the men, were well aware of the danger, the risks involved.

In the field, agents had to rely on London's judgement about what was going on in the forest; they could only make out the leaves on the trees. As it turned out, their own judgements as well as those of the staff directing them, both working more or less in the dark, were sometimes mistaken.

The war was a vast enterprise, and SOE's French Section's part in it was just one small branch of the British war machine, one of countless complex and interweaving efforts all going on at once. We will probably never know exactly who did what and for what reasons in what became the disasters of SOE's French Section in the summer of 1943. There are many possible scenarios that do not require direction from the top at Churchill's underground headquarters in Storey's Gate. But it is conceivable that those responsible for planning and implementing strategy, appraising the consequences of the mistakes that had been made in France, decided to profit from the situation, to use it as a contribution to the military victory that was their aim and the purpose of everything they did. No one then knew how things would turn out, or what would eventually have proved decisive in determining the war's outcome. Trying every desperate thing that had a chance of working towards defeating the Nazis was not a game; at that time it was a matter of life or death for millions. It is easier to say from the perspective of years gone by what did or did not need to be done; nothing was that clear at the time except the overriding necessity of winning the war. The men and women of SOE in France, British and French, contributed significantly in their various ways to that end. Sabotage and subversion, as it turned out, could take many forms.

In the dirt and despair of a prison cell, men and women had scratched names, dates, messages to the world on the walls. Now all that remains of them are these names on a wall. And, for a little time yet, remembrance.

Survivors of the Natzweiler camp and their families come

together there each year to mourn and celebrate. In June 1990 I joined them. The main ceremonies took place on a morning when the mist had not yet dissipated. There were governmental ministers attended by much official pomp and press photographers ready to catch them at the moments of high oratory. There were many official wreaths, much protocol, and some moments of real emotion. They tended to be the wordless moments: the sounding of the bugle over the valley, the singing of the Marseillaise, the Chant des Partisans and the Chant des Marais, the placement of a spray of flowers at the feet of the monument that looms over the camp. The monument is in the shape of a flame, with an elongated human figure sculpted in relief within its concavity.

But the ghosts had been there the night before, at a funeral vigil without the crowds of officials and public that would attend the next day. This ceremony belonged only to the remaining survivors of the camp, who formed a cortège with their families, the leaders holding torches as the first group of them moved ahead to stand on the base of the monument. A trumpet sounded, and was echoed from the lowest level of the camp beside the crematorium and the ash pit and then from above, the site of the cemetery with its rows of crosses and Stars of David. At regular intervals a bugle sounded and the group of elderly men and women handed their torches over to the next group, many of them accompanied by their grandchildren, some of them helping to hold the torches. All the while, recorded voices echoed in the dark valley, their words those of the songs and poems of the resistance. The flames against the night sky, the old faces echoed in those of their young, the view of the gallows still standing in the middle of the camp made speeches superfluous.

The next day, after the oratory and the laying of many imposing wreaths and sprays at the base of the monument, the ministers and prefects, followed by veterans of the resistance and members of the public who had come for the occasion, made their way down the camp steps to the crematorium. It remained as it had been. There was the oven, surprisingly small; on the stretcher that bore the bodies into it someone had placed a single flower. An official wreath was laid beneath the plaque naming the four women who had been among so many killed there. Next to it lay a bunch of wilting poppies that had been picked in a French field earlier that day by an American writer and two Englishmen, all of them too young to have taken part in the battles but old enough to remember the war and why it was fought. One of the two, tall, wearing a bowler hat and carrying a furled umbrella – the stereotype of the Englishman realized in the flesh – had been here before.

In 1971 Nigel Smith, an amateur military historian in the habit of touring battlefields and war memorials where British troops had fought, visited Moussey, where the SAS men killed by the SS had been buried in the churchyard. Nearby was Natzweiler. Hearing about the four women agents of the British who had been killed there and noting that there was no memorial to them, he undertook, with Vera Atkins' help, a campaign to persuade the French government and the Amicale des Déportées de Natzweiler-Struthof to install the commemorative plaque that was finally placed there in 1975. He has come back every year since.

While the trumpet sounds and the scratchy old records of resistance songs play, over and over the aging men and women pass the torches of fire from one to the next and move up there to stand holding the flames with their grandchildren beside them. They know a simple thing – that ceremony is the repetition of the past that keeps it in the present. The flame that keeps burning is the reminder of four women walking down the camp steps, still hoping, as it is of four other women kneeling on the bloodied sand in another place, holding hands, all hope gone. Here they go walking down the steps forever, as they still kneel in that other place. Memory is all we have to connect us, a response to what the historian Marc Bloch, before he was killed by the Nazis, called 'the secret needs of the heart'.

'The man who can most truly be accounted brave is he who knows best the meaning of what is sweet in life and of what is terrible and then goes out determined to meet what is to come . . . Some of them, no doubt, had their faults; but what we ought to remember first is their gallant conduct against the enemy in defence of their native land. They have blotted out evil with good, and done more service to the commonwealth than they ever did harm in their private lives . . . and, in a small moment of time, the climax of their lives, a culmination of glory, not of fear, were swept away from us.'

From Pericles' Funeral Oration, Thucydides,
History of the Peloponnesian War

Notes

(For publication data see Bibliography)

CHAPTER 1

1. The material on Natzweiler is based on the works by Allainmat; Comité national pour l'erection ... Struthof; Hornung; and Klarsfeld; on interviews with Brian Stonehouse in London, August 1988; and interviews with various former prisoners and their families at Natzweiler in June 1990.

CHAPTER 2

1. Foot, *SOE in France*, p. 11.
2. Ibid.
3. Secret War Cabinet memorandum of 19 July 1940, quoted by Foot, op. cit., p. 8.
4. Dalton, Hugh, *The Fateful Years* (London: Muller, 1957), quoted in Foot, op. cit.
5. The existing secret intelligence service – SIS, later known as MI6 – had been part of the Foreign Office for years, its purpose the gathering of secret information from other countries, its agents presumably British 'passport control officers'. Military intelligence was something else. In the new kind of warfare being waged on the Continent, it would be needed in order to plan acts of sabotage and spread propaganda, and several War Office departments were combined in 1939 for the purpose. They were eventually to become SOE, and to remain separate from both MI6 and MI5, the internal counter-espionage service. In its early days directed by civilians, from September of 1943 SOE would be headed by General Colin Gubbins, a wiry Scotsman with the brisk manner and military bearing of a regular soldier. Cultured, well travelled, and seasoned in battle, Gubbins was an expert in guerrilla warfare

and clandestine operations and a natural leader. It was his combination of the military and the imaginative that made him uniquely right to head this innovative organization.

6. Howarth, *Undercover*, p. 5.

7. This chapter's account of recruitment and training procedures is drawn from so many sources, both published and from personal interviews with former agents, that I can only refer the interested reader to the bibliography, almost every item of which contains some discussion of how SOE agents were selected and trained.

8. Persico, *Piercing the Reich*, p. 15.

9. 'Now It Can Be Told', Film Department, Imperial War Museum, London.

10. Goldsmith, *Accidental Agent*, p. 22.

11. Ibid., p. 27.

12. Interview, Crest, August 1991.

13. Goldsmith, op. cit., p. 30.

14. Verity, *We Landed by Moonlight*, p. 65.

15. Interview, London, August 1988.

CHAPTER 3

1. The account of the Special Duty Squadrons and their equipment is drawn primarily from the works by Hugh Verity and Pierre Lorain.

2. Bleicher, *Colonel Henri's Story*, p. 50.

3. Ibid., p. 65.

4. Interview, Crest, August 1991.

5. Goldsmith, op. cit., p. 135.

6. The summer of 1943 saw tragedy descend on the resistance, with mass arrests and deportations of agents in the Paris area and those in touch with them throughout France. At the same time, disaster struck the umbrella organization of resistance groups formed by Jean Moulin, who would become the French resistance's great martyr.

7. Foot, op. cit., p. 421. See also Howarth, op. cit., and Cookridge, *Set Europe Ablaze*. De Gaulle's dismissive treatment of SOE organizers who had led the resistance effort to its final victory has been documented in many memoirs and historical accounts.

8. The material in this chapter is based on several interviews with

Vera Atkins in East Sussex and London from 1988 to 1991, with Brian Stonehouse in London in 1988, and with Odette Hallowes in London in 1988, and on *The Secret Hunters* by Anthony Kemp. Kemp's book is based on research for a television programme of the same name produced by Cinetel Productions Ltd, of Sydney, Australia, and presented on TVS in Britain and by WNET/Channel Thirteen in New York in November 1987 (see Preface) as part of *Memories of War*, a documentary series about the Nazi era.

CHAPTER 4

1. Millar, *Road to Resistance*, pp. 27, 29.

CHAPTER 5

1. Webb, *The Natzweiler Trial*, pp. 45–7.
2. 'Use of SOE Archives', a statement provided to researchers by the Foreign and Commonwealth Office.
3. For information about Vera Leigh's background and her training reports I am grateful to the SOE Advisor, Gervase Cowell, who, as a representative of Her Majesty's Government, patiently combed through the available records to provide factual information in answer to my many queries, in person and in correspondence, from July 1989 until the publication of this book.
4. Ward, *F.A.N.Y. Invicta*, p. 23.
5. Ibid., p. 198.
6. Verity, op. cit., p. 91.
7. Information about INVENTOR's operational instructions provided by the SOE Advisor.
8. Pryce-Jones, *Paris in the Third Reich*, pp. 69–70.

CHAPTER 6

1. Much detailed information about Diana Rowden's life and family was provided by Mark Chetwynd-Stapylton in correspondence, documents and manuscripts and in a meeting with the author at his home in Lewes in July 1990.
2. Letter from Clara Harper to Elizabeth Nicholas, 24 January 1957, in EN papers.
3. Nicholas, *Death Be Not Proud*, p. 57.
4. Ibid., p. 26.

5. Ibid., p. 83.
6. Ibid., p. 27.
7. Ibid., p. 83.
8. For information about Diana Rowden's training reports and operational instructions I am again indebted to HMG's representative Gervase Cowell, the SOE Advisor.
9. Overton Fuller, *No. 13, Bob*, p. 31.
10. Nicholas, op. cit., p. 163.
11. Ibid., p. 139.
12. Churchill, *The Spirit in the Cage*, p. 103.

CHAPTER 7

1. Nicholas, op. cit., p. 40.
2. Information about the life and family background of Andrée Borrel was provided by her sister, Léone Borrel-Arend, in interviews in Paris in 1989 and in letters, documents, and photographs. Information about Andrée Borrel's activities in escape and evasion, her arrival in England, her SOE training and her operational instructions was provided by the SOE Advisor.
3. Foot, op. cit., p. 21.
4. Nicholas, op. cit., pp. 134–5.
5. Interview with Lise de Baissac Villameur in Marseille, September 1988.
6. Foot, op. cit., p. 198.
7. Notes of interview with Renée Guépin, undated, in EN papers.
8. Overton Fuller, *Double Agent?*, p. 142.
9. Foot, op. cit., p. 198.
10. Goldsmith, op. cit., p. 24.
11. Message from Francis Suttill to Baker Street, 24 March 1943, courtesy of the SOE Advisor.
12. Foot, op. cit., p. 310.
13. Overton Fuller, op. cit., p. 122.
14. Ibid., p. 125.
15. Foot, op. cit., p. 317.

CHAPTER 8

1. Odette Hallowes' recollections are from an interview in London on 27 August 1988.

CHAPTER 9

1. Transcript of *The Secret Hunters*. See ibid., Chapter 4, Note 2.
2. The testimony quoted throughout this chapter is from Webb, op. cit.
3. Ibid.

CHAPTER 10

1. *The Times*, London, 8 May 1948.
2. Overton Fuller, *Madeleine*, p. 61.
3. Ibid., p. 73.
4. Foot, op. cit., p. 337.
5. Overton Fuller, op. cit., p. 82.
6. Interview with Vera Atkins, 2 July 1990.
7. Overton Fuller, op. cit., p. 180.
8. Ibid., p. 183.
9. Ibid., p. 185.

CHAPTER 11

1. Overton Fuller had begun her first book when she read about Noor's martyrdom and her subsequent citation for the George Cross, the highest British decoration any of the F Section women agents could receive. It was bestowed only on two others, Odette and Violette Szabo, the dramatic story of whose short time in the field was also the subject of a romantic volume called *Carve Her Name with Pride*.

Like Gerald Tickell, the author of *Odette*, Szabo's biographer R.J. Minney had official help putting together his thoroughly admiring, somewhat sentimental account of heroism and sacrifice. His heroine's story – a young war widow of working-class background determined to serve her country, sent behind enemy lines the day after D Day and performing with daring, captured fighting bravely in an ambush and killed at Ravensbrück before her twenty-fourth birthday, just as the war was about to end – could have been written for the cinema. Like the story of Odette, it did become a film. Violette Szabo was a beauty whose photographs have a striking resemblance to those of her contemporary, the actress Hedy Lamarr. She was a crack shot and by all accounts a courageous agent and a scornful captive who walked to her

313

execution with the panache one associates with tales of aristocrats climbing the scaffold during the Reign of Terror. She was the first British woman awarded the George Cross, which was presented to her four-year-old daughter by King George VI.

Unlike the authors who recorded Odette's and Violette's exploits, Overton Fuller and Elizabeth Nicholas went deeper into the shadowed background of F Section's activities than the official accounts and received little or no official help in doing so.

2. Overton Fuller, *No. 13, Bob*, p. 57.

3. Ibid., p. 58.

4. Overton Fuller, *Déricourt: The Chequered Spy*, p. 14.

5. Interview with Francis Cammaerts, Crest, 26 August 1991.

6. Overton Fuller, *No. 13, Bob*, p. 160.

7. Ibid., p. 179.

8. Kahn, *The Code Breakers*, p. 538.

9. Ibid. p. 536.

10. The late 1940s and early 1950s in England saw a succession of memoirs presenting the exploits of individual agents and the achievements of SOE in the most favourable light. The books about Odette and Violette Szabo were followed by the accounts of Maurice Buckmaster and Peter Churchill among others – upbeat, charmingly ironic, modestly self-effacing, and not entirely reliable. In fact, later disclosures would prove that, if Churchill's narratives were superficial, Buckmaster's were in places actually untrue. The very least one could say about them was that they were – incomplete.

11. In France, the Abbé Paul Guillaume investigated *La Sologne au temps de l'héroisme et de la trahison* under the auspices of the official Commission d'Histoire de l'Occupation et de la Libération de la France while the trail was still warm, providing a source for later researchers into the activities of many of the central *réseaux* and in particular of the events surrounding the PROSPER disaster. And others were at work collecting facts and unearthing documents. Historians of the resistance like Henri Michel and Henri Noguères, whose successive volumes would appear throughout the sixties and seventies, were beginning to reconstruct the past in what over the years would become a monumental national archive.

CHAPTER 12

1. Bleicher, op. cit., p. 90.
2. Ibid., p. 92.
3. Ibid., p. 112.
4. Ibid., p. 133.
5. Ibid., p. 137.
6. Ibid., p. 139.
7. Ibid., p. 157.

CHAPTER 13

1. Report by Wanborough commandant, 30 June 1942, quoted in Foot, op. cit., p. 268.
2. Interview with Pierre Raynaud, Provence, 25 June 1990.
3. Provided by the SOE Advisor.
4. Nicholas, op, cit., p. 19.
5. Ibid., pp. 66–7.
6. Ibid., p. 113.
7. Ibid.
8. Ibid., p. 226.

CHAPTER 14

1. EN papers, courtesy of John Nicholas.
2. Ibid.
3. Nicholas, op. cit., pp. 218–20.
4. Interview with Gaston Collins (formerly Gustave Cohen of ROBIN), Paris, 7 November 1990.
5. Material on Sonia Olschanezky's background, early life, and resistance activities is based on an interview with Serge Olschanezky in Limours, France, 6 November 1990, and on letters, photographs, and documents provided by him.
6. When Noor arrived at the PROSPER headquarters at the agricultural school at Grignon, the Balachowskys 'were both rather concerned', they later told Jean Overton Fuller, 'about what they felt to be her "Semitic type". Not knowing that she was partly Indian, they were sure that she was Jewish.' The Professor thought it was 'something in the cast of her face – in the formation of the bones – which was typically Semitic.' Their concern was that her 'Jewish' appearance might cast suspicion on her cover story,

which would not hold up under close examination by the Gestapo (*Madeleine*, p. 91).

CHAPTER 15

1. Interview with Serge Olschanezky, 6 November 1990.
2. Wighton, *Pin-Stripe Saboteur*, pp. 181–2.
3. Ibid., p. 183.
4. Ibid., pp. 212–15.
5. Weil knew some things he might have learned from the books by Elizabeth Nicholas and Jean Overton Fuller and some things he may have heard from French survivors of the resistance, who were freer to talk about what had happened and speculate on why than their British allies would be for a long time afterwards. That Gilbert Norman, at ease in comfortable circumstances at the Avenue Foch, told newly captured agents that they might as well tell the Germans everything – they knew it all already; that the Germans were operating the sets of captured radio operators and that London was continuing to send weapons straight into their waiting hands – all this was common knowledge by 1959. Weil also knew, to Norman's credit, that while the rue Cambon address of ROBIN headquarters was well known to him, Norman did not seem to have revealed it to the Germans, who never raided it.
6. Wighton, op. cit., p. 218.
7. According to Serge Olschanezky (interview, 6 November 1990), an old school friend of Enoch's had also worked as a subagent for ROBIN. When Enoch was taken out of the nightclub to the waiting Gestapo car, his friend was already in the back seat, and they were handcuffed together. After the war, in 1945, Serge met with Weil and with Enoch's old friend, who Weil accused of being responsible for Sonia's and Enoch's capture. He had been at Sonia's first meeting with the man presumed to be from London and Weil accused him of having mentioned names, including that of Sonia's brother, in an attempt to make himself look important to a British officer, to impress London with the fact that it was he, and not Sonia, who should have been put in charge when Weil left. The friend's very survival, his never having been deported, seemed to Weil to be damning evidence against him. The man insisted that

he had managed an escape from the camp at Compiègne. In the end, no action was taken against him.

CHAPTER 16
1. *Sunday Pictorial*, London, 20 June 1958, p. 6.
2. Ibid., 6 July 1958, p. 8.
3. Ibid., 20 July 1958, p. 10.
4. Overton Fuller, *Double Agent?*, p. 16.
5. Foot, op. cit., p. 303.
6. Ibid., p. 305.
7. Bleicher, op. cit., pp. 124–6.
8. Foot, op. cit., p. 309.
9. Overton Fuller, op. cit., p. 138.
10. Ibid., p. 151.
11. Ibid., p. 159.
12. Ibid., pp. 154–5.
13. Verity, op. cit., p. 167.
14. Overton Fuller, op. cit., p. 165.
15. Ibid., p. 164.
16. Verity, op. cit., p. 164.
17. Ibid., p. 165.
18. Ibid.
19. Ibid., p. 166.
20. See note 13.

CHAPTER 17
1. EN papers.
2. 5 October 1958.
3. *Time*, 15 December 1958, p. 26.
4. Ward, op. cit.
5. Overton Fuller, op. cit., p. 181.
6. EN papers.
7. Nicholas, op. cit., p. 216.
8. Overton Fuller, op. cit., p. 183.
9. Letter to the Editor, signed 'Irene Ward, House of Commons', undated (appears to be sometime in 1966), with no masthead or other identification of publication, in EN papers.
10. Ibid.

11. EN papers.
12. 12 February 1959, pp. 24–6.
13. Foot, op. cit., p. 252.
14. EN papers.
15. See note 9.
16. Foot, op. cit., p. 153.
17. Interview with Francis Cammaerts, Crest, 26 August 1991.

CHAPTER 18

1. Overton Fuller, op. cit., p. 181.
2. Ibid., p. 169.
3. Foot, op. cit.
4. Interview with Francis Cammaerts, Vaison la Romaine, 15 August 1991.
5. Cookridge, *Set Europe Ablaze*, p. 65.
6. The phrase is Foot's. Op. cit., p. 251.
7. Foot, *SOE: An Outline History . . .*, p. 138.
8. Overton Fuller, op. cit., p. 142.
9. Foot, *SOE in France*, p. 310.
10. Ibid., p. 343.
11. Ibid., pp. 329–30.
12. Ibid., p. 348.

CHAPTER 19

1. In 1965 Sweet-Escott, who had held various senior positions on the SOE staff including heading the Gaullist RF Section (his colleague J.G. Beevor, another senior SEO staff officer, called Sweet-Escott 'SOE's most versatile and ubiquitous officer'), was allowed to publish his account of SOE's organization and operations. He had completed the manuscript of *Baker Street Irregular* in 1954, but the Foreign Office had denied him permission, under the Official Secrets Act, to publish it until the redoubtable Dame Irene Ward took up his cause in the early 1960s and, with certain passages cut from the original, the first general survey of SOE saw the light of day. It was written without benefit of the official records, to which Sweet-Escott had been denied access.

There is no way of knowing what he had been required to cut from his manuscript, but the book that Sweet-Escott was allowed to publish referred to an Allied strategic deception plan involving SOE. Its object was to mislead the Germans about the invasion of Sicily set for July 1943 by creating 'the greatest possible diversion in Greece . . . The Germans were completely deceived, and moved into Greece two divisions which might otherwise have been used against us in Sicily.' Sweet-Escott went on to observe that this was 'not the only diversion thought up to deceive the enemy'. His understated remark would be amply corroborated in the flow of books that followed his.

2. Stafford, *Britain and European Resistance*, p. 86.
3. Muggeridge, *Chronicles of Wasted Time: II: The Infernal Grove*, p. 174.
4. Verity, op. cit., pp. 91ff.
5. Masterman, *The Double-Cross System*, p. 10.
6. Ibid., p. 71.
7. The first important plan of organized deception was a cover plan for TORCH, the landings in North Africa in November 1942. The scheme was designed to mislead the Germans about where the assault would take place. It was followed by the success of MINCEMEAT, the code name for the operation described in Ewen Montague's *The Man Who Never Was*. When the book and the film based on it appeared in the early 1950s there was no indication that the story was anything more than a unique instance of an inspired trick played on the enemy. By means of false papers planted on a corpse washed up on the coast of Spain, the Germans had been encouraged in the belief that the invasion actually planned for Sicily would only be a preliminary to an invasion of Greece.

It was a fascinating story, as good as any of those Masterman, an Oxford don, plotted in the mystery novels he wrote before the war. A fictitious staff officer was invented, a corpse, dressed in uniform, was given his identity along with every conceivable bit of corroborating detail (dated London theatre-ticket stubs in his pocket, personal letters in his briefcase along with the highly confidential papers in the briefcase strapped to his wrist), and it was left to the Spanish authorities to remove the papers, photograph them, and turn them over to German intelligence. According to Masterman this plan was approved not only by the Chiefs of

Staff but by the Prime Minister himself. Churchill's penchant for intrigue, his appreciation of deception schemes, and his desire to meet individual agents involved in those schemes from time to time was well known.

8. Masterman's book revealed much that had not been acknowledged before. It did not reveal what was meant by his several references in passing to information from 'secret sources'. That revelation was left to a French army intelligence officer named Gustave Bertrand, whose account of Enigma was published in France in 1973, and to an MI6 officer named Frederick Winterbotham, who in 1974 let the English-speaking world in on *The Ultra Secret* – only after Bertrand had made the facts known in France.

9. Cave Brown, *Bodyguard of Lies*, p. 10.

10. Foot, op. cit., p. 121.

11. Cave Brown, op. cit., p. 319.

CHAPTER 20

1. This chapter is based on talks with Pierre Raynaud at his home in Provence on 25 and 26 June 1990 and on letters and documents in his possession.

2. In *Un Soldat Menteur* Bureau gives his version of the events that overtook Suttill, Norman and the rest. A passionate defender of both PROSPER leaders, he exculpates them on every charge that has been levelled against them, from the accusation of carelessness to that of treason. His explanation of the business of Suttill's demonstrating Sten guns in a night club in Montmartre puts it in an entirely different light to Foot's comment that 'he [Suttill] was not particular about where he made his contacts.' Bureau reveals that the place in question, the Hot Club, had been closed down, was in a relatively isolated street, and was being used as a hiding place for the circuit's arms at the time.

CHAPTER 21

1. Despite the pro forma disclaimer in the front matter of *Fall From Grace*, readers who came to Larry Collins' 1985 novel knowing something of the history of SOE's French Section and the controversies surrounding it had no trouble recognizing it as a *roman à*

clef, historical speculation dramatically presented in the form of fiction.

Echoes of the real story abound. The heroine's field name is Denise. There are renamed but recognizable portraits of Buckmaster and Déricourt (with his actual code name of Gilbert) among others. Some things are not even faintly disguised. There is the butler Park in the 'discreetly luxurious apartment, hidden behind the neo-Georgian façade of Orchard Court,' and the service chiefs and members of the Twenty Committee and the LCS appear under their real names, as do German generals and Nazi Party officials, and Sir Stewart Menzies and his deputy the very fully named Colonel Sir Claude Edward Marjoribanks Dansey.

And there are the code names for various once-secret operations and the text of such once-secret directives, now declassified, as COSC (42)180(0) defining the mission of the Controlling Officer for Deception directing the LCS in preparing plans on a worldwide basis for deception and other strategems to gain military advantage by misleading the enemy. Radio games, agents dropped to waiting German reception committees, desperate messages acknowledged with London's chiding reminder to be more careful to include the second part of the double security check next time, an air operations officer regularly turning the secret courier mail entrusted to him over to the Gestapo before sending it on its way to London, captured agents believing they were betrayed by their own side – in short, all of the elements of melodrama that had in fact been the elements of history.

Collins had first heard about SOE and the French Section/ Déricourt/Prosper affair from Arthur Watt, who had been Déricourt's radio operator. In the 1950s, when Collins and Watt were both working in Paris, the two often met and Watt shared his war stories as they talked over drinks. It was his belief that the barman at the Brasserie Lorraine in the Place des Ternes had been working for MI6 and was Nicholas Bodington's contact with Déricourt, who had been playing a triple game. Collins found all this intriguing and it led him to the (very different) books by Foot and Anthony Cave Brown. Later, after having published several bestselling novels and wanting to write one with a woman as the central character, he thought of SOE's unprecedented use of women in special operations. He decided to use the deception plot and undertook an impressive amount of background research involving interviews with most of those still living who had been involved in one way or another.

Collins' novel was already finished but had not yet appeared when he was approached through his publisher by a producer for a BBC television series of historical documentaries. A generous man, Collins opened his files and turned over the notes of his interviews with former SOE staff members and F Section agents, as well as former German staff officers and people who had worked for them, for use by Robert Marshall in putting together the BBC *Timewatch* programme, which aired in 1988, and Marshall's subsequent book with the same title: *All the King's Men.*

In addition to the material Robert Marshall had from Larry Collins, he shared what each had gathered in the way of research with James Rusbridger, a writer on intelligence in the Second World War who had a hand in several BBC television documentaries. Their cooperation was a two-way street, Rusbridger contributing to the *Timewatch* programme and Marshall being credited by Rusbridger for help with an article entitled 'Bluff, Deceit and Treachery' published in the English magazine *Encounter*. Marshall and Rusbridger seemed to corroborate each other, although actually both were drawing from the same well, and reaching the same conclusions from the same assertions.

Rusbridger does not bring Dansey into it, leaving it an open question 'whether anyone authorised his liaison with the Germans.' But he does say that the F Section agents were briefed with false information about invasion, told to hold out for forty-eight hours if captured, and then dropped to a network already penetrated by the Germans – in effect that they were 'used as tethered goats for COCKADE' – and he goes on to suggest that, while the capture of the exposed agents might seem a small price to have paid for the ultimate success of the invasion, given the failure of the COCKADE scheme, 'it was pointless and unnecessary sacrifice.'

2. Buckmaster interview on *All the King's Men, Timewatch*, BBC.
3. Buckmaster interview with Larry Collins, London, 2 May 1983.

4. Sporborg interview with Larry Collins, London, 21 March 1983.

5. Ibid.

6. Until the publication of the volume on Strategic Deception in the official history of *British Intelligence in the Second World War* in 1990, the most thorough survey of the documents that had come to light and what they signified was David Stafford's *Britain and European Resistance, 1940–1945*.

7. See Note 2, Chapter 20.

8. *Sunday Times*, London 24 January 1988, p. 10.

9. Overton Fuller, op. cit., pp. 137, 151, 157.

10. Marshall, op. cit., p. 161.

11. Overton Fuller, *The German Penetration of SOE: France 1941–1944*, p. 178.

12. Overton Fuller, *Déricourt: The Chequered Spy*.

13. Ibid., p. 367.

14. Ibid., p. 149.

15. Howard, *British Intelligence in the Second World War, Vol. 5: Strategic Deception*, p. 221.

Not until 1990, fifty years after the outbreak of the Second World War in Europe and forty-five years after it ended, and a full decade after the book itself had been completed, did the fifth volume of the official history of British intelligence in the Second World War appear. This should not come as a great surprise to anyone having followed the tortuous path of disclosures on its subject, since this was the volume dealing with strategic deception.

Based on official sources, including confidential files still not released to the public, this work, by an Oxford historian, contains as much as we are ever likely to learn about the uses of strategic deception from 1939 to 1945. Here are set out the details of how Britain made use of the two extraordinary advantages it possessed: the ability to read much of the enemy's communications and the total control of what the enemy believed to be its own network of agents. Coordinating those two unique capabilities made it possible at every stage to assess what effect the misinformation being fed to the Germans was having.

Howard describes the orchestration of the over-all designs of the LCS and the workings of the Twenty Committee coordinating what was being passed through the controlled agents, as well as the way in which such tactics as the creation of fictional armies, the setting up of dummy installations, and the activation of the rumour factory were used to contribute to the final effect.

Little in this volume had not appeared somewhere, in some form, before. Only now it becomes official. This modest-sized volume stands in sober contrast to some of the books it will inevitably be shelved beside. This is the version of those long-ago events behind the headlines and the battles that students of these matters will refer to years from now.

Howard's book deals with deception policies and operations in all of the theatres of the war over all of the years that it lasted. On the events of 1943 and 1944 in France, his considered opinion is that COCKADE, although disappointing in its immediate objective, was 'a valuable rehearsal for the real performance.' It was deception, Howard maintains, that 'made possible tactical surprise which in its turn produced complete and economical victory.'

CHAPTER 22

1. Interviews with Vera Atkins in East Sussex and in London took place at various times from 1988 to 1991.
2. Interview with M.R.D. Foot, London, 4 July 1990.
3. Interview with Brian Stonehouse, London, 27 August 1988.

CHAPTER 23

1. Interviews with Francis Cammaerts in France on 15 and 26 August 1991.
2. Interview with Léone Arend-Borrel, Paris, 28 August 1989 and 15 September 1989.
3. Interview with Odette Mathy Fournier and Georges Fournier, Hyères, 11 September 1989.

Bibliography

Allainmat, Henry, *Auschwitz en France: la vérité sur le seul camp d'extermination nazi en France, le Struthof*, Paris: Presses de la Cité, 1974.

Beevor, J.G. [John Grosvenor], *SOE: Recollections and Reflections, 1940–1945*, London: The Bodley Head, 1981.

Bertrand, Gustave, *Enigma ou la plus grande énigme de la guerre 1939–1945*, Paris: Librairie Plon, 1973.

Bleicher, Hugo, *Colonel Henri's Story*, London: William Kimber, 1954.

Braddon, Russell, *The White Mouse* [American edn of *Nancy Wake*], New York: Norton, 1957.

Brome, Vincent, *The Way Back*, London: Cassell, 1957.

Buckmaster, Maurice, *Specially Employed*, London: Batchworth Press, 1952.

Buckmaster, Maurice, *They Fought Alone*, London: Odhams Press, 1959.

Bureau, Jacques, *Un soldat menteur*, Paris: Laffont, 1992.

Burney, Christopher, *Dungeon Democracy*, New York: Duell, Sloane and Pearce, 1946.

Burney, Christopher, *Solitary Confinement*, London: Clerke and Cockeran, 1962.

Casey, William, *The Secret War Against Hitler*, Washington, D.C.: Regnery Gateway, 1988.

Cave Brown, Anthony, *Bodyguard of Lies*, New York: Bantam, 1976.

Churchill, Peter, *Duel of Wits*, London: Hodder and Stoughton, 1953.

Churchill, Peter, *Of Their Own Choice*, London: Hodder and Stoughton, 1952.

Churchill, Peter, *The Spirit in the Cage*, London: Hodder and Stoughton, 1954.

Cobb, Richard, *French and Germans, Germans and French*, Hanover, N.H.: University Press of New England, 1983.

Collier, Basil, *Hidden Weapons: Allied Secret or Undercover Service in World War II*, London: Hamish Hamilton, 1982.

Comité national pour l'érection et la conservation d'un mémorial de la déportation au Struthof, *Natzwiller Struthof*, Paris: Commission executive de Comité national du Struthof, 1976.

Cookridge, E.H., *Set Europe Ablaze* (American edn of *Inside S.O.E.*), New York: Thomas Y. Crowell, 1967.

Cookridge, E.H., *They Came From the Sky*, New York: Crowell, 1965.

Cowburn, Benjamin, *No Cloak, No Dagger*, London: Jarrolds, 1960.

Cruickshank, Charles, *Deception in World War II*, Oxford: Oxford University Press, 1981.

Deacon, Richard, *A History of the British Secret Service*, New York: Taplinger, 1970.

Epstein, Edward Jay, *Deception: The Invisible War Between the KGB and the CIA*, New York: Simon & Schuster, 1989.

Escott, Beryl E., *Mission Improbable: A Salute to the RAF Women of SOE in Wartime France*, Sparkford, Somerset: Patrick Stephens Limited, 1991.

Fédération nationale des déportés et internés résistants et patriotes, *La Déportation*, Paris: 1978.

Foot, M.R.D., *Resistance*, London: Paladin Books, Granada, 1978.

Foot, M.R.D., *Six Faces of Courage*, London: Eyre Methuen, 1978.

Foot, M.R.D., *SOE in France: An Account of the Work of the British Special Operations Executive in France 1940–1944*, London: Her Majesty's Stationery Office, 1966.

Foot, M.R.D., *SOE: An Outline History of the Special Operations Executive 1940–46*, London: British Broadcasting Corporation, 1984.

Foot, M.R.D. and J.M. Langley, *MI9: The British Secret Service that Fostered Escape and Evasion 1939–1945 and its American Counterpart*, London: Bodley Head, 1979.

Fourcade, Marie-Madeleine, *Noah's Ark*, New York: E.P. Dutton, 1974.

Funk, Arthur L., *Hidden Ally: The French Resistance, Special Operations, and the Landings in Southern France, 1944*, Westport, Conn.: Greenwood Press, 1992.

Ganier-Raymond, Philippe, *The Tangled Web*, London: Arthur Barker, 1968.

Giskes, H.J., *London Calling North Pole*, London: Kimber, 1953.

Goldsmith, John, *Accidental Agent*, New York: Scribner's, 1971.

Goldston, Robert, *Sinister Touches: The Secret War Against Hitler*, New York: Dial Press, 1982.

Grant, R.G., *MI5 MI6: Britain's Security and Secret Intelligence Services*, London: Bison Books, 1989.

Guillaume, Paul, *La Sologne au temps de l'héroisme et de la trahison*, Orléans: Imprimerie Nouvelle, 1950.

Hamilton-Hill, Donald, *SOE Assignment*, London: William Kimber, 1973.

Heslop, Richard, *Xavier*, London: Rupert Hart-Davies, 1970.

Hoehling, A.A., *Women Who Spied*, New York: Dodd, Mead, 1967.

Hornung, Albert, *Le Struthof: Camp de la Mort*, Paris: Editions de la Nouvelle Revue Critique, 1945.

Howard, Michael, *British Intelligence in the Second World War*, New York: Cambridge University Press, 1990.

Howarth, Patrick, *Undercover: The Men and Women of the Special Operations Executive*, London: Routledge & Kegan Paul, 1980.

Hutchison, James, *That Drug Danger*, Montrose, Scotland: Standard Press, 1977.

Johnson, Brian, *The Secret War*, London: BBC, 1978.

Jones, Liane, *A Quiet Courage*, London: Bantam Press, 1990.

Jones, Reginald Victor, *Most Secret War*, London: Hamish Hamilton, 1978.

Kahn, David, *The Code Breakers*, New York: Macmillan, 1967.

Keegan, John, ed., *The Times Atlas of the Second World War*, New York: Harper & Row, 1989.

Kemp, Anthony, *The Secret Hunters*, London: Michael O'Mara Books, 1986.

Kemp, Peter, *No Colours or Crest*, London: Cassell, 1958.

King, Stella, *'Jacqueline': Pioneer Heroine of the Resistance*, London: Arms and Armour Press, 1989.

Klarsfeld, Serge, ed., 'The Struthof Album', New York and Paris: The Beate Klarsfeld Foundation, 1985.

Lacouture, Jean, *De Gaulle: The Rebel, 1890–1944*, Trans. by Patrick O'Brian, New York: Norton, 1990.

Larteguy, Jean and Bob Maloubier, *Triple Jeu: L'espion Déricourt*, Paris: Laffont, 1992.

Le Chêne, Evelyn, *Watch for Me by Moonlight: A British Agent with the French Resistance*, London: Eyre Methuen, 1973.

Lorain, Pierre, *Clandestine Operations: The Arms and Techniques of the Resistance, 1941–1944*, New York: Macmillan, 1983.

Lovell, Mary S., *Cast No Shadow*, New York: Pantheon, 1992.

Marshall, Bruce, *The White Rabbit*, Boston: Houghton Mifflin, 1952.

Marshall, Robert, *All the King's Men*, London: Collins, 1988.

Masson, Madeleine, *Christine*, London: Hamish Hamilton, 1975.

Masterman, J.C., *The Double-Cross System in the War of 1939–1945*, New Haven: Yale University Press, 1972.

Millar, George, *Road to Resistance*, Boston: Little, Brown, 1979.

Minney, R.J., *Carve Her Name with Pride*, London: George Newnes, 1956.

Morgan, Ted, *An Uncertain Hour*, New York: Morrow, 1990.

Muggeridge, Malcolm, *Chronicles of Wasted Time: II: The Infernal Grove*, London: Collins, 1973.

Nicholas, Elizabeth, *Death Be Not Proud*, London: Cresset Press, 1958.

Noguères, Henri, *Histoire de la résistance en France*, Paris: Laffont, 1967–81.

Overton Fuller, Jean, *Madeleine*, London: Gollancz, 1952.

Overton Fuller, Jean, *No. 13, Bob* [American edn of *The Starr Affair*], Boston: Little, Brown, 1955.

Overton Fuller, Jean, *Double Agent? Light on the Secret Agents' War in France*, London: Pan Books, 1961. [Revised edition of *Double Webs*, 1958.]

Overton Fuller, Jean, *The German Penetration of SOE: France 1941–1944*, London: William Kimber, 1975.

Overton Fuller, Jean, *Déricourt: The Chequered Spy*, Wilton: Michael Russell, 1989.

Paine, Lauran, *German Military Intelligence in World War II: The Abwehr*, New York: Stein and Day, 1984.

Peis, Gunter, *The Mirror of Deception*, London: Weidenfeld and Nicolson, 1977.

Persico, Joseph E., *Piercing the Reich*, New York: Viking, 1979.

Pryce-Jones, David, *Paris in the Third Reich: A History of the German Occupation, 1940-1944*, New York: Holt, Rinehart and Winston, 1981.

Rake, Dennis, *Rake's Progress*, London, Leslie Frewin, 1968.

Rodriguez, Ferdinand and Robert Hervet, *L'Escalier sans retour*, Paris: Éditions France-Empire, 1983.

Rossiter, Margaret L., *Women in the Resistance*, New York: Praeger, 1986.

Ruby, Marcel, *F Section, SOE: The Buckmaster Networks*, London: Leo Cooper, 1988.

Rusbridger, James, 'Between Bluff, Deceit and Treachery', in *Encounter*, Vol. LXVI, No. 5, May 1986, pp. 5-13.

Russell of Liverpool, Lord, *The Scourge of the Swastika*, London: Cassell, 1954.

Stafford, David, *Britain and European Resistance, 1940–1945: A Survey of the Special Operations Executive*, London: Macmillan, 1983.

Stevenson, William, *A Man Called Intrepid*, New York: Harcourt Brace Jovanovich, 1976.

Sweet-Escott, Bickham, *Baker Street Irregular*, London: Methuen, 1965.

Taylor, Eric, *Women Who Went to War*, London: Grafton Books, 1988.

Thomas, Jack, *No Banners*, London: Allen, 1955.

Tickell, Jerrard, *Moon Squadron*, London: Allan Wingate, 1956.

Tickell, Jerrard, *Odette: The Story of a British Agent*, London: Chapman & Hall, 1949.

Verity, Hugh, *We Landed by Moonlight*, London: Ian Allan, 1978.

de Vomécourt, Philippe, *Who Lived to See the Day*, London: Hutchinson, 1961.

Walters, Anne-Marie, *Moondrop to Gascony*, London: Macmillan, 1947.

Ward, Dame Irene, *F.A.N.Y. Invicta*, London: Hutchinson, 1955.

Warner, Philip, *The Secret Forces of World War II*, London: Granada, 1985.

Webb, Anthony M., *The Natzweiler Trial*, Volume V of *War Crimes Trials*, ed. Sir David Maxwell Fyfe, London: William Hodge and Company, 1949.

West, Nigel, *GCHQ: The Secret Wireless War 1900–86*, London: Weidenfeld and Nicolson, 1986.

West, Nigel, *Secret War: The Story of SOE*, London: Hodder and Stoughton, 1992.

Wheatley, Dennis, *The Deception Planners: My Secret War*, London: Hutchinson, 1980.

Wheeler, Mark, 'The SOE Phenomenon', in *Journal of Contemporary History*, Vol. 16, 1981, pp. 513-19.

Whiting, Charles, *Ardennes: The Secret War*, Briarcliff Manor, N.Y.: Stein and Day, 1985.

Wighton, Charles, *Pin-Stripe Saboteur*, London: Odhams Press, 1959.

Winks, Robin W., *Cloak and Gown: Scholars in the Secret War*, New York: Morrow, 1987

Winterbotham, F.W., *The Ultra Secret*, New York: Harper & Row, 1974.

Wynne, Barry, *No Drums . . . No Trumpets*, London: Barker, 1961.

Young, Gordon, *Cat with Two Faces*, New York: Coward McCann, 1957.

Index